Introduction to Research Methods and Statistics in

to be returned on or before
below

PSYCHOLOGY

SECOND EDITION

Hugh Coolican

Hodder & Stoughton

A MEMBER OF THE HODDER HEADLINE GROUP

DEDICATION

To Jeevan. Hope you enjoy the family.

British Library Cataloguing in Publication Data
A catalogue record for this title is available from the British Library

ISBN 0 340 67937 9

First edition published 1995
This edition published 1996
Impression number   10 9 8 7 6 5 4 3 2 1
Year   1999 1998 1997 1996

Typeset by Wearset, Boldon, Tyne and Wear.
Printed in Great Britain for Hodder & Stoughton Educational, a division of Hodder Headline Plc, 338 Euston Road, London NW1 3BH by Bath Press, Bath.

CONTENTS

Surveys; Questionnaires, scales, and psychometric tests; Sociometry; Glossary; Exercises

PREFACE

This book is, in a sense, the daughter or son of *Research Methods and Statistics in Psychology*. It covers what you might need at A level including all the concepts covered by any of the current syllabuses, but particularly that of the AEB. This book now contains all the statistical tests for that syllabus and all the amendments brought in by the syllabus revision for 1996. These include, in particular, the concept of the quasi-experiment, more information on content analysis and qualitative research and a set of 15 structured questions which follow the pattern set in the draft syllabus for examination papers. The book retains some of the features of *Research Methods* which have been found useful by several tutors who have been in touch, including the self-test/glossary system at the end of each chapter, help with formulae in statistics, the bogus student report with marker's comments and several of the newer exercises and illustrative diagrams. Tutors may note that in this second edition the language of hypothesis testing has changed somewhat in the light of recent debate. Also, items in this book which are *not* in the AEB's revised syllabus are listed [see page 281].

Teaching in Higher Education has shown me that psychology undergraduates without A level, especially those who may only take psychology as a minor or complementary course, should also benefit from a textbook at this level, along with those on Access, BTEC, nursing, social work and other vocational courses which include some 'hands-on' work in the behavioural and social sciences.

To expand on a point in the preface to the first edition of *Research Methods*, statistics and methods are like the engine room of a luxury liner. Not many people want to go down and visit (and get their hands dirty) but they *do* want to enjoy the cruise. Whatever exciting findings you hear about in your psychology course it must always be remembered that *someone* went out and did the research work. We just can't *have* the fascinating results and support for theory without the data collection and analysis.

This book is firmly rooted in the notion that statistics and methods can be made accessible. Many students still think they are somehow 'non-mathematical' yet continue to be surprised that they can follow and carry out the methods and the consequent data analysis. This is because the ideas are not so far from concepts (such as probability) which have been acquired in everyday life (especially since the lottery!). In my teaching I always try to make this connection and my aim has been to write this book from the same point of view. I hope I have helped in demystifying the subject and in breaking down the fear barriers for all those who think that they cannot do statistics. I really hope it can aid those who fancy psychology, but fear the methods, to roll up their sleeves and get their hands on the practice of finding out about people.

ACKNOWLEDGEMENTS

I would like to thank Anthony Curtis and Richard Gross for their helpful comments during the preparation of this book. My thanks also go to Julie Hill, Louise Tooms and Tim Gregson-Williams at Hodders for all their help and encouragement. Finally, I would like to thank all those students on whom I have tried out this material, for their help in fine-tuning it.

Psychological research

1

PSYCHOLOGY AND RESEARCH

Student: I'd like to enrol for psychology please.
Lecturer: You do realise that it includes quite a bit of statistics, and you'll
           have to do some experimental work and write up practical
           reports?
Student: Oh . . .

When enrolling for a course in psychology, the prospective student is very often taken
aback by the discovery that the syllabus includes a fair-sized dollop of statistics and
that practical research, experiments and report-writing are all involved. My experience as a tutor has commonly been that many 'A' level psychology students are either
'escaping' from school into further education or tentatively returning after years away
from academic study. Both sorts of student are frequently dismayed to find that this
new and exciting subject is going to thrust them back into two of the areas they most
disliked in school. One is maths – but rest assured! Statistics, in fact, will involve you
in little of the maths on a traditional syllabus and will be performed on real data most
of which you have gathered yourself. Calculators and computers do the 'number
crunching' these days. The other area is science.

   It is strange that of all the sciences – natural and social – the one which directly
concerns ourselves as individuals in society is the least likely to be found in schools,
where teachers are preparing young people for life in society, amongst other things! It
is also strange that a student can study all the 'hard' natural sciences – physics,
chemistry, biology – yet never be asked to consider what a science *is* until they study
psychology or sociology.

   These are generalisations of course. Some schools teach psychology. Others
nowadays teach the underlying principles of scientific research. Some of us actually
enjoyed science and maths at school. If you did, you'll find most of this book fairly
easy going.

   Returning to the prospective student then, he or she usually has little clue about
what sort of research psychologists do. The notion of 'experiments' sometimes
produces anxiety. 'Will we be conditioned or brainwashed?' If we ignore images from
the black-and-white film industry, and think carefully about what psychological
researchers might do, we might conjure up an image of the street survey. Think again,
and we might suggest that psychologists watch people's behaviour. I agree with Gross
(1992) who says that, at a party, if one admits to teaching, or even studying,
psychology, a common reaction is 'Oh, I'd better be careful what I say from now on'.
Another strong contender is 'I suppose you'll be analysing my behaviour' (said as the
speaker takes one hesitant step backwards) in the mistaken assumption that
psychologists go around making deep, mysterious interpretations of human actions as
they occur. (If you meet someone who does do this, ask them something about the

evidence they use, after you've finished with this book!) The notion of such analysis is loosely connected to Freud who, though popularly portrayed as a psychiatric Sherlock Holmes, used very few of the sorts of research outlined in this book.

WHERE DOES THE PSYCHOLOGY STUDENT START?

One of the interesting things about teaching psychological research methods and statistics is that people actually *start* their psychology course (I fervently believe) with many of the ideas used in research already in their heads. All the experts in research started out with the same reasoning faculties that most humans share. The tutor's job, I've always thought, is to help the student formalise their thoughts, to add precision, to supply the names for many common notions, and then to take students a little further into the more technical realms of methods and statistics. You already have a good idea, for instance, how many cats out of ten ought to prefer 'Poshpaws' cat food to another brand if the number is to be impressive and not just a 'fluke' majority. You can probably discuss quite competently how to gather a representative sample for a survey on attitudes to eating meat. So, to make my point, let's go straight away into an exercise which you can do alone or with colleagues:

> Suppose you overhear the following statement in conversation in your college canteen:
>
> 'I don't know. You hear about all these wars and they're nearly all in hot countries. I reckon heat makes people aggressive – you know, want to rush to fight instead of thinking about it beforehand.'
>
> As you've started a course in psychology, and therefore presumably want to ask questions about people's behaviour and thinking, I hope you wouldn't be able to accept this gross assumption. Rather than accept this 'armchair' theory, I hope the first thing you'd want to do is to ask for *evidence* for this claim. So let me ask you to take on this problem yourself. How would you design and conduct a study to test the idea that heat makes people more aggressive? That is, what would you do to gather evidence to support or disprove this idea? Try to think of several alternative methods you might use.

You and your colleagues may have come up with one or a few notions rather like those in Box 1.1:

Box 1.1   *Possible research designs testing the idea that heat makes people aggressive*

> 1 We'd take a group of people and put them in a cool room, ask them to discuss a problem and observe whether they got aggressive or not; then we'd make the room hotter and observe them again.
>
> 2 We'd have one group in a hot room and show them a somewhat violent film and ask them to say how aggressive the people in the film were; then we'd do the same with another group of people in the same room when it's cool.
>
> 3 We'd take a group of schoolchildren and observe them in the playground playing and see which is the most aggressive pair, next most aggressive pair and so on. We'd split the pairs to form two equivalent groups for aggression. Then we'd get naive observers

to watch one group playing in a cool room and the other in the same room when it's hotter and compare the pairs of children on their levels of aggression.

4 We'd have this guy and put him into a room and vary the temperature and each time ask him to do a frustrating task like threading a needle with thread that's too large for the eye. We'd measure his aggression with a questionnaire.

5 We'd observe and interview drivers in the rush hour in Iceland and in Mexico.

6 We'd take samples from different areas of the country on one day when the temperature varied across these different areas. We'd ask the people to do things like give prison sentences or say what they'd do if someone hit their little sister.

7 We'd follow a group of boys through the year recording temperature and number of fights they've got into that week/month.

Each of the suggestions in Box 1.1 is a **RESEARCH DESIGN**, a way of setting up conditions to gather data with which to answer a question. The question, originating from the rather sweeping generalisation made by the person in the canteen, is 'Does heat make people more aggressive?'

HOW DO PSYCHOLOGISTS ANSWER QUESTIONS?

Basically, they do research. They decide upon an overall design, such as one of those in Box 1.1 (though with greater precision) and they then need to make several more decisions about their overall research study:

1 *what will be measured* and how, exactly?

2 *who* will be studied?

3 *how* will the data gathered be used to demonstrate a real difference?

Decision 1 concerns the *precise* measurement of **VARIABLES**. For instance, notice that only examples 4 and 7 in Box 1.1 give a specific means by which to measure 'aggression'. Variables are things which vary and need to be precisely defined in any research project. Chapter 3 deals with this topic.

Decision 2 concerns the **PARTICIPANTS** in the study (these used to be known as **'SUBJECTS'** and you will often find this term still used in much psychological writing). For instance, what is the advantage of using the same group for each condition, as in example 1 in Box 1.1, and what is the disadvantage? Conversely, what advantage does example 2 have in using different groups ... and what problems? Further problems are encountered in comparing Mexican and Icelandic drivers. The questions concerning who to study, in what sort of groups, and how to get fair samples of people to study are covered in Chapter 4.

Decision 3 is probably the hardest, and the one that will tax you the most in studying psychological research methods. How do we know when a discovered difference is a *real* one and not just the result of random variation? For instance, when do you become convinced that women really do tend to strike matches away from their bodies whereas men tend to strike towards (as is claimed)? How do researchers convince each other that their data show real effects and not just likely random fluctuations? In the language to which you will become accustomed later in your course, is the difference *significant*? This is the subject of **INFERENTIAL STATISTICS**, which, along with **DESCRIPTIVE STATISTICS**, occupies most of the second part of this book.

> If you are keen to get on with the practical aspects of doing research then you might like to turn to Chapter 2 and carry on from there. The rest of this chapter deals with the questions of why psychologists ask questions and how they justify their scientific approach. You will certainly need to read this section eventually but, for now, your course might be structured in a way which makes it sensible to get on with nitty gritty practical matters first and to leave the heady notions of scientific method, theory and hypothesis testing until later – but don't leave it too long before reading this section!

WHY DO PSYCHOLOGISTS ASK QUESTIONS?

It would be nice if, having decided to study psychology, we could just go to a book and find out all the facts. Unfortunately, life is not so simple. Science is about comparing explanations and looking for the best ones. It is not just about collecting facts. Let me try to explain. Suppose you want some facts about baby development. You might ask 'When does a baby definitely know its mother?' Immediately I have to ask some awkward questions 'What do you mean by "know"?', for instance. I could tell you that babies appear to recognise their mother's smell after a few hours and that they will turn towards her voice after only a few days. But does this count as 'knowing' someone? For certain, by about 8–9 months we know that most infants will get very distressed if separated from their main caregiver. All this information has been gathered from testing carried out under scientific conditions. We will discuss what 'scientific' means in a minute. An important point to note straight away though, is that, just like the incessantly questioning 4-year-old, psychologists usually want to know, not so much *when do children do X* or *what Xs do children do* but *WHY do they do X*? To use a 'hard science' comparison, astronomers are of course interested in *when* heavenly bodies appear and *what* they do but they are *ultimately* interested in *why* the stars and planets move as they do. Observation of the facts of the world (retaining, for later on, some doubt about what a fact *is*) inevitably leads humans to ask why the world is as it is. If we find that heat influences aggression we shall want to know why. The step from known fact to querying why is the step towards **THEORY**. Psychological researchers, for the most part, would agree that their research should be *scientific* and that science, as Allport (1947) argued, has the aims of:

> . . . understanding, prediction and control above the levels achieved by unaided common sense.

What does Allport, or anyone, mean by 'common sense'? Aren't some things blindly obvious? Isn't it obvious that babies are born with different personalities, for instance?

> What do you make of the claim, often described as 'common sense', that: women are less logical, more suggestible and make worse drivers than men?

As it happens, research shows us that women score the same as men on logical tests in general. They are equally 'suggestible', though young boys are more likely to agree with views which they don't hold but which are held by their peer group. Statistically, women are more likely to obey traffic rules and have less expensive accidents. Why else would 'one lady owner' be a selling point? I hope you see why we need evidence to challenge 'common sense'.

WHAT IS A FACT? WHAT ARE DATA?

People often say 'just give me the facts of psychological research'. Well, all research gathers data but data are not (note the plural form) automatically facts. Take a look at Box 1.2. Both papers reported a 'fact'. When we conclude that something is a fact

Box 1.2 *Fearing or clearing the bomb?*

In psychology we constantly challenge the simplistic acceptance of facts 'in front of our eyes'. A famous bomb disposal officer, talking to Sue Lawley on *Desert Island Discs*, told of the time he was trying urgently to clear the public from the area of a live bomb. A newspaper published his picture, advancing with outstretched arms, with the caption, 'terrified member of public flees bomb', whereas another paper correctly identified him as the calm, but concerned expert he really was.

we mostly do this by interpreting data through *theory*. When we lie on the beach and 'spot a satellite' there is a big difference between the actual data before us (black background, thousands of still spots, one moving spot, etc.) and the fact (a satellite) that we report. We use, without thinking about it, our culturally acquired astronomical knowledge to go beyond the immediate data.

DATA are obtained through EMPIRICAL OBSERVATION – that is, information obtained through our senses. Facts are interpretations. So do we have to distrust all facts? Rather than despair of ever acquiring psychological truth, most researchers use some form of the *empirical method* to investigate the world consistently. This method was developed at a historically important stage in the philosophical approach to knowledge and originally had two stages:

Empirical method

1 Collection of data through our external senses with no prejudgement as to how they are ordered or what explains them.
2 Induction of patterns and relationships within the data, where 'induction' means to move from individual observation to general statements of facts or 'laws'.

Humans, though, have a sometimes annoying habit of going beyond patterns of data to ask 'But *why* does that pattern occur?' Finding out, scientifically, involves forming a theory about what causes the pattern to occur and then *testing* it. All the steps in the *full*, traditional scientific method, known as the *hypothetico-deductive approach*, are shown in Box 1.3.

Spotting patterns and testing theories

Let's look at an everyday practical example of how we might note a regular occurrence (observe data, induct pattern), form a THEORY (guess why the occurrence happens so regularly), develop a HYPOTHESIS (a specific effect which *should* exist if the theory is correct) and test that hypothesis with a research project.

Box 1.3 *Traditional scientific (or 'hypothetico-deductive') method*

1 Observation, gathering and ordering of data
2 Induction of generalisations, laws
3 Development of explanatory theories
4 Deduction of hypotheses to test theories
5 Testing of the hypotheses
6 Support or adjustment of theory

Suppose I notice that my child Jeevan keeps getting a rash. I note the occasions when this happens and come to the conclusion that it might have something to do with food additive 243 which is in the contents of a brand of orange juice he likes. How might I check out this theory?

There are several hypotheses which follow logically from the theory. *If* the culprit is additive 243, then orange juice *with* it should produce a rash, orange juice without it should not, *other* products with additive 243 should also produce a rash, keeping him free from additive 243 for one month should result in no new rashes, and so on. The logic and language of hypothesis testing in this case go as follows:

- My *theory* is that additive 243 gives Jeevan a rash
- A *hypothesis* following logically from that theory is that apple juice with additive 243 should give Jeevan a rash
- A *test* of the hypothesis would be to give Jeevan some apple juice with additive 243
- If the apple juice produces a rash my theory is supported
- If the apple juice does *not* produce a rash then the theory appears wrong

Notice that we only claim that our theory is *supported* not *proved*. It could be that the apple juice contains another factor which the orange juice also contains and which is responsible for the rashes. This would be a *confounding variable* – see Chapter 3. This can be ruled out by a further test where we give Jeevan *only* additive 243 or orange juice *without* additive 243.

It is very often the case that, where we think we have isolated a cause and an effect (for instance, that additive 243 causes a rash), the cause might well be some other factor or it can even be that the effect is actually the cause and vice versa. For instance, perhaps Jeevan only calls for this orange juice when he has a rash. This is quite unlikely but we should always consider these alternative explanations.

In psychological research, the theory that mothers talk more to young daughters (than to young sons) because girls are naturally more talkative, and the opposite theory, that girls are more talkative because their mothers talk more to them are both supported by the evidence that mothers *do* talk more to their daughters. Evidence is more useful when it supports one theory and *not* its rival. Ben Elton (1989) is onto this when he says:

Lots of Aboriginals end up as piss-heads, causing people to say 'no wonder they're so poor, half of them are piss-heads'. It would, of course, make much more sense to say 'no wonder half of them are piss-heads, they're so poor'.

Support and challenge not *proof and disproof*

From the orange juice example I hope you can see two important principles. If a theory predicts that a hypothesis should be true, and we test that hypothesis then:

1 *If a prediction from the hypothesis is confirmed then the theory is* **supported but not proven true** *(it is only shown not to be wrong)*

2 *If the prediction is disconfirmed then the theory is* **challenged** *(it's probably wrong or it needs modification)*

Suppose I now conduct several more tests using *other* foods containing additive 243 which produce a rash each time. It is often not a lot of use getting more and more of the same sort of support for your theory. If I claim that all swans are white because the sun bleaches their feathers, it gets a bit tedious if I keep pointing to each new white one saying 'I told you do'. All we need is one sun-loving black swan to blow my theory apart.

Different sorts of evidence supporting a theory do not make that theory true or 'more true'. In the same way as mounting circumstantial evidence against a suspect in a murder case can all be explained away by the defence, so mounting evidence for a theory can always be explained away by the theory's critics. The fact that orange juice *without* additive 243 does *not* produce a rash could be explained by arguing that, in this case, Jeevan drinks less of the juice or takes it down in a different way, and so on.

What is *really* damaging to a theory is *dis*proof, a finding which shows it *must* be wrong as stated. If the apple juice with additive 243 does *not* cause a rash the theory has a problem. In a similar argument to that for the black swan, if we held the theory that older people are more conformist than younger people, and then a researcher comes up with the evidence that, in certain circumstances, younger people can be more conformist than older people, then one of three explanations is possible. Either the theory is completely wrong, *or* it needs revision since it does not take account of the subtlety of differing circumstances, *or* there was something amiss in the research design – for instance these might be a specially biased sample of older and younger people. This last factor is a rationale for much of the first half of this book. We must be fairly certain our research project was sound before rushing to announce the importance of our results.

If our hypothesis is disconfirmed it is not always necessary to ditch the theory from which it was developed. If apple juice with additive 243 does *not* produce a rash perhaps something *else* in the apple juice *prevents* the rash occurring. In scientific research, theories are mostly *adjusted* to take account of new data rather than abandoned. Similarly, however, theories in science don't just get 'proven true' and they rarely rest on totally unambiguous evidence. There is often a balance in favour, with several anomalies yet to explain. Theories tend to 'survive' or not against others depending on the quality, not just the quantity, of their supporting evidence. But for every *single* supportive piece of evidence in social science there is very often an alternative explanation. It might be claimed that similarity between parent and child in intelligence is evidence for the view that intelligence is genetically transmitted. However, this evidence supports *equally* the view that children *learn* their skills from their parents, and similarity between adoptive parent and child is a *challenge* to the genetic theory.

Conventional scientific method

What has been presented so far, summarised in Box 1.3, is generally recognised as the conventional progress of scientific method. It should be noted here though that the traditional scientific method is not without its critics. Some flavour of this will be given in Chapters 2 and 8, but the interested reader might like to consult Gross (1992), Valentine (1992) or Coolican (1994).

Assuming the conventional method is being followed, research projects may take place near the beginning or the end of the steps outlined. They be *exploratory*, seeking data with which to make generalisations and create theories. Most psychological research, however, involves HYPOTHESIS TESTING. The project sets up strict conditions of measurement or experiment and gathers data which test a hypothesis that has been developed from a theory. If successful the resulting findings are fitted into a framework of explanation – that is, a theory about the causes of and reasons for human experience and behaviour. For instance, careful observation and measurement of children's early speech reveals that they produce grammar which they have not imitated and for which they do not appear to have been rewarded. Here, data concerning an existing phenomenon are taken as support for the theory that language learning is a partly innate (unlearned, 'inborn') process.

Hypothesis testing – a psychological example

Let's look at the ever-popular practical experiment in which, for one condition, participants simply repeat every word they hear in a list presented one word at a time, whilst in the second condition they try to form each item (from a different list) into a strong visual image and link it meaningfully (in a story) to the next item. After each condition participants are asked to 'free recall' (retrieve in any order) all the items in the list. Typically, the image-linking condition produces far more correct words than the rehearsal condition. This is an experiment performed to show weakness in the 'dual process' memory theory which holds that items in the short-term store get transferred to the long-term store by being *rehearsed* in the short-term memory 'buffer' (Atkinson & Shiffrin, 1968). If we can show that image-linking produces far better recall than rehearsal alone, then we have a clear challenge to the dual process theory. The theory is either wrong or requires modification. However, as a test of the alternative 'meaningful information processing' theory, the result does *not* 'prove it correct' but it provides *support*. The theory is not proven because the evidence is not absolutely conclusive. No evidence ever is. As we have seen there is always a possible alternative explanation of any set of 'facts'. For instance, in this case, people in the imagery condition may do better because the experimenter's instructions were probably a lot more interesting. Often, such counter arguments seem pendantic. One can say 'Oh it's *obvious* what was going on here.' But this is the stuff of scientific research – it was once *obvious* that the world was flat or that humans (as my father vehemently used to assure me) could not possibly escape the Earth's gravitational pull in a rocket. An extremely important skill to acquire in studying psychology (not just research methods) is the ability to ask 'Ah, but could something *else* explain the results here?'. More of this throughout the book.

What exactly is a hypothesis then?

A hypothesis is a special statement about the world which follows logically from a general theory. We have seen some examples already. A hypothesis must be very precisely stated otherwise it would be hard to see how we can test it. For instance, if I claimed that Helen had psychic powers you would expect me to support my theoretical claim with an exact demonstration. I might claim that she can guess, at better than a chance level, the identity of cards which you hold in your hand. To test this hypothesis precisely we would record her guesses and see whether her responses are *significantly* better than what would occur with mere guessing. Similarly, the memory theory is tested with the hypothesis that image-linking produces more words recalled than does rehearsal and the exact prediction that, if tested, any such difference will be significant. It is important, in practical reports, to state your hypothesis *precisely*. There is an exercise in this on page 227. Note for now, however, that we do *not* include the aim or theory:

1 **Vague hypothesis: (includes theory)**	'People will do better with the imagery words because they need to make information meaningful before storing it.'
2 **Precise hypothesis:**	'More words are recalled correctly with image linking than with rehearsal.'
3 **Expectation from test of hypothesis:**	'There will be a significant difference between the mean number of words correctly recalled in the image-linking condition and the mean number of words recalled in the rehearsal condition.'

Depending on context, researchers either give their general hypothesis to be tested or state what outcome will *support* their hypothesis. In either case, notice that the *exact* means of measuring the outcome is stated. This emphasis on precise definition of what is meant by a term is known as *operationalising* a variable and is dealt with in Chapter 3.

THE NULL HYPOTHESIS – if you are sceptical about psychic powers you may well claim that Helen was just lucky, when she performs at a little better than chance level in guessing the identity of hidden playing cards. You would say that, over very many trials, she would only operate at a chance level. This is, in fact, pretty well what the null hypothesis is all about. It is the view that no actual difference exists in reality between, say, two groups or two conditions. For instance it would be the view that people recall the same number of words, overall, when they use image-linking as they do when using rehearsal. What social scientists usually want to do in their research is to *reject the null hypothesis* and show that their results were highly unlikely to occur *if the null hypothesis is true*. In this way they provide support for their **ALTERNATIVE HYPOTHESIS** – what they want to establish as true.

The reasoning is similar to what would occur if you bought a box of matches and found only 36 inside when across the box it clearly states 'average contents 40'. The shopkeeper, were you to complain, would almost certainly say something like 'Well Guv, it says *average*. Across *all* the boxes it's true, honest – the *average* content is 40. You got 36. That often happens; other people get 44. It's all luck!'. The shopkeeper is saying that yours was a mere random selection from among all boxes. You might disagree if you got only 27 (or if you got 36 four times in succession!). You would want to *reject the null hypothesis* that the boxes average 40. As we shall see in Chapter 10, if the probability of drawing a box of 27 matches at random from a set with an average of 40 is very low, you would be justified in rejecting the null hypothesis. You could claim that a *significant* variation from 40 has occurred. This would support the *alternative hypothesis* that the matches are from a group with a mean less than 40. If the probability is quite high that your matches came from a group with a mean of 40 (e.g. you got 37) then we would *retain the null hypothesis* and just shrug our shoulders and accept some rotten luck.

In the memory experiment example, then, the null hypothesis would be that the mean number of words recalled under image-linking and under rehearsal are equal. Our hypothesis test (the experiment) tries to reject this view by showing that, *if the null hypothesis is* true, then the probability of obtaining the difference between means which we have obtained is fairly low (i.e. getting the difference we did was quite unlikely by chance alone). Ways of working out this probability are the content of Section 4 of this book, and we shall return to the topics of hypothesis testing and significance, fundamental to most psychological research, in Chapter 10.

If our two means are not far enough apart we will have to *retain the null hypothesis*. Holding onto the null hypothesis is rather like being innocent until proven guilty. There's usually *some* sort of evidence against an accused person but if it isn't strong enough we stick, however uncomfortably, to the innocent view. This doesn't mean that researchers give up very easily. They talk of 'retaining' or just 'not rejecting' the null hypothesis. The null hypothesis is not automatically treated as 'true' after a failure to reject it because differences weren't large enough. Have a look at the way we might use the logic of the null hypothesis in everyday life, as described in Box 1.4.

Box 1.4 *The null hypothesis – the truth standing on its head*

Everyday thinking	**Formal research thinking**
Women just don't have a chance of management promotion in this place. In the last four interviews they picked a male each time out of a shortlist of two females and two males	Hypothesis of interest: more males get selected for management. Underlying theory: selectors biased towards males
Really? Let's see, how many males *should* they have selected if you're wrong?	Construct null hypothesis – what would happen if our theory is *not* true?
How do you mean?	
Well, there were the same number of female as male candidates each time, so there should have been just as many females as males selected in all. That's two!	Express the null hypothesis statistically. Very often this is that the difference between the two sets of scores is really zero. Here, it is that the difference between females and males selected will be zero
Oh yeah! That's what I meant to start with. There should have been at *least* two new women managers from that round of selection	Note: if there had been three female candidates and only one male each time, the null hypothesis would predict three females selected in all
Well *just* two unless we're compensating for past male advantage! Now is none out of four different *enough* from two out of four to give us hard evidence of real selection bias?	Conduct a statistical test to assess the probability that the actual figures would differ as much as they do from what the null hypothesis predicts

How do psychologists conduct research and get their results published?

The whole process is outlined in Figure 1.1. Notice that actually *running* an experiment or survey is often a small part of the whole 'research cycle'.

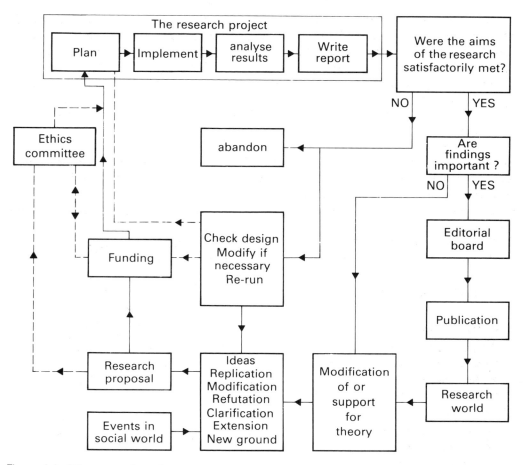

Figure 1.1 *The research cycle*

Psychologists develop projects from a combination of the current trends in research thinking (theory) and methods, other challenging past theories and, within psychology at least, from important events in the everyday social world. The investigator might wish to replicate (repeat) a study by someone else in order to verify it. Or they might wish to extend it to other areas, or to modify it because it has weaknesses. Every now and again an investigation breaks completely new ground but the vast majority develop out of the current state of play.

Politics and economics enter at the stage of funding. Research staff, in universities, colleges or hospitals, have to justify their salaries and the expense of the project. Funds will come from one of the following: university, college or hospital research funds; central or local government; private companies; charitable institutions; and the odd private benefactor. These, and the investigator's direct employers, will need to be satisfied that the research is worthwhile to them, to society or to the general pool of scientific knowledge, and that it is ethically sound.

The actual testing or 'running' of the project may take very little time compared with all the planning and preparation along with the analysis of results and report-writing. The report will be published in a research journal if successful. This term 'successful' is difficult to define here. It doesn't always mean that original aims have been entirely met. Surprises occurring during the research may well make it important, though usually such surprises would lead the investigator to rethink, replan and run again on the basis of the new insights. As we saw above, failure to confirm one's hypothesis can be an important source of information. What matters overall, is that the research results are an important or useful contribution to current knowledge and theory development. This importance will be decided by the editorial board of an academic journal (such as the *British Journal of Psychology*) who will have the report reviewed, usually by experts 'blind' as to the identity of the investigator.

Theory will then be adjusted in the light of this research result. Some academics may argue that the design was so different from previous research that its challenge to their theory can be ignored. Others will wish to query the results and may ask the investigator to provide 'raw data' – the whole of the originally recorded data, unprocessed. Some will want to replicate the study, some to modify . . . and here we are, back where we started on the research cycle.

GLOSSARY

At the end of each chapter in this book there is a set of definitions for terms introduced. If you want to use this as a self-test, cover up the right-hand column. You can then write in your guess as to the term being defined or simply check after you read each one. Heavy white lines enclose a set of similar terms, as with hypotheses, below. If a key term in the chapter does not appear here then consult the index. You'll find the glossary entry on the page number which is printed in bold type.

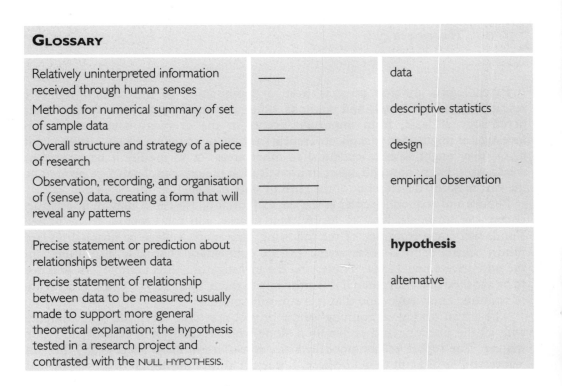

GLOSSARY

Relatively uninterpreted information received through human senses	_____	data
Methods for numerical summary of set of sample data	_____ _____	descriptive statistics
Overall structure and strategy of a piece of research	_____	design
Observation, recording, and organisation of (sense) data, creating a form that will reveal any patterns	_____ _____	empirical observation
Precise statement or prediction about relationships between data	_____	**hypothesis**
Precise statement of relationship between data to be measured; usually made to support more general theoretical explanation; the hypothesis tested in a research project and contrasted with the NULL HYPOTHESIS.	_____	alternative

Statement that data do not vary in the way predicted in the alternative hypothesis. Very often, the statement that population differences or correlations are zero.	_____	null
Activity of checking our predictions from theory and hypotheses with supporting or contradictory data	_____	testing
Methods for assessing the probability of chance occurrence of certain data differences or relationships	_____ _____	inferential statistics
People taking part in a research study	_____	participants
Trying out a prototype of a study or questionnaire on a small sample in order to discover snags or errors in design or to develop workable measuring instrument	_____ _____ _____	piloting; pilot trials
Overall structure of study including general method adopted, composition and type of groups and so on	_____ _____	research design
Method used to verify truth or falsity of theoretical explanations of why events occur	_____ _____	scientific method
Older term for 'participants'	_____	subjects
Proposed explanation of observable events	_____	theory
Phenomenon (thing in the world) which goes through changes	_____	variable

DESIGNS – EXPERIMENTS AND NON-EXPERIMENTAL DESIGNS IN PSYCHOLOGY

Experimental and non-experimental designs

Look back to the possible designs for testing the heat–aggression hypothesis in Box 1.1. Some of these studies (if they were tightened up a bit) would count as experiments. Can you decide which would count and which wouldn't?

Examples 1 and 2 could certainly be experiments as long as people were allocated randomly to groups in example 2. Examples 3 and 4 could be experiments but there are certain reservations. Examples 5, 6 and 7 are certainly *not* experiments. I hope the following description of experiments and non-experiments will help you see why.

The logic of the experiment is one of the most powerful methods at the disposal of the human mind in order to get at the truth about causes of events. We often experiment in everyday life just to sort out practical problems. If your television produces interference it makes sense to turn off each electric appliance in turn, *keeping all the others on*, until the interference stops, in order to identify the offending item. But any old study is not an experiment (see Box 2.1). **INVESTIGATION** is the general term for any study which seeks information (usually to test a hypothesis), experimental or not. An **EXPERIMENT** is a study in which:

> All possible causes of variation in the effect being measured are eliminated
> except the one influence under investigation.

An influence might be heat, for example and the object of the research is its effect on length of a certain metal. In this case we should keep all other possible influences on expansion constant – the room temperature, air pressure, draughts, and so on. I hope the following example from common-sense biology will help with understanding this distinction between experiments and other studies.

Imagine yourself out for a walk one day with your friend Sharon. She points out that the sykik flowers are taller where they receive more light from the sun. The ones nearer the tree trunks, and therefore in the shade, are a lot shorter. Sharon's

Box 2.1 *Common errors in defining an experiment*

The following points are often made when people are asked to define 'an experiment'.

The points below are *not* reasons for calling a study an 'experiment'

Point	Not a good reason because
It tests a hypothesis	so do non-experimental research designs
It is conducted in a laboratory	studies in laboratories are not always experiments and studies *outside* the laboratory (field studies) can also be experiments
It controls measures (or 'variables')	all scientific studies should use some control over as many variables as possible; a study is an experiment only when the independent variable is controlled
It uses impressive technical equipment	so do non-experiments

explanation is that the flowers are affected by light and grow taller because of it. 'Janice', you say (you never can get her name right), 'we were talking about confounding variables (see Chapter 3) in psychology yesterday and you know what? It may seem obvious that light makes the sykik flowers grow taller but think a minute. It *could* be that the ones under the trees grow smaller because of some chemical produced by the tree roots, *or* because those squirrels are up and down the trees all day long and you can guess what *they* drop on the flowers.'

What would you do *exactly* to check that it can only be the *light* that is responsible for the height differences in these flowers?

Most people quite quickly devise a classic example of the true experiment. You probably had this idea: take two trays of sykik seeds. Use identical soil and place both in identical conditions (heat, humidity, etc.) except that one tray gets a good deal more light than the other.

THE EXACT NATURE OF EXPERIMENTS

If you got this as your answer then you understand the basic nature of an experiment. There are two important features which are really two sides of the same coin. In an experiment:

1 Only the **INDEPENDENT VARIABLE** (IV) is manipulated or changed in value.

2 All other variables are held constant.

Earlier, what I called an 'influence' is the independent variable (heat). The thing that it influences or has an effect on (length of metal) is known as a *dependent variable* (DV). We shall have more to say about the IV and DV in the following chapter on variables. If there is a change in the DV as a result of the experiment (the manipulation of the IV) we can be fairly confident that we have isolated a cause–effect relationship – the IV has caused the DV to change. In the flower example, we would expect the light/no light variable (IV) to produce differences in flower height (DV). Nothing else can have done this because everything else was prevented from varying. If everything else is *not* prevented from varying there could be trouble in interpreting results. Imagine, on a hot day, you take your car to the garage with a problem. 'Hmm. That's probably your exomonater playing up', they say, and proceed to fix it, for an exorbitant sum, on the following day, which happens to be quite cool. The 'experiment' has worked; your car runs nicely. However, next time it's fairly warm the same old problem returns. 'Hmm . . .' says the mechanic.

If we *don't* hold every other variable constant then something *other than* the IV could be responsible for any changes observed. Of course, in psychology experiments, unlike biological or physical ones, things are never quite so clear-cut, because people, and all their complications, are involved, but the *logic* of the experiment in psychology is exactly the same as elsewhere. At the simplest level we have an *experimental group* who receive a 'treatment' (say, a hot room) and a *control group* who do *not* receive the treatment (they work in a normally heated room). The change in heating is the *independent variable*. We measure aggression as an *outcome* or *effect* of the independent variable. This outcome measure is the *dependent variable*. It is defined and measured very precisely – participants' responses to a questionnaire; force with which participants hit a 'frustration pad'; number of times participants swear or shout per minute. Variables are further discussed in Chapter 3 and experimental and other groups in Chapter 4.

STANDARDISED PROCEDURE

Holding everything else constant includes each experimenter following a STANDAR-DISED PROCEDURE. In experiments, as in most other investigative research, we would expect researchers to follow a common and very well defined ('standardised') procedure. There are several reasons for requiring an identical procedure to be followed with every participant.

We want to keep unwanted variance in participants' performance to a minimum: if participants are treated at all differently then it's highly likely that their performances will also vary as a result. When conducting student practicals it is quite difficult to run an identical procedure with your dad at tea time and with your boy/girlfriend later that same evening. Paid researchers have to do better but it is still likely that, in some studies, features of the researcher, such as accent, dress, looks, or uncontrolled features of the local testing environment will produce some unwanted variation in participants' performances. If these performances vary a lot, within a group, this increases a statistic known as VARIANCE, which we will encounter in Chapter 10. This, in turn, makes it more difficult to demonstrate that this group differed from another.

On the other hand, if one group is treated differently from another, either because two different researchers were involved or because the researcher behaved differently with all of one group, then we might produce an artificial effect – 'experimenter bias' – see below.

We want our study to be replicable: good scientific procedure includes the possibility of REPLICATION of any study performed.

If you tell me you have shown that, with special training, anyone can be trained to telepathise, I should want to see your evidence and experience the phenomenon for myself. It's not that I don't trust you, but we need others to check our wilder claims or to look coolly at processes which, because we are so excited about them, we are failing to analyse closely enough. I may discover an alternative explanation of what is happening or point out a flaw in your procedure. In the interests of replication, then, it is essential that I can follow your procedure exactly.

This is why you'll find that tutors, along with being strict about your definition of variables, will be equally concerned that you record every essential detail of your procedure and the order in which you carried it out. They're not being pernickety. They're encouraging you to communicate effectively and arming you with skills that will help you to defend your project against critics.

Even with standardised procedures laid down, experimenters do not always follow them, possibly because they do not recognise the experiment as a social situation in which people (experimenter and participant) *interact*. For instance, if the participant is female, male experimenters are more likely to use her name, smile and look directly at her than a female experimenter would, or than they would do if the participant was male.

Standardised procedures and qualitative research

As we shall see in Chapter 7, there are psychological research methods for which the requirement of a rigid standardised procedure would stifle the kind of relationship sought with the people the researcher studies or works with. Such methods tend to sacrifice aspects of a tight design in favour of richer and more realistic data.

RANDOM ALLOCATION OF PARTICIPANTS TO CONDITIONS

One important feature of point 2, (page 17) – holding all other variables constant – requires special mention. How can we be sure that the two trays held an identical set of seeds? If, for instance, we took our first handful from the top of a packet, put them in the first tray and placed the remainder in the other tray, perhaps we'd be putting older or more squashed seeds in one of the trays. For this reason, it is important to RANDOMLY ALLOCATE items to conditions. In psychology, this means allocating people at *random* to any conditions. Chapter 4 will deal with random methods in more detail. For now note that random allocation does *not* mean 'selecting any old how'. 'Random' has a specific meaning and there are particular methods for selecting at random. In a simple two-condition psychology experiment it means, precisely, that *every participant has an equal chance of being in either the experimental or control group.*

QUASI-EXPERIMENTS

Random allocation of participants to conditions is a way to ensure that any differences we find between two groups in an experiment is not caused by *pre-existing* differences between those groups. Sometimes it just is not possible to have control over who goes into which condition of an experiment. For instance, this might occur where, say, a training method is to be used in an organisation where it is not practical or permitted to allocate workers at random to the training condition. Here it might be that the researcher, at best, could submit one group (say the day shift or one department) to the training scheme and treat another shift or department as the control (or 'untreated') group. This sort of design would be called a QUASI-EXPERIMENT. In most respects it is an experiment, but the researcher cannot randomly allocate participants to groups. Unfortunately it does mean that any difference found could be the result of pre-existing differences between the two groups. It is often the case that students are forced to use one group (often a school or college class) for one condition of an experiment and another group for the other. This should be permissible as an experiment for a classwork report, bearing in mind that we should still try to control any other obvious interfering variables if possible or at least recognise their potential *confounding* effects (see page 49).

The fundamental point of quasi-experimental thinking is that we should be able to *analyse design and results in terms of cause and effect.* We should be able to indicate in the discussion of our study just where our design has weaknesses, where we did not have control and, therefore, how limited we are in assuming that our independent variable *really did* affect our dependent variable. We should be able to point out possible differences between our groups, and differences in their experiences, which might be responsible for any differences in the dependent variable which we identify, making it difficult to attribute these differences *solely* to the change in the independent variable. For a thorough review of quasi-experimental thinking see Cook and Campbell (1979).

Natural experiments

The writers just mentioned include as quasi-experiments some occasions where the researcher also does not manipulate the independent variable. An example might be a 'natural experiment' where we can assess the effects of a new reading programme in a school by comparing the group receiving it with a group still on the traditional method. Here it might be the case that the pupil groups experience other differences between the conditions apart from just the variation in the independent variable (the two groups might have different teachers, different classrooms and so on). In addition, there is no random allocation to groups. Examples of natural experiments which have been analysed as quasi-experiments are:

- changes in the regime of one psychiatric ward from nurses as carers and guards to nurses as guides and trainers and patients as autonomous beings
- the introduction of the Breathalyser and its effect on drink-driving behaviour
- educational intervention programmes and their effects on disadvantaged children

Conditions of quasi-experiments

Quasi-experiments, then, involve a *'treatment'* (a manipulated or 'natural' independent variable), a *dependent variable* (a measured result or outcome) and *people*. The people, however, *are not randomly allocated to conditions.* By 'treatment' is meant a specific event assumed to affect the people. This is why studies looking for a difference between males and females, or introverts and extroverts, do not usually count even as quasi-experiments, since there is no identifiable occasion on which the people suddenly got treated differently. These studies are simply group comparisons. Here, Cook and Campbell (1979) talk of 'passive observation' whilst Robson (1993) talks of 'retrospective studies' under the heading of 'passive experimentation', though he is very wary of the term 'experiment' at all in this context. The reader would do best to concentrate on all the variables which may affect say, males and females, or high-anxiety and low-anxiety people, and recognise that any difference between the two groups on some test variable can hardly be attributed to some global independent variable called 'anxiety', 'sex' or even 'gender'. The differences may be caused by *some* variables which are associated with *some* males and females or *some* types of anxiety. The retrospective or *'ex post facto'* testing of two existing groups on one variable seems to lack just about all the basic features of a true experiment.

Commonly used terms

Experiments	Non-experiments
Laboratory experiment	Correlational study
Field experiment	Observational study
Quasi-experiment	Survey
Natural experiment	Interview
	Case-study

THE LABORATORY

Most studies carried out in laboratories are experiments, but not all. It is possible to bring children into a laboratory simply to observe their behaviour in a play setting without subjecting them to any changes in an independent variable.

Control

If an aim of the experiment is to reduce relevant extraneous variables by strict control then this is best achieved in a laboratory setting, particularly where highly accurate recordings of human cognitive functions (such as memory, perception, selective attention) are required. The IV and DV can be very precisely defined and accurately measured.

Bandura's (1965) research used controlled observation to record amounts and types of aggression shown by children after they had watched an adult model being rewarded, unrewarded or punished for aggression. These three conditions represent the strictly controlled IV of an experimental design. Each child was observed in an identical play setting with an identical (now notorious) Bobo doll.

Consider the difference between this experimental setting and the 'field' setting of raters observing the aggressive behaviour of children in a school playground. In the playground, children may move off, be obscured by others or simply lack energy in cold weather. They may wish to play with the observer if he or she isn't hidden.

Bandura had strict control over timing, position and analysis of filmed records of behaviour.

Artificial conditions

In physical science it is often necessary to study phenomena under completely artificial and controlled conditions in order to eliminate confounding variables. Only in this way would we know that feathers obey gravity in exactly the same way as lead. Critics of the laboratory method in psychology however, argue that behaviour studied out of context in an artificial setting is meaningless, as we shall see below.

Later on we shall discuss various criticisms of the experiment as a research method. Here we shall list some related criticisms of the laboratory as a research focus.

CRITICISMS OF THE LABORATORY AS RESEARCH LOCATION

1 *Narrowness of the IV and DV.* The aggression measured in Bandura's experiments is a very narrow range of what children are capable of in the way of destructive or hostile behaviour. Bandura might argue that at least this fraction of aggressive

behaviour, we are now aware, could be modelled. However, Heather (1976) has
argued persuasively:

> Psychologists have attempted to squeeze the study of human life into a
> laboratory situation where it becomes unrecognisably different from its
> naturally occurring form.

2 *Inability to generalise* (lack of ecological validity – see below). A reliable effect in
the laboratory may have little relationship to life outside it. The concept of an
'iconic memory' or very short-term 'visual information store', holding 'raw'
sensory data from which we rapidly process information, has been considered by
later psychologists to be an artifact of the particular experiments which produced
evidence for it.

   Certainly there is a lot less faith now in the idea that experiments on rats or
chimpanzees can tell us a lot about complex human behaviour.

3 *Artificiality.* A laboratory is an intimidating, possibly even frightening place.
People may well be unduly meek and overimpressed by their surroundings. If the
experimenter compounds this feeling by sticking rigidly to a standardised
procedure, reciting a formal set of instructions without normal interactive
gestures such as smiles and helpful comments, a participant is hardly likely to feel
'at home' and behave in an everyday manner.

SOME DEFENCE

In defence of the laboratory it can be said that:

1 In the study of brain processes, or of human performance, stimulus detection,
and so on, not only does the artificiality of the laboratory hardly matter, it may be
the only place where highly technical and accurate measurements can be made.
   If we study human vigilance in detecting targets, for instance, does it matter
whether this is done in the technical and artificial surroundings of a laboratory or
the equally technical and artificial environment of a radar monitoring centre
where research results will be usefully applied? If we wish to discover how fine
new-born babies' perceptual discriminations are, this can be done with special
equipment and the control of a laboratory. The infant, at 2 weeks, is hardly likely
to know or care whether it is at home or not.

2 Physicists would not have been able to split atoms in the natural environment,
and only in a vacuum apparatus could we know that feathers obey gravity just as
lead does. Psychologists have discovered effects in the laboratory which, as well
as being interesting in themselves, have produced practical applications. Without
the laboratory we would be unaware of differences in hemispheric function, the
phenomena of perceptual defence, or the extreme levels of obedience to authority
which are possible even in the absence of any threat. In each case, the appropriate
interpretation of results has been much debated but the phenomena themselves
have been valuable in terms of human insight and further research.

3 Research conducted under laboratory conditions is generally far easier to *replicate*,
a feature valued very highly by advocates of the experimental method.

4 Some effects must surely be *stronger* outside the laboratory, not just artificially
created within it. For instance, in Milgram's famous obedience study (see
Chapter 16) participants were free to leave at any time yet, in real life, there are
often immense social pressures and possibly painful sanctions to suffer if one

disobeys on principle. So Milgram's obedience effects could be expected to operate even more strongly in real life than he dramatically illustrated in his laboratory.

FIELD EXPERIMENTS

The obvious alternative to the laboratory experiment is to conduct one's research 'in the field'. A field experiment is a study carried out in the natural environment of those studied, perhaps the school, hospital, or street, whilst the IV is still manipulated by the experimenter. Other variables may well be tightly controlled but, in general, the experimenter cannot maintain the high level of control associated with the laboratory. It used to be thought that the laboratory should be the starting point for investigating behaviour patterns and IV–DV links. The effects of such studies could then be tried out in 'the field'. The comparison was with the physicist harnessing electricity in the laboratory and putting it to work for human benefit in the community. In the last few decades, many psychologists have become disaffected with the laboratory as solely appropriate for psychological research and have concentrated more on 'field' results in their own right.

Two examples of field experiments are:

1 An elegant design by Friedrich and Stein (1973) involved observation of nursery schoolchildren to obtain a baseline for cooperative, helpful, and friendly behaviour for each child. Children were then randomly assigned to two groups. Over a month, at regular intervals, one group watched 'pro-social' television programmes whilst the other (control) group watched neutral films of circuses and farm activity. The children were observed again at the end of the period and there was a significant rise in cooperativeness and peer-directed affection for the experimental group.

2 Ganster et al. (1982) randomly allocated 79 public service employees to a treatment group and a control group. The 'treatment' involved stress management training sessions and, at the end, this group showed relatively lower levels of adrenaline secretion, depression and anxiety. The effects, though small, were still present some four months later. The control group later received the same training.

Notice the random allocation to 'treatment' or control groups in both these field experiments. Notice also the difficulty of controlling other variables, such as who talks to whom while the experiment is in progress.

ADVANTAGES AND DISADVANTAGES OF THE FIELD EXPERIMENT

By studying effects in the natural environment, the field experiment avoids the criticism that results can't be generalised to real situations, though of course, one may not be able to generalise to real situations markedly unlike this particular field setting. The field experiment, therefore, is likely to have higher ecological validity, though control, and therefore, 'internal validity', is generally lower (see below).

In many cases, participants are unaware of being involved in an experiment until effects have been recorded. The extent to which they are aware of the aims of the experiment determines the extent to which it may be queried for bias from participants and the effects of 'demand characteristics' (see below). Still, even with some distortion through this awareness, it will not involve the apprehension and artificiality of the laboratory.

The field experiment may be more expensive and time consuming than a laboratory experiment. The researcher may require skills of tact and persuasion, not needed in the laboratory, in dealing with those who need convincing that the research is necessary, and in arranging details of the design which will ensure valid results whilst retaining cooperation with personnel such as the teacher or hospital worker.

The major disadvantage, however, is in the lack of control which the investigator can exert over extraneous variables, over strict manipulation of the IV and over careful, accurate measurement of the DV. All these are vulnerable to far more fluctuation in the field setting than in a laboratory.

Table 2.1 compares laboratory and field experiments.

Table 2.1 *Comparison of laboratory and field experiments*

Field experiment	COMPARISON POINT	Laboratory experiment
Natural	Environment	Artificial
Controlled	Independent variable	Controlled
Random	Allocation of participants to conditions	Random
Participants *may* be unaware of study (if so, can't guess design, try to look good, etc.)	Awareness of aims by participants	Participants (except very young children) must be aware of being in experiment (though *not* what the design really is)
Weaker	Control of extraneous variables	Tighter
Higher	Realism	Lower
Harder	Replication	Easier
Usually higher	Expense & time	Usually lower
To real-life field setting – good. To *other* real-life settings – probably weaker	Generalisation (ecological validity)	To real life – often very weak
Perhaps can't be brought to field situation	Equipment	Can be complex and only usable in the laboratory
OTHER DISADVANTAGES		
More confounding possible because of researcher's need to negotiate with field setting personnel and managers		Narrow IV and DV → low construct validity
		Setting more likely to create apprehension, wariness of strange surroundings, etc.

NON-EXPERIMENTAL INVESTIGATIONS

Not fully understanding scientific method, imagine that Sharon says 'I'll *prove* I'm right! Let's look at another wood where sykik flowers grow'. You do this and, sure enough, the sykik flowers are again taller in the sun than under the trees. Unfortunately, though, all the other variables could *still* be affecting the flowers' growth. This is similar to the situation in many psychological investigations. We find already existing groups and we measure something about them, by test, observation, interview, or even by very technical-looking equipment. Imagine a laboratory where extroverts and introverts are tested for perceptual recognition speed and heart rate fluctuation by some very impressive-looking machinery. If we're looking for differences between introvert and extrovert groups, this *still* isn't an experiment. The fact is that the *independent variable* (personality type) is *not* being manipulated. The participants were extroverted or introverted before they came in. We identify flowers in two positions and measure the differences in height between them. We identify a group of introverts and a group of extroverts and measure differences between them. This is a non-experimental investigation. We could, of course, try to eliminate the squirrel *and* tree-root hypothesis by finding sykik flowers in the shade but not under trees. However, this still leaves several other variables uncontrolled and we can't so easily demonstrate a cause–effect relationship.

A particular problem with non-experimental studies concerns demonstrating the *direction* of cause. As we have not held control over an independent variable we cannot therefore be sure whether one of our variables affects the other or whether the relationship is the other way around. For instance, suppose we investigate a proposed theory that watching violent television causes children to be more aggressive. Suppose we observe higher levels of aggression among children who choose and watch more violent television programmes. Does the television promote their aggression or were they initially more aggressive, therefore tending to choose more violent programmes? We need to manipulate TV violence in an experiment.

CORRELATIONAL STUDIES (AND FIELD STUDIES)

This term is often used for studies where two aspects of people are measured, not in an experiment (but possibly in a 'laboratory'), and are related. For instance, we might measure people's level of depression and also their feeling of control over their lives, predicting that these two measures would CORRELATE (see Chapter 12), i.e. go together – the more depressed people are, the less control they might feel they exert over their lives. The trouble with this term is that correlation, as a statistical technique, *could* be used in an experiment. However, if it is used as a term for an *overall design* (as it usually is), the study is *non-experimental* and just investigates whether people high or low on one measure also tend to be correspondingly high or low on a second measure. A *field study* is any research conducted outside a laboratory and, if non-experimental, may well be called 'correlational' if it somehow compares groups and variables.

OBSERVATIONAL STUDIES

Like correlational studies, this term can be misleading. Bandura (as described above; see page 21) used observation as a *technique* in an experimental setting. However, when used to describe an *overall design* this refers to a *non-experimental* study where measures are made by observation only without control of an IV. An example would be a field study in which observers simply rate children for co-operation in a school playground (observation is dealt with in Chapter 5).

INTERVIEWS, SURVEYS, AND CASE-STUDIES

These methods concentrate mainly on the *questioning* of participants. They are dealt with in detail in Chapters 6 and 7. As with correlational or observational studies, interpretation of data from these studies can suffer the weakness that cause and effect cannot be determined. However, in *quasi-experimental* studies they *can* be used to interpret a relationship in terms of cause and effect by eliminating possible *alternative reasons* for the relationship. For instance, suppose the children observed for co-operation, mentioned above, included two groups, one undergoing an experimental teaching programme the other serving as controls. Interviews might help rule out the possibility that the children have discovered co-operation is a key variable or that the two groups differ in home encouragement of co-operation.

Experimental designs

In Chapter 1, I asked you to consider the advantages and disadvantages of examples 1 and 2 in Box 1.1 as research designs. Try that exercise again now (or for the first time!). What is a good idea about having the same people perform *both* conditions in an experiment and what problems does this create? Likewise, what if you use separate groups of people for each condition?

REPEATED MEASURES DESIGN

The design in example 1 is a REPEATED MEASURES design. We use *one* group of people and test them in *both* of our two experimental conditions – hot room and cool room – keeping all other conditions the same. We *repeat* the measure on the people under two values of the IV – hot and cool. We don't compare a 'hot' group with a 'cold' group.

RELATED DESIGNS

The repeated measures design is one of a set known as RELATED DESIGNS – (Table 2.2) – 'related' because, when results are presented, a value in one condition is directly related to a value in the other condition.

What we do in the repeated measures design is to answer the possible criticism that any difference found is caused by differences between the people in our two groups. Instead of a control group to compare experimental results with, we use the same people as their own control, so any differences between conditions *can't* be because the people in conditions were different from one another.

Table 2.2 *Related and unrelated designs*

	In each condition	
Design	**Same people**	**Different people**
Related	Repeated measures	Matched pairs
Unrelated	Single participant	Independent samples

ORDER EFFECTS – A PROBLEM WITH THE REPEATED MEASURES DESIGN

Suppose we found people *were* more aggressive in the hotter room. Why might this be? Because of the heat . . . or because they're getting fed up with the experiment? They might be getting rather tired of arguing in rooms that change in temperature! In general, in repeated measures designs, we have the problem that people may improve through practice, or worsen through boredom or fatigue, in their second condition. This is known as an ORDER EFFECT and it can *confound* (see Chapter 3) any effect we are looking for.

Can you make a list now of some solutions to this problem? How can a researcher design an experiment which avoids the contamination of order effects?

Dealing with order effects

COUNTERBALANCING – If all participants' performances in the hot room are worse because they are tired after the cool room, it makes sense to have half of them perform in the hot room *first* so that tiredness will also affect half the cool room scores. This is known as COUNTERBALANCING the conditions. Would this in fact *eliminate* the order effect? Well, no it wouldn't. Tiredness, if it is effective, will still produce aggression but this will affect only half the scores in the hot room and half in the cool room. Hence, the changes should cancel each other out overall.

In order to counterbalance we must split all our participants into two groups (at random of course) so that one group takes conditions in the order AB (condition A followed by condition B) and the other group perform in the order BA. This gives rise to a warning for tests and exams! If you are told that participants were divided into two groups, it's easy to assume, immediately that the design must be *independent samples* (see below). However, the splitting may only be for the purpose of counterbalancing. If so, we still have, in the end, pairs of related results – one pair from each participant taking both conditions.

Asymmetrical order effects

This neat arrangement of counterbalancing may be upset if the tiredness effect occurring in the AB (cool–hot) order is not equivalent to that produced in the BA order. For instance, people may become quite aggressive when fatigued *and* hot. Switching from hot-but-fresh to cool-but-a-bit-tired, on the other hand, may produce no complementary *decrease* in aggression. Counterbalancing now loses its evening-out effect and we have an artificial effect, a 'constant error' (see Chapter 3), of fatigue increasing aggression in the hot condition only for half the participants. 'Asymmetrical' just means 'not symmetrical' – the effect is not evenly balanced between the two groups.

RANDOMISATION OF STIMULUS ITEMS – This is an elegant way to deal with possible order effects in a two-condition experiment. Suppose we want to see whether concrete words are easier to recall than abstract words. Instead of giving the same group of people a list of concrete words to learn and recall, *then* a list of abstract words, we can give them *one* list with concrete and abstract words mixed randomly together.

ELAPSED TIME – We can leave enough time between conditions for any order effects to dissipate, the problem here being that we may 'lose' several participants between conditions.

Changing the design

If none of these solutions is possible we might have to change to a different type of design – 'independent samples' or 'matched pairs'. The following list gives conditions under which a repeated measures design would either be not advisable or not possible:

1 When order effects cannot be eliminated or are asymmetrical.

2 When testing differences between males and females, extroverts and introverts, and so on, in which case we *must* have two groups!

3 We may need people to be 'naive' in each condition. In 'vignette' studies, for example, participants are shown one of two alternatives, with all other material kept the same. The alternatives are the independent variable. For example, a person committing a crime might be described identically except for race, and participants hearing the descriptions might be asked to choose an appropriate sentence. This often results in a 'black criminal' receiving a significantly longer sentence than a 'white criminal'. Obviously, in such studies, participants cannot serve in both conditions.

4 A *control group* may be essential. For instance, if we pre-test a group of children, give them a programme designed to increase awareness of the needs of people with disabilities, test again and look for improvement, we need a baseline measure from another 'untreated' group in order to rule out the possibility that the children might have changed during the treatment period *without* the programme.

INDEPENDENT SAMPLES DESIGN

Suppose we follow the design in example 2, Box 1.1 – we use a different group of people for each of the two rooms – hot and cool. This will avoid the possibility that the people became more aggressive because they were more fatigued. We are now conducting what is known as an INDEPENDENT SAMPLES design experiment. An entirely different group of people participate in each condition. This kind of experiment belongs to the category of UNRELATED DESIGNS mentioned in Table 2.2 The score of any participant in one group is entirely unrelated to any score in the other group. Other names for this design are: INDEPENDENT GROUPS, INDEPENDENT SUBJECTS, and BETWEEN GROUPS.

Let's suppose we use a psychology A-level class for the hot-room condition, and a class of nursery nurse students for the cool room condition. The cool-room group turns out to be *much* less aggressive. What problems can you see in accepting this result as supporting the view that heat makes people more aggressive?

Of course, of course! Obviously the difference might arise *not* because of the variation in heat but because of the differences between people. The nursery nurses are training to *care*. We might expect them to keep 'cooler' in a tense situation.

PARTICIPANT (OR SUBJECT) VARIABLES AND HOW TO DEAL WITH THEM

This problem of expected differences coming *not* from the effect of the IV but, annoyingly, from the unwanted source of differences between the people in either condition, is known as the problem of PARTICIPANT VARIABLES. (The traditional term was SUBJECT VARIABLES, but, as explained below, the newer, more humanistic term is used here.) This problem of differences *between groups* is the major weakness of the independent samples design.

Group A   Group B

Figure 2.1 *Participant variables might affect experiment on diet*

Random allocation of participants to conditions

As for our sykik seeds, in this type of design, participants are allocated randomly to either the hot room or cool room condition. Recall that the null hypothesis claims that any differences found between the two groups are the result of chance fluctuation only. If the difference is large (significant) we shall want to claim that the cause is the variation in IV. By randomly allocating people to conditions we are anticipating, and ruling out, the alternative interpretation that differences in results are caused by important differences between the types of people in each condition.

Pre-test of participants

We can show that both groups were similar in relevant performance before the experimental conditions were applied. For instance, we could show that the A-level students and nursery nurses were equal in aggressiveness prior to the experiment. There could still be a participant variable problem, though, depending on the nature of the pre-test subject matter and the topic for debate in the actual experiment. If the topic were the issue of whether to use physical punishment in disciplining children, from teaching experience, I can guarantee a 'hot' debate amongst otherwise calm nursery nurses!

Representative allocation

We can ensure that each group contains half the males, a similar age group, a similar range of educational background and, so on. We can't balance for everything, however, and the variables included must be decided upon intuitively, taking into account the nature of the research topic and of prior findings.

In our hot/cool room study, if we can *only* use the A-level and nursery nurse students, then perhaps we should divide these evenly between the two groups, also balancing for age, sex and, perhaps, assertiveness, if we can assess it. Any such division should be carried out on a random basis, as described in Chapter 4.

OTHER DISADVANTAGES OF INDEPENDENT SAMPLES DESIGN

1 To obtain as many scores in each condition we have to find, and test, twice the number of people as in repeated measures. This can be costly and time consuming. We do have the advantage (over repeated measures design), however, that we can't lose participants between conditions and we can run the two conditions simultaneously rather than having to wait until practice effects have worn off.

2 If there is too much difference between the statistical variances of the two groups, we may not be able to proceed with a parametric test – the most powerful of statistical tests (see Chapter 11).

MATCHED-PAIRS DESIGN

What was an advantage of the design suggested in example 3, Box 1.1? Why pair a child in one group with a similarly aggressive child in the other group?

For the independent samples design we suggested making the two groups roughly equal in terms of student type, age, and so on. We can do more than just assure that our two groups are roughly equivalent on relevant variables. We can *pair* a person in one condition with a person in the other condition. The pairing is based on relevant variables.

For example, we might wish to investigate the effect of an experimental preschool programme on children's intellectual development. We would pair children on the basis of, say, exact age, sex, ethnic group, social and economic background of parents, number of siblings, and so on. However, sample totals will limit the extent of what can be matched. It is important to note that the pairs of children are then allocated to the experimental or control groups on a random basis. This would need to occur in the hot/cool example for it to count as an experiment.

The matched-pairs design falls into the category of related designs because each score or rating in one group can be related to a score in the other group. This obviously can't be done where two sets of scores come from two unmatched groups.

One of nature's most useful gifts to psychological researchers is, some believe, the existence of identical (monozygotic) twins. These represent the perfect matched pair – when they're just born at least – and create the perfect natural experiment. Any differences between them later in life can fairly safely be attributed to differences in environmental experience. The converse is not true, however. Similarities cannot be easily attributed to common genetic make-up, as identical twins usually share fairly similar environments too.

SINGLE PARTICIPANT DESIGN

Example 4 in Box 1.1 seems a bid odd. We conduct *all* the experimental trials on just one person. This could make the scientifically minded recoil in horror. Surely this must produce quite unrepresentative results, impossible to generalise with? Quite rightly, they assume, one turns to objective psychological research in order to avoid the many generalisations which the lay person often makes from their own limited experience.

However, consider a physical scientist who obtains just one sample of weird moonrock from a returning space mission. The rock could be tested for the amount of expansion at different temperatures, in a vacuum and in normal atmosphere, in order to detect significant changes in its behaviour. This would yield valuable scientific knowledge in itself.

Further, from our general knowledge of the world of rocks, we could fairly safely assume that similar rock would exist on the moon. In the same way there are some sorts of things which people do which, we know for good reason, are likely to vary according to the same *pattern* (but not necessarily at the same level) for almost everyone. An example of this might be the experimental situation in which someone has to make decisions from an increasing number of alternatives – sorting cards according to colour, then suit and so on.

What really seems odd, at first, about a single participant design is that it should count as an unrelated design. Surely, all the scores come from the same person so they must be related? Well, in a sense, yes, but not for purposes of statistical comparison. Say we have a set of reaction times to recognise words under two conditions – with coffee and without coffee. The first score in the coffee condition is related to all the scores in the without-coffee condition, because the scores come from the same person, but it is not related *uniquely* to any specific score in the second condition. The two sets of scores are *independent samples* of scores in that sense.

CRITICISMS OF THE EXPERIMENT

The criticisms here apply to the experiment *whether it is conducted in a laboratory or in the field*. Barber (1976) has documented many of the possible pitfalls in running experiments, some of these pitfalls are not obvious and have been brought to our attention by often dramatic demonstrations. Barber divides the problems into those relating to the 'investigator' (the person with overall responsibility for the research) and the 'experimenter' (the person who actually deals with the participants). Experimenters may 'fudge' results because they want the research to succeed and hence keep their job, or because they are being compared with other experimenters to

Box 2.2 *Summary of advantages and disadvantages of the various experimental designs*

Design	Advantages	Disadvantages	Remedy (if any)
Repeated measures	Participant variables eliminated	Order effects	Counterbalance/ randomise conditions
	More economical on participants	May not be able to conduct second condition immediately	Leave long time gap between conditions
		Need different stimulus lists etc.	Do independent samples instead
			Randomise stimulus materials
	Homogeneity of variance not a problem (see Chapter 11)	Participants not naïve for second condition and may try to guess aim	Deceive participants as to aim (or leave long time gap)
	Need fewer participants	Loss of participants between conditions	
Independent samples	No order effect	Participant variables not controlled	Random allocation of participants to conditions
	Participants can't guess aim of experiment	Less economical on participants	
	Can use exactly the same stimulus lists etc.	Lack of 'homogeneity of variance' may prevent use of parametric test (Chapter 11)	Ensure roughly equal numbers in each group (see p. 169)
	No need to wait for participants to 'forget' first condition		
Matched pairs	No order effects	Some participant variables still present	Randomly allocate pairs to conditions
	Participant variables partly controlled	Hard to find perfect matches and therefore time consuming	
	No wait for participants to forget		
	Can use same stimulus lists etc.	Loss of one member of pair entails loss of whole pair	
	Homogeneity of variance not a problem		
Single participant	Useful where few participants available and/or a lot of time required for training participant	Can't generalise to other categories of people with confidence	
		Retraining required if original participant leaves project	Treat participant very nicely!

check **EXPERIMENTER RELIABILITY** – the extent to which their results agree. Investigators may set up procedures which are too 'loose', or they may produce a design in accordance with their own theoretical perspective, which then produces results different from those of other designs. We'll now look at some specific unwanted effects.

EXPERIMENTER EXPECTANCY

As psychology experiments are carried out by humans on humans, it has been argued that the necessary social interaction which must occur between experimenter and participant makes the psychological experiment different in kind from any other. Is it possible that the experimenter could unintentionally 'give the game away' to the participant? This effect is known as **EXPERIMENTER BIAS** or **EXPECTANCY**.

Rosenthal (1966) showed that students given groups of 'bright' and 'dull' rats (who were actually randomly mixed for maze learning ability) produced results consistent with the label of their rats. This was originally used to show that experimenter expectancies can even affect the behaviour of laboratory rats. However, Barber argues that the results were almost certainly due to other effects, such as deviation from procedure.

Forty experiments between 1968 and 1976 failed to show evidence of experimenters passing on influence which the investigators tried to produce. However, some studies have shown that experimenters *can* affect participants' responses through facial or verbal cues, and that certain participants are more likely to pick up experimenter influence than others, particularly those high in need of approval. Perhaps this occurred when Raffetto (1967) led one group of experimenters to believe that sensory deprivation produces reports of hallucinations and another group to believe the opposite. The experimenters then interviewed people who had undergone sensory deprivation, with the interview procedure left purposely vague. Guess what? Yes, experimenters reported more or less hallucinations from their interviewees in accordance with the expectation they had been given.

DEMAND CHARACTERISTICS

If participants who need approval are affected by experimenter influence, then it suggests that they perhaps want to 'please the experimenter' and get the 'right' result. To do this they would have to know what was required in the first place.

Orne (1962) argued that there are many cues in an experimental situation which give participants an idea of what the study is about, what behaviour is under study and perhaps even what changes are expected or required of them. These cues may reveal the experimental hypothesis Orne named **DEMAND CHARACTERISTICS**. 'Experimental realism', described on p. 34, was thought by Aronson to *lower* the likely effects of demand characteristics, because participants' attention is entirely grabbed by the interest of the procedure.

Participant reactions

Participants could react to demand characteristics in several ways. They may engage in what is termed **PLEASING THE EXPERIMENTER**.

In fact, Weber and Cook (1972) found little evidence that participants do try to respond as they think the experimenter might wish. Masling (1966) has even suggested that, knowing the experimental aims, behaviour might be altered away from expectancy – the 'screw you' effect. Research suggests, however, that most participants try to appear normal and competent because they are concerned about how their behaviour will be judged. This may well influence them to behave as naturally as possible and show that they cannot be influenced.

EVALUATION APPREHENSION may occur when participants are worried what the researcher may find out about them and this anxiety may affect results. Some may try to 'look good'. This is known as SOCIAL DESIRABILITY. Others may just not concentrate as well on the task at hand. A further problem, sometimes known as 'enlightenment', is the increasing awareness of psychology students (who are most often participants) and the general public about psychological research findings, even if these are often poorly understood.

REMOVING BIAS – BLINDS AND DOUBLE-BLINDS

Investigators usually do not want their participants to be aware of the experimental aim. Deception may well have to be employed to keep them in the dark and the moral implications of this are discussed in the chapter on ethics. Keeping participants in the dark is known as the employment of a 'single-blind' procedure. But it has been argued here that experimenters may transmit cues. Hence, it makes sense to keep experimenters in the dark too. The employment of a 'double-blind' procedure does just that – experimenters, or those who gather results directly from the participants, are not told the true experimental aims. Where a placebo group is used, for example, neither the participants, nor the data gatherers may know who has received the real treatment.

Are problems with experiments unique to the experiment?

It must be noted that *non*-experimental studies can suffer from all the objections so far raised against the experiment, though it is true to say that the experimental design, in general, is far more likely to suffer the problems and to a greater extent than less rigidly controlled studies and those where 'participants' are unaware of their involvement. As we shall see, however, these 'participant-unaware' studies *may* suffer from ethical difficulties.

INTERNAL AND EXTERNAL VALIDITY

We want to attribute any difference found in experimental results unambiguously and confidently to the variation in the independent variable. Imagine a critic who just keeps picking holes in the design, procedure, measures, and results ('Ah, but your researchers might have *expected* differences', 'The control group just might have been less skilful than the experimental group to start with', and so on). The critic is highlighting what are known as 'threats' to the study's INTERNAL and EXTERNAL VALIDITY.

Note The far more common (and related) use of 'validity' refers to whether a test is measuring what it was constructed to measure and is dealt with on page 52.

Threats to internal validity

As the name suggests, these are factors *within* the study which will cause the overall result to be wrongly interpreted. Many of the things we've covered in this chapter are included – any (such as order effects or biased allocation to groups) that cause us to think the independent variable affected the dependent variable when, actually, it didn't. It also includes factors that made us think there *wasn't* an effect when, in fact, there was. Further, it includes the issue of using the wrong statistical test and getting apparently significant differences which shouldn't be counted – covered from Chapter 11 onwards.

Threats to external validity

These all concern the possibility of *generalising* from the study conducted. It is usual, in scientific studies, to wish to be able to generalise from one study to more general circumstances. Newton wasn't particularly concerned about an individual apple; he was pondering *general* rules of gravity. Obviously though, in psychology, generalisation must often be limited. Will this effect work on nurses in the same way as it does on geography students? Will it work on Colombians as it has done with Welsh people? Will the difference be found with actual aggression in the home as it has using our questionnaire? These sorts of generalisation can be broken down as follows:

1 Will the effect occur with all similar people or with other groups and types?

2 Will the effect occur in other places?

3 Will the effect occur at other times? (Would Asch's conformity effects work today?)

4 Will this effect occur if we use different measures (e.g. observed behaviour rather than a questionnaire)?

Ecological validity

Item 1 in the above list is known as 'population validity' and item 2 as ECOLOGICAL VALIDITY. This second term is very commonly used nowadays, but it has several meanings. It was originally coined by Brunswick in 1947, and referred to whether perceptual effects in the laboratory could be generalised outside it. When it came into general use, though, in the context of external validity, it was intended to refer to the extent to which any study's findings could be generalised to other settings. It is common to find textbooks referring to *any* naturalistic study as having 'ecological validity' (just because it is conducted in a natural setting). However, if the study's results do not generalise, it has little ecological validity. Of course, it *is* true to say that very many laboratory studies lack ecological validity because, without doubt, one could not generalise the findings to many other situations, if any.

Laboratory studies *can* possess ecological validity and this just depends on whether we *would* find the effects occurring elsewhere. Ainsworth et al.'s (1971) study used careful video and audio recording in a laboratory to study infants' reactions to strangers and to separation from their mothers. Ten-month-old infants are very often in places as strange as the laboratory (which, anyway, was set out as a nursery play area); the park and the doctor's surgery are equally strange to a 10-month-old. What mattered to the infant was whether mother was there or not. If the infant behaved in the study as it would at home then ecological validity was high. Equally, 'real life' does not always occur in what, for the individual, is a 'natural' environment – consider the inside of an aeroplane or a police station.

A better term for research situations that are close to real life is MUNDANE REALISM (Carlsmith et al., 1976).

Some studies lack ecological validity but are so gripping and engaging for the participant that any artificiality is compensated for. This is known as EXPERIMENTAL REALISM. Examples would be Asch's (1956) and Milgram's (1963) studies where, again, film evidence shows participants certainly taking the situation as genuine and very serious. For more detail on internal and external validity, see

Coolican (1994) for a brief account or, in much greater depth, Cook and Campbell (1979).

THE HUMANIST OBJECTION

I pointed out in Chapter 1 that people involved in psychology experiments have traditionally been referred to as 'subjects', though this is now changing. Humanist psychologists have argued that this is a reflection of the experimentalists' attitude to humans and human research. 'Subject' implies that the researcher holds, perhaps implicitly, a 'mechanistic' model of humans. Heather (1976) has claimed that 'Human beings continue to be regarded by psychologists as some kind of helpless clockwork puppet, jerked into life only when something happens to it.' Hampden-Turner (1971) states '. . . power over people in a laboratory can *only* lead . . . to a technology of behaviour control' (italics in original). Such objectors to the experimental method would normally be found in the qualitative research method 'camp', to be discussed in Chapter 8.

There is, of course, a composite position, well put by Baars (1980): 'Without naturalistic facts, experimental research may become narrow and blind: but without experimental research, the naturalistic approach runs the danger of being shallow and uncertain.'

GLOSSARY

Note: *confounding variable, constant error, dependent variable* and *independent variable* are defined in the glossary in Chapter 3; *control group* is defined in Chapter 4.

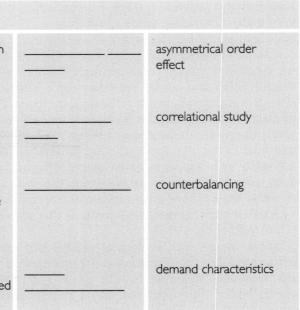

GLOSSARY

Order effect which has greater strength in one particular direction and where, therefore, counterbalancing would be ineffective	_____ _____ _____	asymmetrical order effect
Study of the extent to which one variable is related to another, often referring to non-manipulated variables measured outside the laboratory	_____ _____	correlational study
Half participants do conditions in a particular order and the other half take the conditions in the opposite order. This is done to balance (not eliminate) any order effects	_____	counterbalancing
Features of a study which help the participant to work out what is expected of him/her	_____ _____	demand characteristics

		designs
Two or more separate groups take the various conditions of the independent variable	_____ _____	independent samples (or *independent groups* or *between groups*)
Each participant in one group/condition is paired on specific variable(s) with a participant in another group/condition	_____ _____	matched pairs
Each participant takes part in all conditions of the independent variable	_____ _____	repeated measures (or *within groups*)
Design in which scores in one condition are paired with scores in other conditions	_____	related
Design in which only one participant is tested	_____ _____	single participant (single subject)
Design in which particular scores in one condition cannot be paired (or linked) in any way with particular scores in any other condition	_____	unrelated
Procedure in an experiment where neither participants *nor* data gatherer (experimenter or assistants) know which treatment participants have received (i.e. which conditions they were in)	_____	double-blind
Participants' concern about being tested, which may affect results	_____ _____	evaluation apprehension
Study in which an independent variable is manipulated	_____	**experiment**
Experiment carried out in a natural setting outside the laboratory	_____ _____	field experiment
Experiment carried out in controlled conditions in experimenter's own habitat	_____ _____	laboratory experiment
Design which exploits the occurrence of a naturally occurring independent variable	_____ _____	natural experiment
Design in which researcher does not have control over random allocation of participants to conditions nor, in some cases, over the independent variable	_____-_____	quasi-experiment
Extent to which research conditions 'grab' participant and focus attention irrespective of representation of real life (especially, outside the laboratory)	_____ _____	experimental realism

Person who deals directly with participant in an experiment	_____	experimenter
Tendency for experimenter's knowledge of what is being tested to influence the outcome of research	_____ _____	experimenter expectancy
The extent to which the results produced by two or more experimenters are similar	_____ _____	experimenter reliability
Any study outside a laboratory	_____	field study
Person with overall responsibility for research study	_____	investigator
An enquiring experimental or non-experimental piece of research	_____	investigation
Extent to which research conditions represent real life	_____ _____	mundane realism
Research which simply measures characteristics of how people are or behave but doesn't intervene or (more narrowly) research in which the main data gathering technique involves looking directly at behaviour as it occurs and categorising or measuring it	_____ _____	observational study
A confounding effect caused by experiencing one condition, then another, such as practice or fatigue	_____ _____	order effects
Variables which differ between groups of people and which may need to be controlled in order to demonstrate an effect of the IV	_____ _____	participant (or 'subject') variables
Tendency of participants to act in accordance with what they think the experimenter would like	_____ _____	pleasing the experimenter
Assign people to conditions of an experiment so that each person has an equal chance of being in any of the groups in the study	_____ _____	randomly allocate
Procedure in an experiment where participants do not know which treatment they received (i.e. which condition they were in)	_____ _____	single blind
Tendency of participants in research to want to 'look good' and provide socially acceptable answers	_____ _____	social desirability
Way of testing or acquiring measures from participants which is repeated in exactly the same way each time for all common steps of the method	_____ _____	standardised procedure

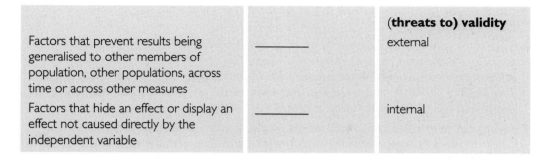

		(threats to) validity
Factors that prevent results being generalised to other members of population, other populations, across time or across other measures	_____	external
Factors that hide an effect or display an effect not caused directly by the independent variable	_____	internal

EXERCISES

1 State whether the following are laboratory experiments, natural experiments, field experiments or non-experimental investigations:

   a) A ladder is placed against a street wall to see whether more males or females will avoid it

   b) Boys with no brother and boys with two brothers are observed under laboratory conditions to see which group exhibits greater aggression

   c) A researcher, dressed either casually or smart, approaches passengers at a station to ask for directions. The aim is to see whether smart dress elicits greater help

   d) Under laboratory conditions, people are asked to make a speech, contrary to their own view, first alone and then in front of others

   e) One psychology class is given a distance learning package to see whether it improves test results over another class serving as controls

   f) Researchers visit various grades of worker at their place of employment and take them through a questionnaire on their attitude to authority. It is thought the more highly paid will express greater respect for authority

   g) One of two very similar homes for the elderly passes from local government to private control. Workers in each are compared on job satisfaction before and after the change, using informal interviews

2 Of the designs outlined in **1**:

   a) Which are not likely to be affected by demand characteristics?

   b) Which are subject to researcher bias?

   c) In which could 'blind' procedures be employed?

3 You are discussing with a colleague two methods of measuring 'conformity'. One involves recording how often people will answer a simple question wrongly when several other people in the room have already answered wrongly (laboratory study). The other involves stopping people in the street who have infringed a traffic light or litter regulation and taking those who agree to do so through a short questionnaire (field study). Find arguments for and against each proposal – I hope you can think of at least three for and three against each. Pages 26 to 32 of this chapter, and Chapter 6 should provide the general information you need.

4 In Fantz's famous 'looking-chamber' experiment, in each trial a baby is shown two patterns and the researcher records how much time is spent looking at either pattern. The idea is to see whether the baby prefers complex patterns to simpler ones. What is the IV, the DV and what sort of design is this?

5 In one version of the 'visual cliff' experiment, infants are observed while their mothers try to entice them to come to them across a glass sheet with a large drop beneath it. What condition can be added to make this a true experiment and what sort of design would the experiment then be?

6 Your tutor conducts an experiment on your class. Each student is given a set of anagrams to solve and the time to solve each one is taken. You find that some of the anagrams were of concrete words and the others were of abstract words, in no particular order. This was the IV. What design was this, and what special precaution, associated with this design, has your tutor wisely taken and why?

7 Again your tutor conducts an experiment. Students are in pairs. You time your partner while she learns a finger maze, first with the left hand, then with the right. She then times you while you learn first with the right, then the left. What design is this? What special precaution is taken and why?

8 Each child from several pairs of 8-year-old twins is randomly allocated either to a special reading support programme or to a control group. After six months the two groups are compared on reading ability. What sort of design is being employed here?

PSYCHOLOGICAL MEASURES – VARIABLES IN PSYCHOLOGICAL INVESTIGATIONS

In our hot room/cool room experiment I have so far been very quiet indeed about how 'aggression' is to be measured. In the examples given in Box 1.1 the weakest aspect is the measurement of aggression, and this is very common. Defining variables with precision is very often the most neglected part of early psychology practical projects. Yet how are we to observe changes in aggression and record these as public evidence – the heart of our project – if we do not state exactly how aggression is to be measured?

> In which examples in Box 1.1 is the measure of aggression more clearly defined? Which is the most exact definition?

I hope you agree that examples 1, 3, and 5 are the vaguest in defining their proposed measure of aggression – in fact, they give no measure at all. Example 2 is a little better. It gives a focus for people to express aggression but it says nothing about *how* people will state their assessment of aggression and how these might be compared. Example 4 gives a precise focus for the expression of aggression, states that a questionnaire will be used but does not give details of the questionnaire or how it is to be scored. Example 6 is similar to example 4. The first measure could be quite precise – number of years in prison, for instance. However, what are we to do with the answers people give to the second suggestion – what people would do if someone hit their little sister? How can we compare the answers of 'go and hit them' and 'smash their car to pieces'? Is one more aggressive than the other? Finally, example 7 gives the most precise definition of the lot.

MEASURING VARIABLES

The essence of studying anything (birds, geology, emotion) is the observation of change. If nothing changed there would be nothing to observe – think about it. If something changes it 'varies' – it is variable; in the language of science it is a VARIABLE. The basic aim of science is to relate changes in variables to changes in other variables. A variable, then, is any feature of the world which varies, be it plant growth, rock formation or people's behaviour. Let's list some things which vary:

Height	varies as you grow older and between individuals.
Time	to solve a set of anagrams.
Political party	these vary in name and composition.
Feelings	toward your partner or parents.
Attitude	towards vandals, for instance, or towards people with disabilities.
Anxiety	different levels in different people?

We can measure these variables across time, in one individual, or between different individuals. Variables can take several or many values across a range. The value given is often numerical but not necessarily so. In example 3, for instance, the different values are names.

Some of the variables above are easy to measure and we know just what instruments to use. Height is one of these and so is time. Some variables are familiar in concept but the suggestion of *measuring* them leaves people stumbling for ideas. Extroversion, anxiety, or attitude fall into this category. However, we often make estimates of these things when we say, for instance, 'She gets anxious over nothing' or 'She doesn't care anything about the future of the health service in this country'.

If we are to make estimates of these variables in research we must be able to answer the question 'Well, how do you *know*?' with precise definition of what we are measuring. This way, we can confidently report our findings to others and expect to be taken seriously. In the interests of science, or, at least, objective research, others must be able to replicate and agree our findings. So what *are* extroversion, anxiety, and attitude?

DEFINING PSYCHOLOGICAL VARIABLES

First, try to write down your *own* definition of:

a extroversion
b anxiety
c attitude

Perhaps that was difficult. Now, give some examples of people producing *evidence* of having these dispositions.

You probably found the definitions quite hard. Why do we have difficulty in defining terms we use every day with good understanding? There is usually no problem with:

1 Our tutor is quite extroverted. I think most psychology tutors are.

2 Bob gets anxious whenever a dog comes near him.

3 His attitude on race is quite obnoxious.

PSYCHOLOGICAL CONSTRUCTS

I hope you found it a bit easier, though, to give examples of people displaying evidence of extroversion or anxiety. Remember, information about people *must* come somehow from what they say or do. When we are young we are little psychologists.

We build up a concept (or 'construct') of extroversion or anxiety or attitude from learning what are signs or manifestations of it. Biting lips and trembling voice may show anxiety, for instance. The important question is, does our internal (mental) 'construct' of extroversion relate to any *real* identifiable phenomenon which affects people's behaviour in a regular or predictable manner?

We do not observe something called 'extroversion' as such – we observe what we assume is evidence of it in a person – unafraid of complaining in shops, first to dance at parties and so on. So how are we to establish that the 'psychological construct' of extroversion is a scientifically valid one?

Scientists validate their constructs using the 'black box' approach, which argues: 'We can't see X but *if* it exists then Y should happen when we do Z'. For instance, we can't see oxygen, but if it's a constituent of air and it gets burnt up by fire then a lighted candle, covered by a glass, should soon go out. Psychologists might argue: 'We can't *observe* extroversion directly but if it is a real factor in human behaviour, people with more of it (as measured by this test) should differ from people with lower levels in certain ways: extroverts (high scorers) should go to bed later, work better in the afternoon and evening, get bored more quickly, and so on'. (These are real predictions.) This is not exactly the same as the oxygen argument – I've introduced the idea of psychological tests (see Chapter 6) – but I hope you get the general point. We can argue that our assumed psychological variables (which we can't observe directly) *do* have some sort of reality if hypothesis tests, based on the assumption that these concepts *are* real, come out positive.

Physicists do this with constructs like the 'quark'. So long as evidence generally supports the concept of quarks, with not too much contradictory evidence, the concept can survive as part of an overall theory. Theoretical psychologists (those in research) carry on their business in much the same way. They *assume* that concepts like extroversion or intelligence are factors that can somehow explain observable patterns of human behaviour. If, after research that attempts both to support and refute the existence of these concepts, the explanations remain feasible, then they can remain as theoretical entities.

ORGANISATION OF CONSTRUCTS

A construct can be linked to others in an explanatory framework from which further predictions are possible and testable. We might, for instance, infer low self-esteem in people who are very hostile to members of minority ethnic groups. The low self-esteem might, in turn, be related to authoritarian upbringing, which could be checked up on. We might then look for a relationship between authoritarian rearing and prejudiced behaviour as shown in Figure 3.1.

If psychologists are to use such constructs in their research work and theorising, they must obviously be very careful indeed in explaining how these are to be treated as variables. Their definitions must be precise. Even for the more easily measurable variables, such as short-term memory capacity, definitions must be clear.

OPERATIONAL DEFINITIONS

In search of objectivity, scientists conducting research attempt to **OPERATIONALISE** their variables. An **OPERATIONAL DEFINITION** of variable $\underline{X}$ gives us *the set of activities required to measure X*. It is like a set of instructions. For instance, in physics, pressure is precisely defined as weight or mass per unit area. To measure pressure we have to find out the weight impinging on an area and divide by that area.

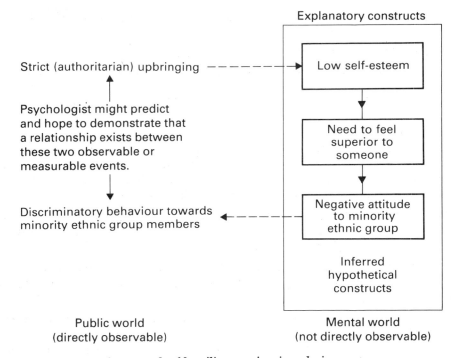

Figure 3.1   *Explanatory framework of hostility to minority ethnic groups*

Even in measuring a person's height, if we want to agree with others' measurements, we will need to specify conditions such as what to take as the top of the head and how the person should stand. In general though, height and time present us with no deep problem because the units of measurement are already clearly and universally defined.

In a particular piece of memory research we might define short-term memory capacity as 'the longest list of digits on which the participant has perfect recall in more than 80% of trials'. Here, on each trial, the participant has to try to recall the digit string presented in the order it was given. Several trials would occur with strings from three to, say, 12 digits in length. At the end of this it is relatively simple to calculate our measure of short-term memory capacity according to our operational definition.

For any particular piece of research we must state exactly what we are counting as a measure of the construct we are interested in. As an example, consider a project carried out by some students who placed a ladder against a wall and observed men and women walking round or under it. For this research, 'superstitious behaviour' was (narrowly) operationalised as the avoidance of walking under the ladder.

Imagine you were about to start testing the hypotheses stated below. In each case, try to provide operationalised definitions for the variables involved. If it helps, ask yourself 'What will *count* as (aggression) in this study? How exactly will it be measured?' Think carefully, and then state the exact procedure you would use to carry out the measurement of the variables.

1 Physically punished children are more aggressive

2 Memory deterioration can be the result of stress at work

3 Language development is advanced in infants by parents who provide a lot of visual and auditory stimulation

4 People will be more likely to comply with a request from a person they trust

5 People told an infant is male will be more likely to describe the infant according to the popular male stereotype than will those told it is female

Here are some ideas:

1 *Physical punishment*: number of times parent reports striking per week; questionnaire to parents on attitudes to physical punishment. *Aggression*: number of times child initiates rough-and-tumble behaviour observed in playground at school; number of requests for violent toys in Santa Claus letters.

2 *Stress*: occupations defined as more stressful the more sickness, heart attacks, etc. reported within them. *Memory* could be defined as on page 44, or participants could keep a diary of forgetful incidents.

3 *Language development*: length of child's utterances; size of vocabulary, etc. *Stimulation*: number of times parent initiates sensory play, among other things, during home observation.

4 *Compliance*: if target person agrees to researcher's request for change in street. *Trust*: defined in terms of dress and role. In one case, the researcher dressed smart with doctor's bag. In the other, with scruffy clothes. We could also use post-encounter assessment rating by the target person.

5 *Stereotype response*: number of times participant, in describing the infant, uses terms coming from a list developed by asking a panel of the general public what infant features were typically masculine and typically feminine.

INDEPENDENT AND DEPENDENT VARIABLES

In our hot/cool room experiment there are two important variables. One (the independent variable – IV) is manipulated by the experimenter – hot or cool room. This can be defined operationally by the exact temperature. The other variable (the dependent variable – DV) is the level of aggression. There are several ways to measure this but the closest to an operational definition we have seen is number of fights per month, as in example 7 of Box 1.1. Learners in psychology often find it very difficult to distinguish between the independent and dependent variable so I hope the following exercise may help to make the relationship clearer.

Considering these two variables, which of the following statements makes more sense to you?

I The temperature depends on the number of fights per month.

2 The number of fights per month depends on the temperature.

Not too difficult I hope? I hope it's obvious that, if there is any effect at all, the number of fights will depend on temperature, and that temperature could hardly depend on number of fights! Hence, the number of fights, in this hypothesis, is the *dependent* variable because it *depends on* the temperature. The variable *depended on* is

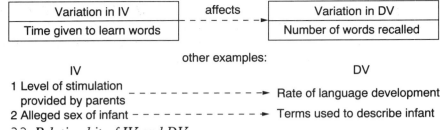

Figure 3.2 *Relationship of IV and DV*

known as the *independent* variable. It isn't affected by the DV; it is independently varied and this variations we hope, directly affects the DV.

Suppose we give participants a list of words to learn under two conditions. In one, they have 30 seconds to learn and in the other they have 1 minute. The time given for learning (IV) will be related, we expect, to the number of words correctly recalled (DV). This is the hypothesis under test, as depicted in Figure 3.2.

DEFINING THE DEPENDENT VARIABLE IN PRACTICAL PROJECTS

Generally, learners have little problem defining the independent variable in practical projects. A general rule is to look for the *conditions*: effects of coffee compared with tea, or of left-hand and right-hand mirror drawing; otherwise look at the two *groups* being tested: males and females, anxious and non-anxious participants, etc. What very often suffers, however, is the description of the *dependent variable*.

> Consider these fictitious extracts from practical reports, where students are trying to describe the dependent variable in their statement of the hypothesis to be tested:
> - '...*aggression* will be greater in the hot room group'
> - '...the group with more practice will have *better memories*'
> - '...males will be *more sexist* in their attitudes'
>
> Why might a tutor write 'What *exactly* was the measure?' by the italicised terms?

The tutor is not being awkward and hasn't got it in for you individually. What is needed here is the *operational definition* of the dependent variables concerned. Why? The practical is, in general, about aggression, for instance, but the hypothesis you're testing specifically is *only* about your particular measure of aggression. We must always remember that, in our practical studies, a simple measure, such as a questionnaire, can hardly do justice to the full meaning and richness of a concept like 'aggression'.

'Better memories' needs narrowing down to *the way this will be measured in the experiment* – for instance, 'number of words correctly recalled' or 'number of items ticked in the final checklist'.

'Sexist' has enormous implications and is often misused when no discrimination is implied. Here, it might have been measured only as '. . . will use a greater number of masculine than feminine terms to describe a new-born baby (or occupation)'.

We should also always remember that we can't generalise from one *method* of measuring a concept to others. Measures taken on paper cannot be directly generalised to people's actual behaviour in their life outside the classroom or laboratory. A person answering a questionnaire may be affected by *social desirability*, that is, attempt to 'look good', for instance by following liberal social norms on homosexuality, yet continue to discriminate in daily life, tell 'homophobic' jokes and so on. It is argued that the narrower the measure we take of a construct, the weaker is our *construct validity* – to be described later in this chapter.

EXTRANEOUS VARIABLES

In our hot/cool room experiment, assuming we used a different but equivalent group in each condition (participant variables are not a problem) and asked each group to rate aggression in a film:

1 What variables might affect aggression ratings in either condition?

2 What might be responsible for higher aggression ratings in the hot room, *other than the heat itself?*

'Extraneous variables' is a general term referring to any variable, other than the IV, which might have an effect on the measured DV. It tends to be used in reference mainly to experiments where we would normally be interested in controlling the unwanted effects of all variables except the IV, so that we can compare conditions fairly.

If all variables are controlled – kept from altering – then any change in the DV can more confidently be attributed to changes in the IV.

The unwanted effects of extraneous variables are often known as 'errors'. Look at Figure 3.3. Imagine each picture shows the deliveries of a bowler. In Figure 3.3b

a 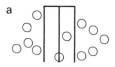   b

high random error; low/no constant error   low random error; low/no constant error

c 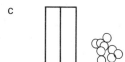   d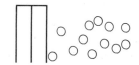

low random error; high constant error   high random error; high constant error

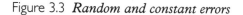

Figure 3.3 *Random and constant errors*

there are few errors. In Figure 3.3c there seems to be one systematic error. If the bowler could correct this, all the deliveries would be accurate. In Figure 3.3a there seems to be no systematic error but deliveries vary quite widely about the wicket in a seemingly random pattern. In Figure 3.3d we can only sympathise! Deliveries vary randomly *and* are systematically off the wicket. We will now look at the way these two sorts of CONSTANT (systematic) ERROR and RANDOM ERROR (having inconsistent effects) are dealt with in research.

RANDOM ERROR (OR RANDOM VARIABLES)

Your answers to question 1 in the exercise above might have included:

- a noisy heater going on and off and interfering with concentration
- a varying fault in the television monitor showing the film
- a flickering neon light

The heater may go on and off by thermostat. Experimental apparatus may behave slightly differently from trial to trial. A technician may cough when you're trying to concentrate. Some of the variables above affect only you as participant. Others vary across everyone. Some people will pay more attention than others. This is a 'people' difference – the problem of PARTICIPANT VARIABLES, which we met in the last chapter.

All these variables are unpredictable (well, something could have been done about the heater!). They are sometimes called 'nuisance variables'. They are random in their effect. They do not affect one condition more than the other, we hope. In fact, we assume that they will just about balance out across the two groups, partly because we *randomly allocated* participants to conditions (see Chapter 2).

Where possible, everything is done to remove obviously threatening variables. In general though, random errors cannot be entirely eliminated. We have to hope they balance out. Random errors, then, are unsystematic extraneous variables.

CONSTANT ERROR

For question 2 in the previous exercise you could have suggested, among other things:

- humidity might also increase with the heat and *that* might raise aggression, not temperature
- there may be less air circulating generally in the hot room condition
- a noisy heater may be on throughout this condition and not in the cool condition

In these examples an extraneous variable is operating *systematically*. It is affecting the performances in one condition more than in the other. This is known as a CONSTANT ERROR.

If the effect of an extraneous variable is systematic it is serious because we may assume the IV has affected the DV when it hasn't.

Suppose babies lying in a cot look far more at complex visual patterns (they *do*). Suppose though, the complex patterns were always presented on the right-hand side, with a simple pattern on the left. Maybe the cot makes it more comfortable to look to the right. Perhaps babies have a natural tendency to prefer looking to the right (Figure 3.4). This is a constant error which is quite simple to control for. We don't have to know that left or right *does* make a difference. To be safe we might as well

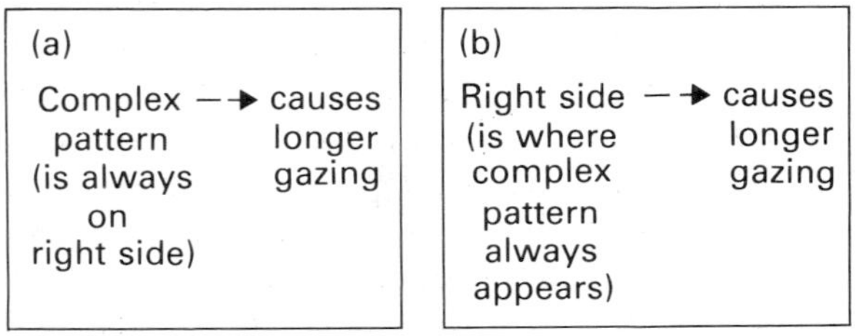

```
(a)                          (b)

Complex  ──▶ causes          Right side ──▶ causes
  pattern       longer        (is where      longer
 (is always     gazing        complex        gazing
    on                        pattern
 right side)                  always
                              appears)
```

Figure 3.4 *Alternative explanations of gazing effect*

present half the complex designs to the left, and half to the right, unpredictably, in order to rule out the possibility. This is an example of RANDOMISATION of stimulus position, rather like the randomisation of items seen in the previous chapter. Essentially, participants should not be able to develop an *expectancy* of what is coming next.

CONFOUNDING (OR CONFOUNDING VARIABLES)

The fundamentally important point made in the last section was that, *whenever differences or relationships are observed in results, it is always possible that a variable, other than the independent variable has produced the effect.* In the example above, left or right side is acting as an IV that has not been accounted for. By making the side on which complex and simple designs will appear *unpredictable* the problem would have been eliminated. This *wasn't* done, however, and our experiment is said to be CON-FOUNDED.

Confounding is a regular feature of our attempts to understand and explain the world around us. Some time ago, starting a Christmas vacation, a friend told me that switching to decaffeinated coffee might reduce some physical effects of tension which I'd been experiencing. To my surprise, after a couple of weeks, the feelings had subsided. The alert reader will have guessed that the possible confounding variable here is the vacation period, when *some* relaxation might occur anyway.

There is a second possible explanation of this effect. I might have been expecting a result from my switch to the far less preferred decaffeinated coffee. This alone might have caused me to reappraise my inner feelings – a possibility one always has to keep in mind in psychological research when participants know in advance what behaviour changes are expected. This is known as a PLACEBO EFFECT and is dealt with in Chapter 4.

Confounding is said to occur, then, whenever the true nature of an effect is obscured by the operation of unwanted variables. Very often these variables are not recognised by the researcher but emerge through critical inspection of the study by others.

The confusing effect of confounding variables is far higher in non-experimental work, where there is little influence over most variables. Children who watch violent TV may become aggressive, but many uncontrolled variables, *other than TV viewing*, may be responsible.

RELIABILITY, VALIDITY, AND STANDARDISATION OF PSYCHOLOGICAL MEASURES

We have been discussing the fact that, in order to conduct research, psychologists must find ways of measuring things. Think of the measuring instruments with which you are already familiar. You might come up with a ruler, a car speedometer, a set of bathroom scales. What do you expect of any good example of these measures? First, you wouldn't want any of them to give different readings for the same amount at different times. A variable speedometer might create problems with the police, and a changing set of scales might produce arguments in the family! Second, you want them to measure what they're supposed to. The police probably won't be sympathetic if you tell them, after doing your own repairs, that your speedometer was actually measuring oil pressure. Third, you want them to *transfer*. Again, it's no use

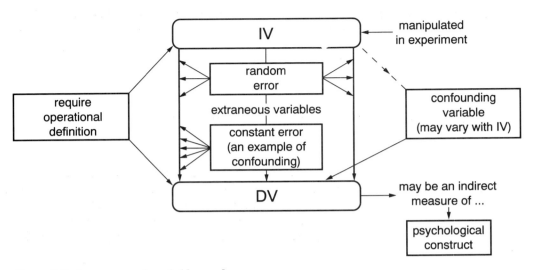

Figure 3.5 *Summary of variables and errors*

telling the police that you were only doing 30 *nautical* miles an hour, and you can't get away with saying your weight is only 100 pounds and, for you, a pound is the weight of the stone just outside your back door. We want our scales of measurement to be transferable from one public situation to another. We want any measure worth its salt to be:

- **RELIABLE** – it is consistent and stable
- **VALID** – it measures what is intended
- **STANDARDISED** – we can make comparisons with other people measured on the same scale

Notice that a measure could be reliable (i.e. consistent) but not valid. That is, it can do a job well but it's the wrong job! It is harder to imagine a measure which is valid but not reliable. However, it is possible to argue that a set of scales generally measures weight (and not height, pressure or temperature) yet they are a bit unreliable because they stick unpredictably. In the same way, some psychologists use methods, especially the more 'qualitative' ones, which provide rich 'valid' data on one occasion but it would be hard to obtain similar data again in the same circumstances.

RELIABILITY

Many measures of psychological variables are made using questionnaires, scales or tests containing a number of separate items. These are dealt with in some detail in Chapter 6. For any of these measures we can ask two questions concerning reliability. These are:

1 Is it consistent within itself? (the issue of **INTERNAL CONSISTENCY** or **INTERNAL RELIABILITY**)

2 Does it vary from one use to another? (the issue of **STABILITY** or **EXTERNAL RELIABILITY**)

To make this clear (I hope), imagine giving a statement to the police. You might contradict yourself *within* the statement, damaging your *internal* reliability, or you might contradict yourself from one statement to the next, affecting your *external* reliability.

METHODS FOR CHECKING INTERNAL RELIABILITY

Split-half method

As a psychological test contains several items (see Chapter 6), these can be split so that they are divided randomly, or by odd and even numbers, into two sets each comprising half the test. If the test is reliable then people's scores on each half should be similar (Figure 3.6) and the extent of similarity is assessed using *correlation* (see Chapter 12). Positive correlations near the top of the possible range (0–1) would normally be expected.

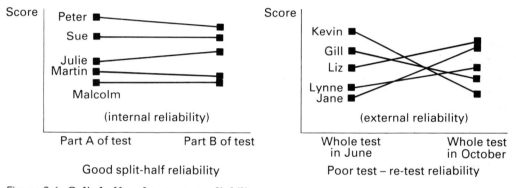

Figure 3.6 *Split-half and test-retest reliability*

Item analysis

A way to *improve* reliability is to employ some form of *item analysis*, explained briefly on page 93.

CHECKING EXTERNAL RELIABILITY

Test–retest reliability

This term tells you what is done to check whether a psychological measure is consistent from one testing occasion to the next. Participants are tested once, say in June, and again, say in October. The two sets of scores are then correlated (see Chapter 12) to determine the extent to which pairs of test scores from the same person at the two different times remain similar. It is important to remember that *the same group of people will be tested on each occasion*. If we tested different groups we could not compare individual old results with new results.

VALIDITY

A test or effect may well be rated as excellent on reliability but may not be measuring what was originally intended. This criticism is often levelled at tests of intelligence which, though quite reliable, measure only a narrow range of intellectual ability, missing out, for instance, the whole range of creative thought which the public language definition would include. The VALIDITY of a psychological measure is the extent to which it *does* measure what it is intended to measure.

Suppose you gave some 7-year-old children a list of quite difficult words to remember and recall. You may actually be testing their reading ability or word knowledge rather than their memory. Early experiments on perceptual defence, which seemed to show that people would take longer to recognise 'taboo', rude, or emotional words, were criticised for the validity of the effect on the grounds that what may well have been demonstrated was people's unwillingness to report such words to a strange experimenter or their disbelief that such words could occur in a respectable scientific experiment. The effect was quite reliable but confounded, so that the variable actually measured was later held to be (conscious) embarrassment and/or social expectation. The following are methods for checking validity.

FACE VALIDITY

The crudest method for checking a test's validity is simply to inspect the contents to see whether it does indeed measure what it's supposed to. When a test has face validity, it will be obvious to the test-taker what, in general, is being measured.

CONTENT VALIDITY

A researcher may ask colleagues to evaluate the content of a test to ensure that it is representative of the area which it is intended to cover. They will carry out this task using their expertise in the topic area to judge whether the collection of items has failed to test certain skills or is unduly weighted towards some aspects of knowledge compared with others. Content validity is, in fact, simply a more sophisticated version of face validity.

CRITERION VALIDITY

The validity of a test of neuroticism might reasonably be established by using it on a group of people who have suffered from a neurotic condition and comparing scores with a control group. Use of the neurotic group would be an example of what is called a KNOWN GROUPS CRITERION. There are two types of criterion validity differing only in terms of the timing of the criterion test:

Concurrent validity

If the new test is validated by comparison with a currently existing criterion, we have CONCURRENT VALIDITY. Very often, a new IQ or personality test might be compared with an older but similar test known to have good validity already.

Predictive validity

A prediction may be made, on the basis of a new intelligence test for instance, that high scorers at age 12 will be more likely to obtain university degrees or enter the professions several years later. If the prediction is born out then the test has PREDICTIVE VALIDITY.

CONSTRUCT VALIDITY

None of the methods above are very useful when we deal with a new and relatively 'invisible' psychological construct, such as 'extroversion' or 'locus of control'. How could I get you to believe that such a construct has meaning or some form of reality or that it is required in order to understand people's behaviour?

Construct validity entails demonstrating the power of such a construct to explain a network of research findings and to predict further relationships. Rokeach (1960) showed that his test for dogmatism distinguished between different religious political groups, as well as having relationships with tackling new problems and accepting new artistic ideas. Eysenck (1970) argued that extroversion was related to the activity of the cerebral cortex and produced several testable hypotheses from his theory.

If a construct is sound then it should be possible to support the argument for its existence with a variety of measures of its effects on other variables. If 'locus of control', for instance, is a genuine, common psychological factor, then we should be able to predict effects from a variety of different sorts of experiment and non-experimental measures, in the laboratory and the field, with a variety of different groups of people performing a number of qualitatively different tasks.

STANDARDISATION

The process of standardising a psychological measure involves adjusting it, using reliability and validity tests to eliminate items, until it is useful as a measure of the population it is targeted at, and will enable us to compare individuals with confidence. To make such comparisons the test must be used on a large sample of the target population, from whom the mean and standard deviation (see Chapter 9) are established. This will tell us what percentage of people tend to fall between certain scores and what is the value which most of the population centre around. Psychometric tests (see Chapter 6) are used in research but also on an applied basis in education, psychotherapeutic treatment, or job selection. Therefore, it is of the utmost importance that these measures do not discriminate, in a particular way, against some groups of people, which anyway reduces their scientific value. Standardisation has, therefore, both scientific and ethical importance.

An extremely important point here is that a test standardised on a particular population can obviously not be used with confidence on a different population. This criticism has been levelled at those who claimed a difference existed between white and black populations in intelligence. There *was* a difference in IQ score but, until 1973, the Stanford–Binet test had not included black people in its sample for standardisation. Hence, the test was only applicable, with any confidence, to members of the white population.

GLOSSARY

Systematic error in measurement, i.e. affects measurement always in one direction only	_____ _____	constant error
Definition of variable in exact terms of the steps taken to measure it	_____	operational definition
Unobservable psychological factor which is assumed to be responsible for observed behaviour. Retained so long as evidence supports it	_____ _____	psychological construct
Any error possible in measuring a variable, excluding error which is systematic	_____ _____	random error
Consistency or stability of a measure	_____	**reliability**
Stability of a test. Its tendency to produce the same results when repeated	_____	external (also *stability*)
Consistency of a test. Extent to which items agree with one another	_____	internal (also *internal consistency*)
Comparing scores on two halves formed by a random and equal, or odds-evens division of the items in a test	_____ ____	split half
Adjusting test until scores on it form a normal distribution and calculation of norms for the distribution from a large sample	_____	standardisation
Extent to which a test measures what was intended	_____	**validity**
Extent to which test results conform with those on some other measure, taken at the same time	_____	concurrent
Extent to which a proposed psychological variable is supported by a network of research evidence	_____	construct
Extent to which test covers the whole of the relevant topic area	_____	content
Extent to which test scores can be used to make a specific prediction on another measure	_____	criterion
Extent to which the measurement object of a test is self-evident	____	face
Test of criterion validity involving groups between whom scores on the test should differentiate	_____ _____	known groups

Extent to which test scores can predict scores on another variable or group differences	_____	predictive
Anything which can somewhow be observed to change in value	_____	**variable**
Variable which is uncontrolled and obscures any effect sought, usually in a systematic manner	_____	confounding
Variable which is assumed to be directly affected by changes in the IV	_____	dependent
Anything other than the IV which could affect the dependent variable; it may or may not have been allowed for and/or controlled	_____	extraneous
What the experimenter manipulates in an experiment; assumed to have a direct affect on the DV	_____	independent

EXERCISES

1 Identify the assumed independent and dependent variables in the following statements:
   a) Attitudes can be influenced by propaganda messages
   b) Noise affects efficiency of work
   c) Time of day affects span of attention
   d) Performance is improved with practice
   e) Smiles given tend to produce smiles in return
   f) Aggression can be the result of frustration
   g) Birth order in the family influences the individual's personality and intellectual achievement
   h) People's behaviour in crowds is different from behaviour when alone

2 In exercise 1, what could be an operational definition of: 'noise', 'span of attention', 'smile'?

3 Two groups of six-year-old children are assessed for their cognitive skills and sociability. One group has attended some form of preschool education for at least a year before starting school. The other group has not received any preschool experience. The preschool educated group are superior on both variables.
   a) Identify the independent and dependent variables
   b) Identify possible confounding variables
   c) Outline ways in which the confounding variables could be eliminated as possible explanations of the differences

4 A scale measuring attitude towards nuclear energy is given a test–retest reliability check. It is found that correlation is 0.85. However, it is also found that scores for the sample have risen significantly.
   a) Should the test be used as it is?
   b) What might explain the rise in sample scores?

5 A student friend has devised a test of 'Attitude towards the British' which she wants to administer to a group of international students just about to leave the country.
   a) How could the test be validated?
   b) How could the test be checked for reliability?

6 A friend says 'My cat hates Whitney Houston's music. I've put the record on ten times now and each time she goes out'. Is this a reliable test, a valid test, or neither?

PEOPLE – GROUPS, SAMPLES, AND COMPARISONS IN PSYCHOLOGICAL INVESTIGATIONS

SAMPLES

Suppose you had just come back from the airport with an Indian friend who is to stay with you for a few weeks and she switches on the television. To your horror, one of the worst imaginable game shows is on and you hasten to tell her that this is not typical of British TV fare. Suppose, again, that you are measuring attitudes to trade unions and you decide to use the college canteen to select people to answer your questionnaire. Unknown to you, the men and women you select are mainly people with union positions on a training course for negotiation skills. In both these cases an unrepresentative sample has been selected. In each case our view of reality can be distorted.

POPULATIONS AND SAMPLES

One of the main aims of scientific study is to be able to generalise from examples. A psychologist might be interested in establishing some quality of all human behaviour, or in the characteristics of a certain group, such as those with strong self-confidence or those who have experienced preschool education. In each case the POPULATION is all the existing members of that group. As the population itself will normally be too large for each individual within it to be investigated, we would normally select a SAMPLE from it to work with. A population need not consist of people. A biologist might be interested in a population consisting of all the cabbages in one field. A psychologist might be measuring participants' reaction times, in which case the population is the times (not the people) and is infinite, being all the times which could ever be produced.

The particular population we are interested in (managers, for instance), and from which we draw our samples, is known as the TARGET POPULATION.

SAMPLING BIAS

We need our sample to be typical of the population about which we wish to generalise results. If we studied male and female driving behaviour by observing drivers in a town at 11.45 a.m. or 3.30 p.m. our sample of women drivers is likely to contain a larger than usual number driving cars with small children in the back.

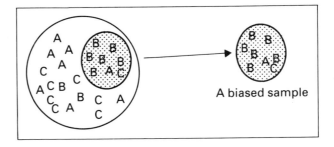

Figure 4.1 | *A biased sample*

This weighting of a sample with an over-representation of one particular category is known as **SAMPLING BIAS** or **SELECTION BIAS** (Figure 4.1). The sample tested in the college canteen was a biased sample, if we were expecting to acquire from it an estimation of the general public's current attitude to trade unions.

According to Ora (1965), many experimental studies may be biased simply because the sample used are volunteers. Ora found that volunteers were significantly different from the norm on the following characteristics: dependence on others, insecurity, aggressiveness, introversion, neuroticism and being influenced by others.

A further common source of sampling bias is the student. It is estimated that some 75% of American and British psychological research studies are conducted on students (Valentine, 1992). To be fair, the estimates are based on studies occurring around the late 1960s and early 1970s. Well over half of the UK participants were volunteers. To call many of the American participants 'volunteers' is somewhat misleading. In many US institutions the psychology student is required to participate in a certain number of research projects. The 'volunteering' only concerns which particular ones. This system also operates now in some UK establishments of higher education.

SAMPLING

REPRESENTATIVE SAMPLES

To avoid bias, what we need are samples that are representative of the population from which they are drawn. The target population for each sample is often dictated by the hypothesis under test. We might need one sample of men and one of women. Or we may require samples of 8-year-old and 12-year-old children, or a group of children who watch more than 20 hours of television a week and one watching less than 5 hours.

Within each of these populations, however, how are we to ensure that the individuals we select will be representative of their category? The simple truth is that a truly representative sample is an abstract ideal unachievable in practice. The practical goal we can set ourselves is to remove as much **SAMPLING BIAS** as possible. We need to ensure that no members of the target population are more likely than others to get into our sample. One way to achieve this goal is to take a truly **RANDOM SAMPLE,** as this is strictly defined as *a sample in which every member of the target population has an equal chance of being included.*

WHAT IS MEANT BY RANDOM?

Random is not just haphazard. The strict meaning of random sequencing is that no event is ever predictable from *any* of the preceding sequence. Haphazard human choices *may* have some underlying pattern of which we are unaware. This is not true for the butterfly. Evolution has led it to make an endlessly random sequence of turns in flight (unless injured) which makes prediction impossible for any of its much more powerful predators.

RANDOM SAMPLES

Which of the following procedures do you think would produce a group of people who would form a random sample?
a) Picking anybody off the street to answer a questionnaire
   (Target population: the general public)
b) Selecting every 10th name on the school register
   (Target population: the school)
c) Sticking a pin in a list of names
   (Target population: the names on the list)
d) Selecting slips from a hat containing the names of all Wobbly College students and asking those selected to answer your questionnaire on sexual behaviour
   (Target population: Wobbly College students)

The answer is that none of these methods will produce a tested random sample. In item (a) we may avoid people we don't like the look of, or they may avoid us. In item (b) the definition obviously isn't satisfied (this is a SYSTEMATIC SAMPLE, but is not random). In (c) we are less likely to drop our pin at the top or bottom of the paper. In (d) the initial selection is random but our sample will end up not containing those who refuse to take part.

If no specific type of person (teachers, drug addicts, 4 to 5-year-olds . . .) is the subject of research then, technically, a large random sample is the only sure way to acquire a fully representative sample of the population. Most psychological research, however, does not use random samples. A common method is to advertise in the local press; more common still is to acquire people by personal contact, and most common of all is to use students. A very common line in student practical reports is 'a random sample was selected'. This has never been true in my experience unless the population was the course year or college, perhaps.

What students can reasonably do is attempt to obtain as random a sample as possible, *or* to make the sample fairly representative, by selecting individuals from important subcategories (some working class, some middle class and so on) as is described under 'stratified sampling' below. Either way, it is important to discuss this issue when interpreting results and evaluating one's research.

HOW TO SAMPLE RANDOMLY

Computer selection

The computer can generate an endless string of random numbers. These are numbers which have absolutely no relationship to each other as a sequence and which are selected with equal frequency. Given a set of names the computer would use these to select a random set.

Random number tables

Alternatively, we can use the computer to generate a set of random numbers which we record and use to do any selecting ourselves. Such a table appears as Table 1 in Appendix 2. Starting anywhere in the table and moving either vertically or horizontally a random sequence of numbers is produced. To select five people at random from a group of 50, give everyone a number from 1 to 50 and enter the table by moving through it vertically or horizontally. Select the people who hold the first five numbers which occur as you move through the table.

Manual selection

The numbered balls in a Bingo session or the numbers on a roulette wheel are selected almost randomly, as are raffle tickets drawn from a barrel or hat so long as they are all well shuffled, the selector can't see the papers and these are all folded so as not to feel any different from one another. You *can* select a sample of 20 from the college population this way, but you'd need a large box rather than the 'hat' so popular in answers to questions on random selection.

These methods of random selection can be put to uses other than initial sample selection:

Random allocation to experimental groups

We may need to split 40 participants into two groups of 20. To ensure, as far as possible, that participant variables are spread evenly across the two groups, we need to give each participant an equal chance of being in either group. In fact, we are selecting a sample of 20 from a population of 40, and this can be done as described in the methods above.

Random ordering

We may wish to put 20 words in a memory list into random order. To do this give each word a random number as described before. Then put the random numbers into numerical order, keeping each word with its number. The words will now be randomly ordered.

Random sequencing of trials

In the experiment on infants' preference for simple and complex patterns, described in Chapter 2, we saw a need to present the complex figure to right and left at random. Here, the ordering can be decided by calling the first 20 trials 'left' and the rest 'right'. Now give all 40 trials a random number. Put these in order and the left–right sequencing will become random.

ENSURING A REPRESENTATIVE SAMPLE

If a researcher, conducting a large survey (see Chapter 6), wanted to ensure that as many types of people from one town could be selected for the sample, which of the following methods of contacting people would provide the greatest access?
a) Using the telephone directory
b) Selecting from all houses
c) Using the electoral roll
d) Questioning people on the street

I hope you'll agree that the electoral roll will provide us with the widest, unbiased section of the population, though it won't include prisoners, the homeless, new residents and persons in psychiatric care. The telephone directory eliminates non-phone owners and the house selection eliminates those in residential institutions. The street will not contain people at work, those with a severe disability unless they have a helper, and so on.

If we use near-perfect random sampling methods on the electoral roll then a representative sample, for the locality, should, theoretically, be the result. We should get numbers of men, women, over 60s, diabetics, young professionals, members of all cultural groups and so on, in proportion to their frequency of occurrence in the town as a whole. This will only happen, though, if the sample is fairly large as I hope you'll agree, at least after reading the section on sample sizes later.

STRATIFIED SAMPLING

We may not be able to use the electoral roll or we may be taking too small a sample to expect representativeness by chance. In such cases we may depart from complete random sampling. We may pre-define those groups of people we want represented (Figure 4.2).

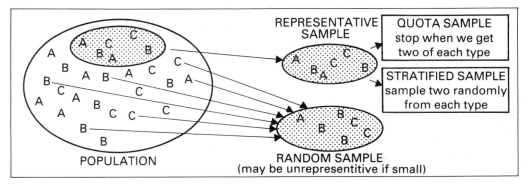

Figure 4.2 *Random, stratified and quota samples*

If you want a representative sample of students within your college you might decide to take business studies students, art students, catering students and so on, in proportion to their numbers. If 10% of the college population comprises art students, then 10% of your sample will be art students. If the sample is going to be 50 students then five will be chosen randomly from the art department.

The strata of the population we identify as relevant will vary according to the particular research we are conducting. If, for instance, we are researching the subject of attitudes to unemployment, we would want to ensure proportional representation of employed and unemployed, whilst on abortion we might wish to represent various religions. If the research has a local focus, then the local, not national, proportions would be relevant. In practice, with small scale research and limited samples, only a few relevant strata can be accommodated.

QUOTA SAMPLING

This method has been popular amongst market research companies and opinion pollsters. It consists of obtaining people from strata in proportion to their occurrence in the general population but with the selection from each stratum being left entirely to the devices of the interviewer who would be unlikely to use pure random methods, but would just stop interviewing 18- 21-year-old males, for instance, when the quota had been reached.

CLUSTER SAMPLES

It may be that, in a particular town, a certain geographical area can be fairly described as largely working class, another as largely middle class and another as largely Chinese. In this case 'clusters' (being housing blocks or whole streets) may be selected from each such area and as many people as possible from within that cluster will be included in the sample. This, it is said, produces large numbers of interviewees economically because researcher travel is reduced, but of course it is open to the criticism that each cluster may not be as representative as intended (Figure 4.3).

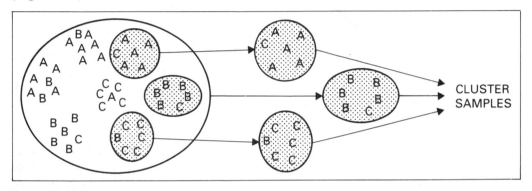

Figure 4.3 *Cluster samples*

THE SELF-SELECTING SAMPLE

You may recall some students who placed a ladder against a wall and observed how many men and women passed under or around it. In this investigation the sample could not be selected by the researchers. They had to rely on taking the persons who walked along the street at that time as their sample. Volunteers for experimental studies are, of course, a self-selecting sample.

THE OPPORTUNITY OR CONVENIENCE SAMPLE

Student practical work is very often carried out on other students. For that matter, so is a lot of research carried out in universities. If you use the other students in your class as a sample you are using them as an opportunity sample. They just happen to be the people you can get hold of (Figure 4.4).

The samples available in a 'natural experiment' (see Chapter 2) are also opportunistic in nature. If there is a chance to study children about to undergo an educational innovation, the researcher who takes it has no control over the sample.

SAMPLE SIZE

One of the most popular items in many students' armoury of prepared responses to 'Suggest modifications to this research' is 'The researcher should have tested more participants'. If a significant difference has been demonstrated between two groups

Figure 4.4 *An opportunity sample?*

this is not necessary unless: (1) we have good reason to suspect sampling bias; or (2) we are replicating the study.

If the research has failed to show a significant difference we may well suspect our samples of bias. But is it a good idea simply to add a lot more to our tested samples?

Large or small samples?

It is easier to produce a biased sample with small samples. I hope this example will make this clear. If you were to select five people from a group containing five Catholics, five Muslims, five Hindus and five Buddhists, you'd be more likely to get a religious bias in your sample than if you selected 10 people. For instance, if you select only five they could all be Catholics, but with 10 this isn't possible.

In general, the larger the sample the less the likely sampling bias.

Does this mean then that we should always test as many people as possible? Well, apart from the economic and time difficulties involved in always testing very large samples there is also a theoretical argument (detailed in Coolican, 1994) against large samples in experimental work. Put simply, it says that if you need *very* many people to demonstrate an experimental effect then the design is probably sloppy. Tightening up the design and procedure should eliminate the confounding or participant variables obscuring the effect you believe exists. The argument doesn't hold for survey work, attitude studies, or non-experimental work where extraneous variables cannot be controlled and evidence of a 'small but significant trend' (often mentioned in newspapers) is valuable, though usually ambiguous, evidence.

It has been argued that the optimum sample size, when investigating an experimental IV assumed to have a similar effect on most people, is about 25 to 30. If significance is not shown then the researcher investigates participant variables and the design of the study.

GROUPS

CONTROL GROUPS AND EXPERIMENTAL GROUPS

Suppose we were interested in attempting to reduce racial prejudice in children by use of a specific training programme. After one year the children's attitudes are indeed more positive than they were at the start. Can we say that the procedure obviously works? Is there an alternative explanation of the prejudice reduction? Where's the confounding variable?

Well, perhaps the children would have reached this greater maturity in thought without the treatment, through the increasing complexity of their encounters with the environment. We need to compare these children's development with that of a group who do not experience the programme. This latter group would be known as a CONTROL GROUP and the group receiving the programme as an EXPERIMENTAL GROUP or TREATMENT GROUP.

In selecting these two groups we must be careful to avoid confounding by participant variables and ensure that they are equivalent in composition. We can select each entirely at random or on a stratified basis. In studies like this, the children might be chosen as matched pairs so that for each child in one group there was a child to compare with in the other, matched on their initial prejudice score and on relevant characteristics such as age, sex, social class and so on.

PLACEBO GROUP

The experimental group in the example above may have lowered their output of prejudice responses because they knew they were in an experimental programme, especially if they knew what outcomes the researchers were expecting. In trials of new drugs some people are given a salt pill or solution in order to see whether the *expectation* of improvement and knowledge of having been given a cure alone will produce improvement. Similarly, psychologists create PLACEBO GROUPS in order to eliminate the possibility that results are confounded by expectancy variables.

A common experimental design within physiological psychology has been to inject participants with a substance that stimulates the physiological reactions which occur when individuals are emotionally aroused. A control group then experiences everything the injected (experimental) group experience, except the injection. The placebo group receives an injection of a harmless substance with no physiological effects. Performances are then observed and if both the control and placebo groups differ in the same way from the experimental group we can rule out expectancy as the cause of the difference. Some of the children in the prejudice study above could be given a programme unrelated to prejudice reduction, and also informed of expected results, in order to serve as a placebo group.

DESIGNS THAT COMPARE GROUPS

In many investigations a comparison is made between existing groups of people, usually in a non-experimental manner. In cross-sectional and cross-cultural studies, these are *different* groups of people. In longitudinal studies, the *same* groups are studied, at intervals, over a longish period, as in example 7 of Box 1.1.

CROSS-SECTIONAL DESIGNS

We often compare two or more groups on a particular variable. We might investigate differences between men and women on verbal reasoning, or between depressed and non-depressed people on 'external locus of control' (a tendency to see events that happen to you as not under your own control). Any such comparison between two or more groups is, in a sense, a cross-sectional design. We might study a cross-section of occupations or ethnic groups within the same area. The term is used most often, however, for studies in which an age comparison is required and several groups of people (often children) of different ages are studied at the same time. Comparisons may reveal age-related changes and are often used in developmental work. For example, Williams et al. (1975) asked 5-, 7-, and 9-year-old children to guess the sex of heavily stereotyped story characters. Five-year-olds showed some stereotyping but 7- and 9-year-olds showed far more.

LONGITUDINAL DESIGNS

As a cross-sectional study uses a kind of independent samples design, we can never be sure that any differences found were not the result of uneven sampling from the groups specified. Longitudinal studies get around this problem by studying the *same* people over a period of time, often many years. An example is the study by Eron et al. (1972), who followed 100 boys from age nine to 19 and demonstrated a correlation between early viewing of violence on television and later aggression. A longitudinal study may use a *control group* over the period, as did Kagan et al. (1980) in demonstrating that day-care children did not suffer in their development compared with home-reared children, so long as the day-care facilities were of good quality. Very large samples of children, followed through in the investigation of national trends, are known as a COHORT.

The relative advantages and disadvantages of these studies are given in Table 4.1.

Table 4.1 *Relative advantages and disadvantages of cross-sectional and longitudinal studies*

Advantages	Disadvantages
Cross-sectional	
Few people will be 'lost' during the study	If groups selected are not equivalent this may confound the results – for instance, if one group has a higher educational level and this is not the variable under investigation
Relatively less costly and time consuming, hence evidence is acquired more quickly and replications or alterations can be dealt with much earlier	Different experiences of one group (say, 30-year-olds who experienced extreme levels of unemployment) may confound the comparisons of all groups together
Longitudinal	
Differences in behaviour at various ages cannot be the result of sample differences	More costly and time consuming. Data for comparison take a long time to arrive. Once the study is under-way it is difficult or impossible to alter unwise decisions. Replication will also take a long time, if possible at all
Useful for following through the effect of some 'treatment' (e.g. educational intervention programme) on one group compared with a control group	The whole of the generation followed may share a unique experience, making generalisation to other generations invalid
Results are not confounded by very different experiences for a group of one specific age (because the group, at all ages, is the same one)	Samples studied are usually small and it is easier to 'lose' participants

CROSS-CULTURAL STUDIES

If you look back to example 5 in Box 1.1 you'll see that it poses something of a design problem. It may be that the drivers in Mexico act more aggressively than those in Iceland, or the reverse, but the results may be confounded by the fact that most of the drivers in Mexico will be Mexican and most in Iceland will be Icelandic!

Suppose, instead, our researchers were interested in driving behaviour differences between Mexicans and Icelanders. This would now qualify as a CROSS-CULTURAL study. In fact, the study would now be *confounded* by the factor of differing heat. In addition, we have a rather serious problem of CULTURAL BIAS in our measuring instrument. British drivers are often astounded by the apparent aggressiveness of drivers in Rome or Bombay, where hooting is pretty well constant. However, if, as would often occur in Britain, one were to take offence and respond aggressively *back* to the hooting, the drivers in those cities might be surprised – hooting is *normal* behaviour – it isn't aggressive by local norms.

This is an example of ETHNOCENTRISM – interpreting the behaviour of another culture as one would interpret that behaviour in one's own culture. A further example is interpreting a tribe's religious beliefs as 'superstitious' whilst assuming one's own are somehow the absolute truth, whereas, members of an outside culture would see them as equally superstitious. Westerners sometimes describe Eastern greetings, involving a bowed head and no eye contact, as 'deferential' or 'shy' but this is simply a Western *interpretation* and not any kind of absolute 'truth'. Similarly ethnocentric is the notion that other, exotic, or different groups are 'ethnic', whereas white Westerners are not. Everyone in the world belongs to at least one ethnic group.

Generalising about *any* culture is fraught with difficulty. Fortunately not many psychologists have been as racist as C.G. Jung (1930) who claimed:

> The inferior (African) man exercises a tremendous pull upon civilised beings who are forced to live with him, because he fascinates the inferior layers of our psyche, which has lived through untold ages of similar conditions.

Africans, he argued, had a 'whole evolutionary layer less', psychologically speaking.

Our assessment of the behaviour and beliefs of cultures different from our own, then, are likely to be biased both by the measures we use, if they have not been *standardised* in that culture, and by the interpretations we make of the results of those measures. As an example consider the IQ test which asked, of a picture of a boy holding an umbrella at the wrong angle to the rain, 'What is wrong with this picture?'. Puerto Ricans mostly scored no points at all on this item as for a boy to carry an umbrella *at all* in their society was (at least then) considered seriously effeminate!

Modern cross-cultural studies are nowhere near as 'Euro-centred' and ethnocentric as they once were. The methods used, and philosophy employed, have been very much influenced by the anthropologists, of whom Margaret Mead (1928, 1930) and Ruth Benedict (1934) were early pioneers, although Mead has since been severely criticised for bias in her methods, probably influenced by her preresearch notions of what she wanted to find in an 'idyllic' non-Western society (Freeman, 1983). An important modern area for application of these studies is that of 'acculturation' – the process of becoming used to another culture (as a result of emigration or of being a refugee) and having one's own culture change as a result (see Williams and Berry, 1991; also Berry et al., 1992, which is an excellent source book for the modern cross-cultural approach). Some researchers are developing 'indigenous psychologies', which reject Western origins and attempt to start afresh with psychological theory and research methods entirely rooted in the local cultural base.

STUDYING CULTURES WITHIN ONE SOCIETY – THE 'RACE PROJECT'

Very often, and for the best possible reasons (reducing prejudice, fascination with another culture) students will wish to carry out a study focusing on ethnic difference, attitude, or belief. This is a highly sensitive area and my advice would be to seek advice from tutors and members of the ethnic group(s) in question and think and plan very carefully before proceeding. Language and concepts used in innocence may well offend many members of the group(s) concerned. Many black people do not like being called 'coloured', for instance, and for obvious reasons. 'Coloured' is a euphemism carrying the implication 'not naturally un-coloured like us', whereas, in fact, everyone has a colour. There will be exceptions and this is because 'other' cultures are not as homogenous as they might seem at a distance. People vary a lot *within* cultures and so one needs the greatest sensitivity, tact and prepared knowledge not to alienate the very people one wishes to find out about.

GLOSSARY

Large sample of people, often children, identified for longitudinal or cross-sectional study	_____	cohort
		comparison studies
Comparative study of two or more different societies or social subgroups	_____ _____	cross-cultural study
Comparative study of several groups measured at a single time point	_____ _____	cross-sectional study
Comparative study of one group over a relatively long period (possible including a control group)	_____ _____	longitudinal study
Effect of specific culture on psychological instrument, especially where the measure was not developed in or for that culture	_____ _____	cultural bias
Bias of viewing another's culture from one's own cultural perspective	_____	ethnocentrism
		groups
Group used as baseline measure against which performance of experimental, treatment, or criterion group is assessed	_____	control
Group who receive values of the IV in an experiment or quasi-experiment	_____ or _____	experimental or treatment

Group who don't receive the critical 'treatment' but everything else the experimental group receive and who are (sometimes) led to believe that their treatment will have an effect; used to check expectancy effects	_____	placebo
Effect on participants simply through knowing they are expected to exhibit changed behaviour	_____ _____	placebo effect
All possible members of a group from which a sample is taken	_____	population
Number which has absolutely no relationship with the other numbers in its set	_____ _____	random number
Group selected from population for study of experiment	_____	**sample**
Sample in which members of a subgroup of the target population are over- or under-represented	_____	biased
Sample selected from specific area as being representative of a population	_____	cluster
Sample selected because they are easily available for testing	_____	opportunity
Sample selected so that specified groups will appear in numbers proportional to their size in the target population; selection ceases when enough of specific subgroup has been found	_____	quota
Sample selected in which every member of the target population has an equal chance of being selected	_____	random
Sample selected so that specified groups will appear in numbers proportional to their size in the target population	_____	representative
Sampling selected for study on the basis of their own action in arriving at the sampling point	_____	self-selecting
Sample selected so that specified groups will appear in numbers proportional to their size in the target population; within each subgroup cases are selected on a random basis	_____	stratified
Sample selected by taking every nth case	_____	systematic

| Systematic tendency towards over- or under-representation of some categories (of people) in a sample | _____ ____ | sampling bias (or selection bias) |
| The (often theoretical) group of all possible cases from which, it is hoped, a sample has been taken | _____ _____ | target population |

EXERCISES

1 A researcher shows that participants in a conformity experiment quite often give an obviously wrong answer to simple questions when six other confederates of the experimenter have just given the same wrong answer by prearrangement. What else must the researcher do in order to demonstrate that the real participants actually are conforming to group pressure?

2 The aim of a particular investigation is to compare the attitudes of working-class and middle-class mothers to discipline in child rearing. What factors should be taken into account in selecting two comparable samples (apart from social class)?

3 A psychologist advertises in the university bulletin for students willing to participate in an experiment concerning the effects of alcohol consumption on appetite. For what reasons might the sample gathered not be a random selection of students?

4 A truly random sample of business studies students in the county of Suffex could be drawn by which one of these methods?
   a) Selecting one college at random and using all the business studies students within it.
   b) Group all business studies students within each college by surname initial (A, B, . . . Z). Select one person at random from each initial group in each college.
   c) Put the names of all business studies students at all colleges into a very large hat, shake and draw out names without looking.

5 A psychologist visits a group of 20 families with a 4-year-old child and trains the mother to use a special programme for promoting reading ability. Results in reading ability at age six are compared with those of a control group who were not visited and trained. A research assistant suggests that a third group of families should have been included in the study. What sort of group do you think the assistant is suggesting?

6 A psychology lecturer requires two groups to participate in a memory experiment. She divides the students in half by splitting the left side from the right side of the class. The left side get special instructions and do better on the problem-solving task. The lecturer claims that the instructions are therefore effective. Her students argue that a confounding variable could be operating. What are they thinking of, perhaps?

Non-experimental investigation methods

5

OBSERVING – OBSERVATIONAL DESIGNS AND TECHNIQUES

Look back once again to our suggestions for research into the heat–aggression relationship in Box 1.1. Decide (again) which ones are *not* experimental studies. Note which ones involve some form of direct observation of behaviour.

By now you should be able to tell that examples 5, 6, and 7 are not experiments. No independent variable is manipulated by the researchers. Nevertheless we *are* interested here in trying to investigate the effect of one variable on another. Remember that in non-experimental studies we often *do* investigate the effect of one variable (cause) on another (effect) and we *do* test hypotheses objectively, and with as much control as possible. In some non-experimental approaches, however, rigid control is sacrificed in the interests of maintaining more natural behaviour in the participants, as we shall see.

OBSERVATION AS A TECHNIQUE

Notice that in example 3, which *is* an experiment (so long as pairs are split randomly) observation is used as a *technique* in order to measure the dependent variable of aggression. (I'm referring to the *second* observation of the two groups, by the naive observers on the hot and cold day.) The study would *not* be termed an *observational study* as such, but an experiment which happens to use observation for measurement of a variable. Bandura's (1965) studies of children imitating adult models follow this pattern. Amongst other things the following variables were manipulated very carefully – status of the model, reward or punishment of the model, amount by which each child was deliberately frustrated prior to the observation – and Bandura's assistants were able to record the child's amount of copying behaviour using observation techniques. The studies, though, were quite definitely experimental in overall nature.

In an **OBSERVATIONAL STUDY** the emphasis is on the overall nature of the study being *non-experimental* and on simply observing the naturally and freely occurring behaviour of people, *with or without* their knowledge. Simply observing the two groups of children, one on a hot day and one on a cool day, would serve as a non-experimental, observational study.

WHY CONDUCT AN OBSERVATIONAL STUDY?

Can you think of some good reasons why a researcher might decide *not* to use an experiment but to observe people's naturally occurring, freely chosen behaviour?

Some common reasons are these:

1 The researchers may feel that an experiment will create behaviour which is too artificial. It might be difficult, for instance, to imagine how one could, in a laboratory, get people to react as they normally would towards a street beggar.
2 Observation may be the only answer – we can't ask babies to behave in a certain way when we're trying to record their language utterances.
3 Again, we can't *create* maternal or educational deprivation in children. We must go out, find deprived children and either observe their behaviour or, if they're old enough, ask them questions.

SYSTEMATIC OBSERVATION

DEVICES FOR GATHERING DATA IN OBSERVATIONAL STUDIES

The raw data gathered in an observational study can take the following forms:

Visual – moving (video) picture or still
Audio – tape recording of spoken observations as behaviour occurs
Written – notes; ratings made on the spot

In all cases data can be further categorised or 'coded' after the event but visual recordings provide the greatest amount of information for analysis at any later pace. Participants may be unaware of the recording process, creating ethical issues, or they may be aware but unable to perceive the equipment. Researchers use screens, hidden cameras, or 'one-way mirrors', which act as a viewing window for observers but a mirror for participants.

SYSTEMS FOR GATHERING OBSERVATIONAL DATA

Observers will usually classify behaviour according to a system such as that shown in Table 5.1. Here, recordings are made of infants' behaviour in a playground. The *frequency* of occurrence of each behaviour pattern would be noted, and possibly the *time* spent in shouting, for instance. With a larger recording grid, facial gestures might also be recorded. Other recording systems might be:

• a RATING SCALE where observers have to assess, say, the emotional strength of a child's reunion with its mother
• a CODING system where particular positions of parts of the body are matched with a set of graphic symbols

SAMPLING BEHAVIOUR FOR OBSERVATION

Observers can't observe everything. They may have to conduct 'time sampling'

Table 5.1   *Categorisation system for observation of aggressive behaviour*

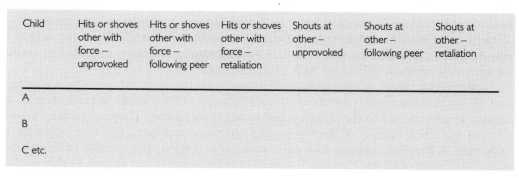

Child	Hits or shoves other with force – unprovoked	Hits or shoves other with force – following peer	Hits or shoves other with force – retaliation	Shouts at other – unprovoked	Shouts at other – following peer	Shouts at other – retaliation
A						
B						
C etc.						

(observe for certain periods), 'point sampling' (observe each individual's current category of behaviour before moving straight on to the next individual), or 'event sampling' (observe a specific event each time it occurs, e.g. a playground fight).

RELIABILITY OF OBSERVATIONAL TECHNIQUES

We need to obtain *reliable* records from observers and this can be achieved by correlating (Chapter 12) their results with those of other observers to produce an estimate of **INTER-OBSERVER** (or **INTER-RATER**) **RELIABILITY**. This reliability estimate may be low if there is **OBSERVER BIAS**. We know that each person's view is unique and that our perception is affected by innumerable factors. A trained observer might report a hard blow where a novice might report it as 'vicious'. Jenny might be mistakenly described as 'copying' when she looks into a box to see what Sarah is looking at. To deal with this, the researcher must *operationalise* any measures using a tightly and clearly defined rating scale. If this is vague or ambiguous, reliability will be poor. The rating or coding system will be standardised by rigid training of observers prior to the commencement of observation proper.

CONTROLLED AND NATURALISTIC OBSERVATION

Remember that we have said that, although non-experimental studies lack control over the independent variable and extraneous variables, nevertheless, researchers usually try to *control* their data gathering as far as possible. Ways to exert this control are:

- control over the assessment system, as described above
- creating good inter-rater reliability with further training and practice if necessary
- control over the environment in which the observation takes place, perhaps using a laboratory as did Ainsworth et al. (1971; mentioned in Chapter 2)

ALTERNATIVES TO CONTROL – NATURALISTIC OBSERVATION

Observational studies in the laboratory can be criticised on the same grounds as was the laboratory experiment in the last chapter. Behaviour can be artificial and does not occur in its normal social context. By contrast, a NATURALISTIC OBSERVATION study can produce observation of everyday behaviour in, say, the nursery or workplace. Because this behaviour would have occurred anyway, as long as the observer is discreet, then realism and ecological validity are likely to be high. However, where a researcher or video camera, for instance, follows family members around the house for extended periods, behaviour might be distorted.

To avoid this effect of the observers' presence, researchers can become a familiar part of the environment. Charlesworth and Hartup (1967) made several visits to a nursery school, talked to the children and learnt their names. They found they could also test out the reliability of their proposed observation scheme prior to formal data gathering. A familiar example of a naturalistic observation study might be Brown et al.'s (1964) study of three children's speech in their family home almost weekly for 10 years.

ARGUMENTS AGAINST SYSTEMATIC OR STRUCTURED OBSERVATION

Even researchers conducting observation in the naturalistic setting usually use a clearly defined system for recording and categorising observed behaviour. This approach still runs into a more general criticism of this kind of research, which argues that *any* strict classification system severely limits our appreciation of the full richness and meaning of human behaviour in its social context. A growing number of psychologists in the social and applied areas of research and practice have argued for a quite different approach to studying human behaviour and experience, using some ideas inherited from sociology and anthropology. As an example of the objection, consider how much of what we normally call aggression in a child would be missed by the classification system in Table 5.1. The objectors to rigid classification are not arguing that there could be *better* classification systems in cases like these. They are saying that the attempt to classify *in itself* destroys our ability to appreciate fully or realistically the true meaning and context of human behaviour.

> List the strengths and weaknesses, as you see them, of:
> - observation studies in general, compared with experiments
> - controlled observation
> - naturalistic observation
>
> See Table 5.2 for a summary.

PARTICIPANT OBSERVATION

The last thing left for this chapter is to appreciate an important distinction, already hinted at, between two types of observational study. So far we have talked only of observing other people where the observer is not part of the group. Most of our observations of people in everyday life are made when we *are* part of the group. Some researchers follow the principle that, if you can't 'observe 'em' (as a spectator) 'join 'em'. Others argue that one should not *anyway* observe as a spectator, so join 'em. The latter group follow arguments about realism and genuine information gathering similar to those outlined briefly above.

The *participant observer* joins the group to be investigated but the extent of the involvement can vary. The observer might not *disclose* the observer role but might play a full part in group activities as an ordinary and accepted member. On the other hand the observer might disclose their role and either let every member of the group relate to him/her as a researcher temporarily visiting or, more subtly, the researcher might declare a research interest and role yet still hope to be taken as one of the group, for instance, by becoming a temporary member of a school's teaching staff with a full timetable.

UNDISCLOSED AND DISCLOSED PARTICIPANT OBSERVATION

An example of an **UNDISCLOSED** approach is Rosenhan's (1973) study, in which researchers presented themselves at out-patients' departments complaining of hearing voices and noises in their heads. During their subsequent stays in psychiatric wards they observed the reactions of staff and patients towards them. Other patients in the wards detected their 'normality' before doctors, and one researcher's note-taking was recorded as 'excessive writing behaviour'. In an older 'classic', Whyte (1943) joined a Chicago street gang saying he was writing a book about the area. Hence, his role was not entirely undisclosed. He described his transition from a 'non-participating observer' to a 'non-observing participant'.

Becker (1958) used a **DISCLOSED** approach, having his observers join groups of medical students for their working day and in the social atmosphere of their dormitories.

ETHICAL ISSUES IN UNDISCLOSED PARTICIPANT OBSERVATION

Participant observation can suffer from the same strong humanist criticism of experiments – it deceives the people studied. The researcher must decide what can be published without consent and must be aware that the people studied will not be able to recall everything they have divulged or done during the research period. They must therefore be permitted to review relevant material and to veto any which might identify them. Lack of this consent-seeking will lead to mistrust of the distant and elite research community.

List the strengths and weaknesses, as you see them, of participant observation studies. See Table 5.2 for a summary

Methods for the analysis and interpretation of data from relatively unstructured or participant observation methods are discussed in general terms in Chapter 7.

Table 5.2 *Strengths and weaknesses of types of observational study*

Strengths	Weaknesses
Observation studies in general (compared with experiments)	
Less intrusive	Control over extraneous variables less rigid
Less likely to create artificial behaviour unless performed in the laboratory	Harder to establish clear evidence for cause–effect relationship
Controlled observation (especially in the laboratory)	
Some control over: • extraneous variables • observer variation and bias	Artificiality of e.g. laboratory Rigid classification system may miss important aspects of observed behaviour
Naturalistic observation	
Behaviour observed is naturally occurring and should be unaffected by target's anxiety or need to impress (but not so if, say, video camera obviously present)	Extraneous variables poorly controlled Observer bias more likely because target's behaviour and the environment in general are more unpredictable
Includes full social context of behaviour	Equipment required for good recordings is hard to transport and use discreetly
Greater ecological validity	
Useful where experimentation would be impossible or unethical	Intrusion of, e.g. video camera, may create artificial behaviour
Useful where individuals would be unlikely to cooperate with direct approaches (e.g. patients in a casualty ward)	Difficult to remain hidden Replication is harder Rigid classification system may miss important aspects of observed behaviour
Participant observation	
Flexible, non-structured data gathering system may produce greater richness of information and higher ecological validity	Unstructured data gathering system creates: • problem with observer bias and distortion • difficulty of verifying data with other researchers • difficulty of replication or generalisation to other settings
Participants act completely naturally if undisclosed	
Rapport gained with group produces authentic behaviour and ideas – true meaning of participants' behaviour more readily available	Difficult to make notes on the spot if undisclosed – relies on memory which can easily be distorted over time
Researcher gains first hand experience of the roles and interactions of those under investigation	Ethical issues if undisclosed Emotional involvement of researcher may cloud objectivity

GLOSSARY

System used to categorise observations	_____	coding
Letting people know that they are the object of observation	_____	disclosure
Recording of individual's relatively freely chosen behaviour with or without their knowledge of the observation process	_____	**observation**
Observation in which many variables are kept constant	_____	controlled
Study which is solely observational and does not include any experimentation	_____ _____	observation design (study)
Observation without intervention in observed people's own environment	_____	naturalistic
Observation in which observer does not take part or play a role in the group observed	_____	non-participant
Observation in which observer takes part or plays a role in the group observed	_____	participant
Observation which uses an explicitly defined framework for data recording	_____	systematic
Effect causing unwanted variations in data recorded which are produced because of characteristics of the observer	_____ ____	observer bias
Extent to which observers agree in their rating or coding	_____ _____	inter-observer (or inter-rater) reliability
Scale used in assessment of observed behaviour – observed unit is placed at appropriate point along a numerical dimension	_____ ____	rating scale
Observation study (especially participant) in which observation process is not disclosed to persons being observed	_____ _____	undisclosed observation

EXERCISES

1 Outline a research study which would use observation to investigate the following hypotheses:

   a) During exploratory play, mothers allow their sons to venture further away from them than their daughters

   b) When asked personal, or slightly embarrassing questions, people are likely to avert their gaze

c) Women are safer drivers than men

d) There are common patterns of behaviour among individuals in groups which are asked to produce volunteers for an unpopular task

Ensure that: variables are operationalised;

the *exact* method of data gathering is described, including the location, sample selection, data collection method and equipment used.

2 A student decides to carry out participant observation on her own student group. She is interested in the different ways her classmates cope with study demands and social commitments. Discuss the ways she might go about this work, the problems she might face and the ways in which she might surmount difficulties.

3 Describe ways in which Bandura's hypotheses, including those which investigate the influence of different types of child and adult model, could have been investigated using naturalistic observation rather than the laboratory.

4 A researcher is concerned that the rating scale in use is not producing good inter-rater reliability. The observations of two observers are as follows:

Observation for child X: altruistic acts in 5-minute intervals:									
	0–5	6–10	11–15	16–20	21–25	26–30	31–35	36–40	41–45
Observer A	1	3	4	2	5	12	9	4	8
Observer B	2	10	8	7	1	3	5	5	6

Would you say this represents good reliability or not? What statistical procedure could tell us the degree of reliability (see Chapters 3 and 12)?

5 Work with a colleague and decide on a variable to observe in children or adults. Make the variable something which is likely to occur quite frequently in a short observation period (10 minutes), such as one person smiling in a two-person conversation in the college refectory. Make your observation of the same person at the same time separately and then compare your results to see whether you tend to agree fairly well or not.

6

QUESTIONS – INTERVIEWS, SURVEYS, QUESTIONNAIRES, AND PSYCHOLOGICAL SCALES

There are really only three overall ways to investigate people directly – we observe them, ask questions, or meddle. By 'meddle' I mean experiment. We have dealt with experimenting and observing. Perhaps the reader has asked by now 'Why don't psychologists just go and ask people directly about themselves?' A general term used for a method which asks people to give information about themselves is **SELF-REPORT METHOD**.

> In which of our heat-aggression examples in Box 1.1 are we asking questions directly concerning our participants?

I hope you agree that this only occurs in examples 4, 5, and 6. in example 2 we ask questions but the participants have to answer about the film, not themselves (though we are assuming that this gives us *indirect* information about how aggressive they're feeling – something like projective tests to be covered later in this chapter). In example 6 the first question is also about a fictitious person receiving a prison sentence, not about the participant directly. I'm not at all sure that the interview suggestion in example 5 is workable or even safe!

How do psychologists ask questions?

There are two major approaches to asking questions, first, by **INTERVIEW**, and second by **QUESTIONNAIRE** or **PSYCHOMETRIC TEST** (or 'scale'). Some interviews will incorporate the use of a test, scale, or questionnaire. Some experiments may involve the use of a questionnaire or scale, often to measure the dependent variable. We might, for instance, ask two randomly selected groups to complete a scale measuring participants' attitude towards people with disabilities. We might then give one group some training designed to heighten awareness about disabilities and subsequently measure the two groups' attitudes again, looking for change in the trained group. An experiment might even use interviews to measure such a dependent variable. Interviews can also provide information *additional* to the main data from an experiment. The interviews conducted by Asch (1956) and Milgram (1963) after their celebrated demonstrations of seemingly bizarre human behaviour give some of the most fascinating and rich data one can imagine and certainly formed the springboard for a huge volume of further illuminating and productive research.

However, an INTERVIEW STUDY is one in which the overall design is to use interviews to gather information as opposed to the formality and possible artificiality of the experiment. A *correlational* study might measure and compare people on two or more scales or tests.

> With example 5 from Box 1.1 in mind, make a brief set of notes now on what you might ask in an interview with a driver in the rush hour about their feelings of aggression. More importantly, list all the problems you can see with *any* interview or other questioning method. In what ways would we be likely to obtain distorted, unreliable information and in what ways could we compare one set of information with another?

GENERAL ISSUES

STRUCTURE AND DISGUISE
Structure

As with observational studies, these self-report methods can range across a dimension from:

Unstructured	to	**Structured**

Where the relevant advantages are:
- Rich information
- Interviewee says what they want to say
- High ecological validity
- Interviewer can be flexible in order to get greatest amount of relevant information

- More objectively verifiable or generalisable
- Interviewer needs less training or preparation in interpersonal skills
- Interviewer bias less likely from (emotional) involvement
- Interviewer can take more distant and objective view of proceedings

Disguise

Several techniques used by researchers in questioning participants are constructed so that their real or main purpose is disguised.

> 1 Why might a researcher wish to disguise the true aim of their questioning?
> 2 How might a researcher disguise the true aim of their questioning?

1 Some possible reasons are:
  - Participants might guess the real aim and act accordingly – either 'pleasing the researcher' by giving the answers expected or by acting contrary in order to prove that they are not too conventional in their behaviour.
  - The information required, or the reasons for obtaining it, may be potentially embarrassing for the participant.

Disguising the true aims of a research project is known as 'deception' and, as with undisclosed participant observation or when it occurs in experiments, it raises serious ethical issues, which are dealt with in Chapter 14.

2 Some ways to disguise questioning are:
- Bury the important questions among many other unrelated and irrelevant ones.
- Give fixed choice answers, e.g. I could ask you 'By how much did the government raise taxes in the UK in 1994?' a) 5% b) 10% c) 20%, and your answer might give an indication of how favourable you are towards the government or not, the true answer being irrelevant to the main aim.
- Some researchers ask questions and simultaneously record the participant's galvanic skin response – an indication of anxiety if high.
- Use of a 'projective' test – to be described later on in this chapter.

FACTORS AFFECTING SELF-REPORT METHODS

When you considered the difficulties of asking people questions in the exercise above you may well have noted two important problems. First, it will matter to some extent who the interviewer is. Hence, *personal* variables are relevant. Second, an interviewing or questioning approach produces an interpersonal situation in which certain well-known social or *interaction* variables will have an effect. The experiment is also a social situation and you may recall that it has been argued that *demand characteristics* may affect results. It is highly likely that interviewees *too* will attempt to discern what the interviewer is after. The advantage in an interview is that the interviewer can talk about this and try to get at genuine attitudes and ideas. But, on the downside, this increased intimacy may make it *more* likely that people's behaviour will be affected, as in any social situation, by 'social desirability'. Participants may also respond to *conformity pressures*, feeling they should say what is expected, not what they really think or do.

My list of possible factors *more* likely to have an effect than in other research designs, is given in Table 6.1.

Table 6.1 *Factors affecting self-report situations*

Personal factors	
Gender	Research supports the suggestion that people respond more positively to members of the opposite sex whom they find attractive
Ethnic origin	Research also supports the hypothesis that members of different groups react more formally, at least initially, than do members of similar groups
Formality of role	Even if the interviewer is relatively relaxed, interviewees may still react to her or him as an important figure, and search for somehow 'correct' language
Personality	The 'chemistry' of the interaction between the two people may be useful or detrimental to the production of full, genuine research data
Interaction factors	
Social desirability	See Chapter 2

Table 6.1 *cont.*

Evaluative cues	Linked to social desirability is people's constant searching for 'cues' about 'correct' responses. The interviewer needs to avoid responding in ways likely to be interpreted as criticism or disagreement

These are only some examples I thought worth including. Don't worry if you thought of others not mentioned here. They almost certainly are likely to affect questioning sessions. You could raise these in class discussion with your tutor. The whole area is a massive one and space limits our discussion here. There is a bit more detail in Coolican (1994).

INTERVIEWS

Face-to-face interviews can range from being pretty well unstructured to the complete structure of the survey. A description of types in the range is given in Table 6.2. The data from the less structured methods will be originally in *qualitative* form and will require some form of analysis. Dealing with such qualitative data is dealt with briefly in Chapter 7.

Table 6.2 *Types of interview*

Non-directive	Very much used by counsellors and 'client-centred' therapists where the aim is not so much to gather data as to help the client. No direction is given but the interviewer gives support intended to help the client solve their own problems, gain self-awareness and grow in personal confidence
Informal	Quite unstructured but with an overall data gathering aim. Interviewee is prompted to talk and the interviewer listens patiently and sympathetically and offers intelligent comments but no advice or argument. Interviewer may prompt further expansion on a point and offer a direction or support in further exploration by the interviewee
Informal but guided	The interviewer has a set of topics to cover and perhaps some specifically worded questions to ask but the interview is conducted as a friendly, natural conversation. The interviewer 'plays it by ear' and works in the various questions and topics as the discussion progresses. Also known as 'semi-structured', Piaget used a version of this in his **CLINICAL METHOD** (or interview), which has a specific goal (to test a hypothesis or demonstrate an ability) but follows up a child's answers to set questions with spontaneous new enquiries which hope to do justice to his/her pattern of thought

Table 6.2 *cont.*

Structured but open-ended	There is a fixed set of questions to ask but replies are 'open-ended'. The interviewee may answer in any terms they wish
Fully structured	There is a fixed set of questions and a fixed set of possible responses for the interviewee to choose from. This is the type of interview mostly used in surveys

SURVEYS

A survey consists of asking a lot of people for information, usually using a completely structured questionnaire with mostly fixed-choice questions. Interviewers usually work as a team and so procedures, including the introductory statement, are standardised.

DESCRIPTIVE AND ANALYTIC USE OF SURVEYS

Surveys can be used simply to obtain descriptive data about populations. A notorious one was that of Kinsey et al. (1953) on American sexual behaviour. Jowell and Topf (1988) gathered information on British social attitudes including Aids, the country-side, education, the North–South divide, and opinions on sharing household chores.

Used analytically, survey and interview data can be used to test hypotheses. Ross (1973, in Cook and Campbell, 1979) demonstrated from traffic data that there was a marked drop in the accident rate during weekend nights immediately after the introduction of a breathalyser 'crackdown' in October 1967. However, the cause could have been a reduction in amount of driving, less alcohol consumption or safer driving. Ross used surveys by the British Road Research Laboratory in order to rule out some of these explanations. For instance, he showed that there was a decrease in *accidents per mile driven* not just accidents. Sales of alcohol on weekend nights had not dropped significantly. Interviews showed that for ten months *post*-breathalyser introduction more people reported walking home after drinking than they did in the ten months **preceding** the breathalyser.

SAMPLING

We dealt with sampling in Chapter 4. Note that the survey is more likely than other methods to use *stratified*, *quota*, or *cluster sampling* and that it is extremely important here to try to obtain as representative a sample as possible. If the sample is the whole of the population then the research is known as a CENSUS.

THE MODE OF QUESTIONING

There are three obvious ways of communicating with RESPONDENTS (people who are questioned in a survey): face-to-face, telephone, and letter. Of these, telephones are rarely used, though they will often be used for making the initial contact and are increasing in use during the 1990s. The postal method is cheaper, less time consuming and will probably produce more honest answers (since personal interaction is avoided). However, non-return is likely to be high and instructions must be exceptionally clear. In a face-to-face interview, the interviewer can clear up any misunderstandings.

QUESTIONNAIRES, SCALES, AND PSYCHOMETRIC TESTS

Psychologists use a variety of questionnaires, scales, and tests in order to obtain information from people. In general, borrowing terminology from the natural sciences and technology, these measures are often known as *instruments*. Table 6.3 lists and defines the general categories of measure which a psychologist might use:

Table 6.3 *Categories of measurement*

Questionnaire	The correct name for a measure which does ask several questions, unlike many *attitude* and *personality* scales which are described below. Often used for survey work in order to obtain current views on a particular issue. Also used to obtain information (especially with a 'yes/no' answer) about regular behaviour, for instance, modes of child discipline, sexual habits, typical leisure activities, moral principles, voting behaviour
Attitude scale	Intended to measure a relatively permanent and habitual position of the individual on a particular issue (rather than an opinion). These often employ a set of *statements* with which the respondent indicates their level of agreement or disagreement
Personality scale	Intended to measure a relatively enduring feature of a person's regular behaviour (such as their general anxiety level, extroversion or typical approach to crises). These also mostly use statements with which to agree or disagree. They may also use a set of descriptive terms from which the respondent has to select those most closely describing him or her. A few use questions with only 'yes' or 'no' as possible responses
Psychometric tests	These are instruments of 'mental measurement' and include personality scales along with measures of mental ability such as intelligence, creative thinking, linguistic ability and so on. It's important here to distinguish between measures of: • *personality trait* – what you are normally like most of the time, e.g. your friendliness • *personality state* – what you're like at this moment, e.g. your current state of anxiety • *ability* – what you are generally able to do, for instance, your numerical ability • *achievement* – what you have achieved so far, for

Table 6.3 *Continued*

> instance, your performance in a school or college test
> in psychology
> - *aptitude* – your *potential* performance, for instance a
> general logic test which aims to predict how good you
> would be at computer programming

TYPES OF SCALE OR QUESTIONNAIRE ITEM

> Examples 4, 5, and 6, in Box 1.1, are designs in which participants will be questioned,
> directly or indirectly, about their current level of aggression, rather than their *general*
> aggressiveness (known as their 'state' rather than their 'trait' of aggression). Try to
> devise some questions or statements, for participants to agree or disagree with, which
> might help measure this level of aggression.

Some examples could be:

1 'Tell me about how aggressive you feel right now'
2 'Do you feel aggressive right now?'
3 'On a scale of 1–100, where 50 represents your *normal* level of aggression, could
you estimate how aggressive you feel right now?'
4 A set of items including, for example, *at this moment*:
If someone pushed in front of me in a ticket queue I would shout at them
If someone cut me up on the road I'd hoot at them hard
1 = very like me; 2 = like me; 3 = unsure; 4 = not like me; 5 = not at all like me

OPEN-ENDED QUESTIONS

Example **1** is an OPEN-ENDED item and will produce 'qualitative' data. The value
here is in the richness given. Also, there is less chance of ambiguity because the
respondent can say what he or she thinks exactly, not respond to a fixed item. They
will feel less frustrated with this lack of constraint and the whole approach is more
realistic. We rarely have to just agree or disagree without comment. However, the
information from each individual is harder to compare with other people's answers.

FIXED-CHOICE QUESTIONS

Examples **2**, **3**, and **4** are FIXED CHOICE items.

Example **2** is not terribly useful since the only answers we get are 'yes' or 'no' – just
two categories of response permitting us only to divide people into two major groups.
If there are *several* (*n*) items then *total* scores will place people on a scale from 0 to *n* if,
say, just the 'yes' responses are added.

Example **3** has some potential for permitting us to make finer comparisons
between people.

Example **4** gives two items from a Likert-type scale (see below) and, with several
items like this, we can get an even finer estimate of a person's current level of
aggression – perhaps.

Some other examples of fixed-choice items likely to be found in a survey are:

1 I voted in the last election   YES/NO

2 I would describe myself as:
   a) employed full time   ☐
   b) employed part time   ☐
   c) unemployed   ☐
   d) self-employed   ☐

3 At what age did your baby start crawling?   .... months

Questionnaire items must be phrased very clearly in order to avoid ambiguity in answering. Ideally, everyone interprets the item in the same way. Certainly, what should be avoided is any overlap, such as that in item **2** above, where a) and d) could *both* be ticked.

CONSTRUCTING SURVEY QUESTIONNAIRES AND ATTITUDE SCALES

At this level of learning psychology you will not be involved in the long, technical process of creating a fully standardised and usable psychometric test. This process can take several years, involves testing and re-testing versions on large numbers of people and requires some fairly serious statistical number crunching and analysis.

You may well, however, get involved in the construction of a 'home grown' attitude scale or survey questionnaire, and I hope you do, because it is usually an enlightening process. It is impossible, in the space provided here, to take you through all the advice possible on questionnaire and scale construction. I have included what, from my experience, are common sources of difficulty and important areas to check before gathering data. Please take a lot of time over your construction because it is sometimes soul destroying for eager students to come back to class with quite untestable or ambiguous data.

Survey construction

1 *Decide on fixed-choice or open-ended questions.* Remember that open questions may well deprive you of the opportunity to present any statistical details or analysis. Don't be drawn into 'What do you think about . . .' type questions if you want to be able to report how many people thought *X*.

2 *Be careful with fixed-choice questions.* Watch out for overlap, as in 'Your age is . . . d) 22–35; e) over 35'. Make sure *all* possibilities are covered and that respondents don't find themselves having to add their own categories. How would a self-describing 'housewife' answer item **2**, above?

3 *Avoid leading questions.* A question like 'Do you agree that student grants should be increased' can easily carry with it, from the respondent's point of view, the implication that they should agree with the questioner. It is anyway harder to disagree. One could imagine starting with 'Weeell . . .' or 'Yes but . . .' where the 'but' really amounts to disagreement.

4 *Ask for the minimum of information required for the research purpose.* A respondent's time is precious so why ask for information obtainable elsewhere? Personal details may be available from company or school records. The respondent's time spent answering questions has a bearing on mood, and mood will certainly be altered if the interviewer asks what sex the respondent is! Other details, such as whether married and number of children may well be drawn from an introductory relaxing chat and, if not, during final checking.

A further argument concerns the principle of *parsimony*, that is, limiting effort to the necessary whilst maintaining efficiency. Too much information may not be useful. Some questions may have been included only because they 'seemed interesting', which is too vague a basis for inclusion.

5 *Make sure questions* can *be answered.* 'How many times have you visited a doctor this year?' may be quite difficult for many people to answer at all accurately.

6 *Make sure questions will be answered truthfully.* The question in point 5 is unlikely to be answered truthfully because of its difficulty. Other difficult or wide-ranging questions are likely to receive an answer based more on well-known public opinion than on the individual's real beliefs. Questions on child-rearing, for instance, if not phrased very explicitly, are well known for producing, where wide error is possible, answers more in accord with prevailing 'expert' views on good practice.

7 *Invasion of privacy.* A question such as 'Do you have a criminal record?' requests information which, along with sexual habits and so on, is material which most people would prefer to keep private, and they have every right to do so. It should be fairly obvious, before starting out, what will be seen as such an invasion and, to avoid very embarrassing and difficult situations, do think carefully when planning your questions. If in doubt seek advice. If you *are* asking sensitive questions, make sure you announce them carefully and justify their inclusion.

ATTITUDE SCALE CONSTRUCTION

Scales as measuring instruments

It is important to note that, unlike surveys, attitude scales, personality scales and other psychometric tests are considered to be *scientific measures of a psychological construct.* Unlike most surveys, a psychological scale is intended to measure a relatively enduring characteristic of the person, in a similar way to that in which we measure a person's height or typical blood pressure. As the measure is intended for repeated use with different people in different places, it needs some publicly checkable credibility as a measure. Similarly, you expect your local pub's drinks measures to be checkable – calibrated to a standard size, inspected and unlikely to vary much whilst in use. These are the issues of *reliability*, *validity*, and *standardisation* described in Chapter 3. We will now look at three common scale types.

Equal appearing intervals (Thurstone, 1931)

Two of the most commonly used scale designs employ statements. People being assessed on the scale indicate their agreement or disagreement, or level of agreement, with each statement. The first of these, a THURSTONE-type scale, is constructed as follows:

1 Produce a large set of statements, both positive and negative towards the attitude object. If the attitude object were equal opportunities, one item might be: 'Companies should provide more crèche facilities'.

2 Engage a panel of judges to rate each item on a scale of one (highly negative on the issue) to 11 (highly positive on the issue). They are urged to use all of the scale and not to bunch items into a few categories.

3 Take the mean value, for each item, of all the judges' ratings. Our item above might get an average rating of 8.7 for instance. This is its SCALE VALUE.

4 In the interests of reliability, reject items which have a high variance (see Chapter 9). These items are those on which judges are least in agreement.

5 In the finished scale, respondents now score the scale value of each item they agree with. Hence, people favourable to equal opportunities measures will tend to score only on items above the average value and thus end up with a high overall score.

A sample of items which might appear in a Thurstone type scale is shown below, along with each item's scale value. The values, of course, would not be visible to the respondent.

	Please tick *if you agree*	
Women are less reliable employees because they are likely to leave through pregnancy.	☐	(2.1)
Interview panels should scrutinise all questions before interviewing to ensure that none are discriminatory.	☐	(5.8)
Companies should provide more crèche facilities.	☐	(8.7)

Box 6.1 *Weaknesses of the Thurstone method*

1 The judges rating the items initially cannot be completely neutral and may, on occasion, and depending on the issue, produce a distorting bias in the rating system.

2 It may be difficult to choose the best items from those with the same scale values.

Summated ratings (Likert, 1932)

A Likert-type scale is constructed as follows:

1 Produce an equal number of favourable and unfavourable statements about the attitude object.

2 Ask respondents to indicate, for each item, their response to the statement according to the following scale:

5	4	3	2	1
Strongly agree	Agree	Undecided	Disagree	Strongly disagree

3 Use the values on this scale as a score for each respondent on each item, so that the respondent scores five for strong agreement with an item favourable to the attitude object, but one for strong agreement with an unfavourable item. Thus, a high overall score will indicate a positive attitude towards the attitude object.

4 Add up the scores for each item to give the respondent's overall score.

5 Carry out an item analysis test (discussed later) in order to determine the most discriminating items – those on which high overall scorers tend to score highly and vice versa.

6 Reject low discriminating items, keeping a balance of favourable and unfavourable items.

Step 5 here is the Likert scale's greatest strength relative to other scales. It means that, unlike in a Thurstone scale, an item does not need to relate obviously to the attitude issue or object. It can be counted as *diagnostic* if responses to it correlate well with responses overall. For instance, we might find that respondents fairly hostile to equal opportunities issues also tend to agree with 'Women have an instinctive need to be near their child for the first two to three years of its life'. This could stay in our attitude scale since it might predict negative equal opportunities attitude fairly well.

Box 6.2 *Weaknesses of the Likert method*

1 For each respondent, scores on the scale only have meaning *relative* to the scores in the distribution obtained from other respondents. Data produced is therefore best treated as **ORDINAL** (see Chapter 8), whereas Thurstone considered intervals on his scale to be truly equal

2 The 'undecided' score, 3, is ambiguous. Does it imply a neutral position (no opinion) or an on-the-fence position with the respondent torn between feelings in both directions?

3 Partly as a consequence of 2, overall scores, central to the distribution (say 30 out of 60) are quite ambiguous. Central scores could reflect a lot of 'undecided' answers, or they could comprise a collection of 'strongly for' and 'strongly against' answers, in which case, perhaps the scale measured two different attitudes

The semantic differential (Osgood et al., 1957)

The original intention behind this scale was to use it for measuring the *connotative* meaning of an object for an individual, roughly speaking, the term's associations for us. Thus, we can all give a denotative meaning for 'nurse' – we have to define what a nurse is, as in a dictionary. The *connotation* of a nurse may, however, differ for each of us. For me, a nurse is associated with caring, strength, and independence. For others, by popular stereotype, he or she may be seen as deferential and practical.

On a semantic differential the respondent is invited to mark a scale between bipolar adjectives according to the position they feel the object holds on that scale for them. For 'nurse' on the following bipolar opposites, I might mark as shown:

good	√	—	—	—	—	—	—	bad
weak	—	—	—	—	—	√	—	strong
active	—	√	—	—	—	—	—	passive

Osgood claimed that *factor analysis* (see Coolican, 1994) of all scales gave rise to three general meaning factors, to one of which all bipolar pairs could be attached.

'Active' (along with 'slow–fast', 'hot–cold') is an example of the ACTIVITY factor.
'Strong' (along with 'rugged–delicate', 'thick–thin') is an example of the POTENCY factor.
'Good' (along with 'clean–dirty', 'pleasant–unpleasant') is an example of the EVALUATIVE factor.

Box 6.3 *Weaknesses of the semantic differential*

> 1 Respondents may have a tendency towards a 'position response bias' where they habitually mark at the extreme end of the scale (or won't use the extreme at all) without considering possible weaker or stronger responses. This can occur with a Likert scale too, but is more likely here since the scale points lack the Likert verbal designations (of 'strongly agree', etc.)
>
> 2 Here, too, we have the problem of interpretation of the middle point on the scale

ATTITUDE SCALE ITEMS

What to avoid in statement construction

Attitude scale items, like survey questions will need to avoid invasion of privacy and extreme difficulty. In addition there are several other pitfalls.

> What do you think is unsatisfactory about the following statements, intended for an attitude scale?
>
> 1 'We should begin to take compensatory action in areas of employment and training where, in the past, members of one ethnic group, sex or disability type have suffered discrimination or experienced disadvantages as a direct result of being a member of that category.'
>
> 2 'Society should attempt to undo the effects of institutional racism wherever possible.'
>
> 3 'Immigrants should not be allowed to settle in areas of high unemployment.'
>
> 4 'Abortion is purely a woman's choice and should be made freely available.'
>
> 5 'It should not be possible to ask a woman about her spouse's support, when husbands are not asked the same questions.'
>
> 6 'The present Tory government is callously dismantling the welfare state.'

1 *Complexity*. Not many respondents will take this in all in one go. The statement is far too complex. It could possibly be broken up into logical components.

2 *Technical terms*. Many respondents will not have a clear idea of what 'institutional racism' is. Either find another term or include a preamble to the item which explains the special term.

3 *Ambiguity*. Some students I taught used this item once and found almost everyone in general agreement, whether they were generally hostile to immigrants or not. Hence, it was not at all discriminating. This was probably because those positive towards immigrants considered their plight if new to the country *and* unemployed. Those who were hostile to immigrants may well have been making racist assumptions and either mistakenly thinking most immigrants were black, or equally incorrectly, thinking most black people were immigrants.

4 *Double-barrelled items*. This quite simple item is asking two questions at once. A person might well agree with free availability – to avoid the dangers of the back-street abortionist – yet may not feel that only the woman concerned should choose.

5 *Negatives*. In the interests of avoiding *response set* (see below), about half the items in a scale should be positive towards the object and about half negative. However, it is not a good idea to produce negative statements simply by negating a positive one. It can be confusing to answer a question with a double negative, as I hope the example shows.

6 *Emotive language*. A statement such as this may not get an attitude test off to a good start, particularly in affluent constituencies. If there are emotive items at all it might be best to leave these until the respondent is feeling more relaxed with the interviewer or with the test itself.

It is worth warning people about the positive and negative statements. Respondents often think the interviewer *believes* the statements presented. If there are several statements which the respondent dislikes then this may well set up emotional defences. Again, this is an argument for starting off with less controversial items.

Organisation of items

1 *Response set or bias*. An effect called RESPONSE ACQUIESCENCE SET often occurs when responding to questionnaires. This is the tendency to agree rather than disagree ('Yeah saying'). To avoid a constant error from this effect, items need to be an unpredictable mixture of positive and negative statements about the attitude object. This has the effect either of keeping the respondent thinking about each item or of giving the inveterate 'yeah' sayer a central score, rather than an extreme one.

2 *Social desirability*. Defined in Chapter 2, this factor involves respondents guessing at what is counted as a socially acceptable or favourable answer and giving it in order to 'look good'. A further reason for guessing might be to 'please the researcher' by giving the results it is assumed are required. Some questionnaires attempt to deal with this problem by including items which only an angel would agree or disagree with. If too many such items are answered in the 'saintly' manner, the respondent's results are excluded from the research though of course they may not actually be lying.

Number of items

This needs to be kept manageable. A larger number of items increases reliability through ironing out random errors caused by individual interpretations and mis-understandings. However, you'll find it difficult, in terms of time and respondents' patience, to use more than about 30 items with your friends and relations!

Item discrimination

Items that are worth keeping in a scale are those which *discriminate* between people. The ambiguous item 3, above, does not discriminate, because people who were hostile to immigrants and those who were positive all answered in much the same way. The more our items tend to discriminate (the higher their DISCRIMINATORY POWER), the better will be the *reliability* of our scale. Methods for checking discriminatory power (known as ITEM ANALYSIS) compare each person's response on each item with their score overall. Most require sophisticated statistical programmes or a lot of number crunching. One relatively crude way to highlight non-discriminating items is as follows:

1 Select the top 10% and bottom 10% of scorers overall (or 15% or 20%).

2 For each item add up what each of these groups scored on the item.

3 If the two totals are relatively close the item does not discriminate between people who score high on the test (in its original, unanalysed state) and those who score low.

The problem here is, of course, that we're using the original unrefined set of items as an overall gauge of 'high' and 'low'. This means we may end up with a discriminating scale but one which discriminates on a different measure from the one intended – a problem of *validity*, which we discussed in Chapter 3.

In the formal process of constructing a scale, researchers would *pilot* the scale and then conduct some form of item analysis. New items would then be found and the whole procedure repeated over again (. . . and again). This is extremely time consuming and the student practical cannot usually approach this standard. However, it *is* a good idea to try out your initial collection of items on just a few people in order to highlight ambiguous or tricky items and possibly to spot items which are similar and do not add anything to the overall differences in scores.

PROJECTIVE TESTS

These are based on the Freudian notion that, when confronted by ambiguous stimuli, we tend to reveal our inner, normally defended thoughts, by projecting them onto the display. Those who interpret what we report claim to be able to assess such factors as concealed aggression, sexual fantasy, anxiety, and so on. Being unstructured and disguised, they are seen as providing rich data with no bias from people guessing the researcher's intentions.

Figure 6.1 *Rorschach ink blot*

An example of a *Rorschach* ink blot is given in Figure 6.1. A *Thematic Aperception Test* (TAT) is a generally ambiguous picture, or one of people with their expressions hidden. In both cases people are asked what they see and, for the TAT, what may happen next.

Box 6.4 *Weaknesses of projective tests*

> **I** The tests produce initially qualitative data and are therefore suspect for their reliability. This is usually tackled with the use of a comprehensive coding scheme used by raters ignorant of the research hypothesis or of the source of the responses.
>
> **2** Raters can be highly consistent yet the assumed measure can be quite invalid. For instance, a person who says 'I can't quite tell if they [the people in a Rorschach blot] are male or female' is not necessarily confused about their own sex image!

SOCIOMETRY

Sociometry analyses connections between people in small groups. Typically, people are asked who their best friends are, with whom they would share a room and so on. Questions can also ask for least preferred members or who should be group leader.

Information generated is in the form of positive or negative person choices. This can be represented on a **SOCIOGRAM**, like the one in Figure 6.2, where it is obvious

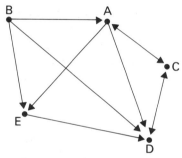

Figure 6.2 *Sociogram or directed graph*

that B is an 'isolate', D is very popular (though chooses colleagues carefully), and C chooses only those people who reciprocate the choice. The approach is useful in practical applications, such as classroom interaction or work groups, rather than in research, where links are too numerous for a clear diagram.

GLOSSARY

Paper measure of participants' attitudes, usually standardised and often consisting of statements with which to agree or disagree	_____ _____	**attitude scale**
Scale on which respondent can choose from a dimension of responses, usually from strongly against/disagree to strongly for/agree	_____	Likert

Scale measuring meaning of an object for the respondent by having them describe it using a point between the extremes of several bi-polar adjectives	_____ _____	semantic differential
Scale in which raters assess the relative 'strength' of each item and respondents agreeing with that item receive the average rated value for it	_____	Thurstone

Survey of whole population	_____	census
Interview method using structure of questions to be asked but permitting tailoring of later questions to the individual's responses; also seeks to test specific hypothesis or effect	_____ _____	clinical method (or interview)
Extent to which items, or the test as a whole, separate people along the scoring dimension	_____ _____	discriminatory power
Dimension of design which is the extent to which interviewees are kept ignorant of the aims of the questioning	_____	disguise
Question where respondent can only choose from a given set of answers	_____-_____ _____	fixed-choice question
Method in which participants are seen individually and asked questions in a manner which can be either structured or not	_____	interview (study)
Checking each item in a scale by comparing its relationship with the total scores on the scale	____ _____	item analysis
Question where respondent can say anything they like as an answer	____-_____ _____	open-ended question
Test in which participants' hidden attitudes, anxieties or personality traits are inferred from their responses to ambiguous material, often visual	_____ ____	projective test
Tests which attempt to quantify psychological variables: skills, abilities, character, etc.	_____ _____	psychometric tests
Set of questions for obtaining respondents' views, opinions and reports of behaviour	_____	questionnaire
Person who is questioned in interview or survey method	_____	respondent
Tendency for people to agree with test items as a habitual response	_____ _____ ___	response acquiescence set (or bias)

A general term for methods in which people provide information about themselves	____ _____	self report
A visual representation of a sociometric matrix	_____	sociogram
Dimension of design which is the extent to which questions and procedure are identical for everyone	_____	structure

EXERCISES

1 Without looking back at the text, try to think of several advantages and disadvantages the survey has compared with the informal interview.

2 Suppose you decide to conduct a survey on attitudes towards the environment in your area. Outline the steps you would take in planning and conducting the survey, paying particular attention to:

  • the sample and means of obtaining it
  • the exact approach to respondents you would use
  • the types of question you would ask

3 You are about to conduct an interview with the manager of the local, large supermarket. He is 43 years old, quite active in local politics and is known to be fairly friendly. Make a list of all the variables, especially those concerning your own personality and characteristics, which might influence the production of information in the interview.

4 A researcher wishes to survey young people's attitudes to law and order. Interviewers complete questionnaires with sixth formers who volunteer from the schools which agree to be included in the study. Families are also selected at random from the local telephone directory. Young people are also questioned at the local youth club. Discuss several ways in which the sample for the complete study may be biased.

5 Comment on any flaws in the following potential attitude scale or questionnaire items:
  a) Do you feel that the government has gone too far with privatisation?
  b) What do you think is the best way to punish children?
  c) How many times were you late for work in the last two months?
  d) People from other countries are the same as us and should be treated with respect.
  e) It should not be possible to avoid taxation and not be punished for it.
  f) Women are taking a lot of management posts in traditionally male occupational areas (in a scale to measure attitude to women's rights).
  g) Tomorrow's sex role models should be more androgynous.

6 A researcher administers Rorschach tests to a control and experimental group of psychiatric patients. She then rates each response according to a very well-standardised scale for detecting anxiety. Could this procedure be improved?

7

QUALITATIVE RESEARCH AND DATA – MEANING VERSUS NUMBERS

INTRODUCTION

The early chapters of this book have presented a conventional and traditional approach to the investigation of human experience and behaviour. The student who progresses with the subject will very quickly discover, however, that all is not peace and harmony in the world of psychological research. For a variety of philosophical and political reasons there are several strands of research philosophy which challenge the traditional 'positivist' (or 'scientific', or 'hypothetico-deductive') approach that psychology developed largely under the influence of nineteenth-century advances in the natural sciences. The challenges come from groups known collectively as 'qualitative' or 'new paradigm' researchers.

THE ARGUMENT AGAINST PURELY QUANTITATIVE DATA

Why is there often such an emotional reaction to the concept of an IQ test? Part of this reaction is usually concerned with the non-psychologist's realisation that a single number cannot do justice to the richness and variability of people's cognitive abilities. Similarly, memory studies often assess our long-term storage abilities in terms of number of words correctly recalled from a list. How often, in everyday life, do people have to recall lists of words? Our everyday memory seems to operate in quite a different fashion from that tested in the laboratory for the convenience of a strictly controlled experiment producing simple numerical data. POSITIVISM, a philosophy associated with great advances in natural science, is the assumption that what cannot be observed and numerically measured is not amenable to scientific investigation. Harré (1981) has argued that positivism in psychological experiments has lead to a great deal of shallow, irrelevant data and theory. In one experiment, designed to investigate G.H. Mead's concept of self, women were asked to look at themselves in a video monitor for 1 minute. They then heard a lecture on venereal disease either immediately or 4 minutes later (the IV). They were then asked whether they would contribute to a venereal disease remedial programme under certain circumstances (the DV). Harré argues that the device to create 'heightened self-focus' (and expected to facilitate 'helping behaviour') completely trivialises Mead's original and much broader concept of self.

The traditional research 'paradigm' (a term introduced by Kuhn, 1962) has the following features, which are objected to by those looking for a 'new paradigm' approach, that is, a more 'qualitative' approach to human investigation:

1 Traditional research isolates people, and bits of people (e.g. their memory), from the surrounding context. 'Subjects' are thought of as identical units manipulated in and out of the research situation.

2 Researchers are expected to remain cool and distant, and the effect of their personal attitudes, qualities, and motives on the research process and participants go unrecognised. The assumed objectivity here is mythical, as the research setting is a social situation where people interact. Respondents to a student questionnaire, for instance, usually want to know why or whether the student actually *believes* all the statements to which they have responded.

3 The tight, artificial experimental context can only permit the gathering of superficial information. 'Subjects' lack their usual freedom to plan, react naturally, and express appropriate social behaviour, yet the data is taken as realistic and generalisable, resulting in a simplistic and mechanistic model of the person.

4 Deception falsifies research and is an insult. The researcher–participant relationship is dominating and elitist so the consequent behaviour will reflect this.

5 Highly structured tests and category systems impose a preordained structure on what data can be obtained, often missing the most important information available.

WHAT DO QUALITATIVE RESEARCHERS PROPOSE?

There is not one unitary group that finds serious fault with quantitative research principles. There are a number of strands of thought and types of alternative too numerous to outline here but I hope the 'further reading', at the end of this chapter, will be a useful guide for the interested reader. However, there are a number of principles which most objectors to the traditional paradigm share. These are:

1 Research should concentrate on the meanings of actions and interaction in a social context, not on isolated units and processes. Attribution, for instance, is not the work of one person but a product of negotiation between observer and observed.

2 Research needs to be naturalistic and qualitative because meanings cannot be sensibly isolated from natural social contexts.

3 Research is conducted as closely as possible *with* participants and, at the most radical end, the participants themselves should be involved in the running and analysis of the research project ('collaborative research').

4 Participants' own terms and interpretations are the most relevant data. For instance Marsh (1978) extracted the 'rules' of football terrace behaviour directly from fans' own accounts.

5 Theories are allowed to 'emerge' rather than be constructed before the research is carried out. Consequently, theories tend to be 'local' (tied to the specific research context) rather than global theories about (all) human behaviour.

Qualitative (or 'new paradigm') research tends to use the following approaches already discussed:

- open-ended questionnaires
- unstructured, or, at most, semi-structured interviews
- relatively unstructured observation
- participant observation

FURTHER METHODS

Diary methods

The researcher or individual participants keep a personal account of daily events, feelings, discussions, interactions and so on.

Role-play and simulation

Participants may be asked to play a role, as in Zimbardo's prison study (see p. 212) or they may be asked simply to observe a role-play, followed by rating the actors' behaviour, reporting feelings, predicting further events and so on. They may be asked to read scripts, as when Mixon (1979) asked participants to predict what would happen next in Milgram's studies of obedience (see p. 209).

Case-study

This is an in-depth study of just one person (usually) or group. The study may be intrinsically interesting, for instance, the study of a severely deprived child and his/her rehabilitation and progress. Such studies also, however, often shed light on general psychological issues, such as the nature–nurture debate in language development or intelligence. There are several uses and values of case-studies:

1 *Outstanding cases.* There may be very few examples of the phenomenon under study available. Osgood et al. (1976), for instance, studied the rare but genuine experiences of a person with three quite separable psychological identities.

2 *Contradicting a theory.* As with my example of the one black swan in Chapter 1, a single instance can seriously damage a theory. If one maternally deprived child develops normally we must reconsider the global view that damage *must* occur to such children.

3 *Data pool.* Whilst few cases exist of an interesting or problematic syndrome, qualitative studies can gather what data is available. Once more reports are gathered, quantitative study might progress towards some overall explanation or summary.

4 *Insight.* Whether or not case-studies lead to more formal, quantitative studies, the insights gained from them can lead to quite unpredicted lines of investigation. Their richness is their strength. Often we could not possibly imagine even the appropriate questions to ask before studying an individual in depth. The experience may help us to identify more closely with, say, an Aids sufferer, adding to our overall psychological knowledge without testing a specific hypothesis.

ACTION RESEARCH

Initiated by Kurt Lewin in the mid-1940s, this approach calls for psychological research to deal with practical social issues: to enter a situation, attempt to change it, and to monitor results. An important guiding principle is to involve the participants (often members of a work group) in the process of change.

PARTICIPATIVE AND COLLABORATIVE RESEARCH

In applied areas of psychology (especially occupational, health, and educational) in the 1980s and 1990s it has become more common for research to include participants as active enquirers in the research process, as Lewin would have recommended. At the extreme, 'collaborative' end of this approach the researcher takes the role of 'consultant' whilst facilitating work group members to conduct their own production of theories, data gathering, analysis and recommendations for change.

Feminist psychology

As with ex-colonial cultures that have attempted to shrug off inherited theoretical approaches that distort that culture, so women writers and researchers have attempted to develop alternative approaches to the traditional paradigm. This is because the traditional paradigm can be seen as a product of a male dominated academic context in which women historically played only bit parts. Consequently, men were able to develop quite unchallenged views of women's character, often producing models that supported the prevailing stereotypes of weakness and intellectual inferiority. It is argued that the methods preferred by the majority of male researchers helped present these models as relatively unquestionable 'fact'. The interested reader could try Sue Wilkinson's *Feminist Social Psychology* (1986).

DEALING WITH QUALITATIVE DATA – INTERPRETING INTERVIEW, OBSERVATION AND CASE STUDY RESULTS

There are basically three major approaches to the issue of interpreting what is originally qualitative data obtainable from observation, interview or a case study (the latter is often a mixture of interview and observation). One way is to categorise and quantify it as it occurs. These methods have been covered to some extent in earlier chapters. The preferred method for many *qualitative researchers*, however, is to leave the data in qualitative form. Other researchers may do this or, on different occasions, reduce at least some of the previously gathered qualitative data to quantitative form by a method such as CONTENT ANALYSIS, which we shall discuss below.

LEAVING THE DATA IN QUALITATIVE FORM

It is important to point out here that most qualitative researchers do not 'have it in for' numbers as such. Obviously, feminist researchers will want to advertise the fact that a significantly lower percentage of female psychologists, for instance, obtain senior positions in academic research or administration. However, the term 'qualitative research' tends to signify that data will be dealt with qualitatively, i.e. not reduced to numerical form.

It is true that not all statisticians agree on one 'correct' interpretation of quantitative data in every case, but it is true to say that there is a good measure of public agreement on what can and can't be said about numeric data. With qualitative data, where interpretation is based on *meanings* not numbers, there is obviously far greater room for disagreement among different researchers, and far more potential for individual investigators to come to quite different subjective conclusions about what has been gathered. Some qualitative researchers would respond that *all* data interpretation is to some extent subjective and that quantitative researchers like to hide behind a myth of complete objectivity in publishing their results. Qualitative researchers might also argue that there is no absolute truth and that different interpretations are natural and inevitable rather than a cause for concern. Nevertheless, there are various ground rules for analysing qualitative data in a qualitative manner. The budding psychological researcher wishing to try a qualitative approach should be aware that results *must* be analysed and discussed at a level beyond that of mere journalism or of unsupported personal speculation.

Data and interpretation

Some researchers argue that *any* observation we make is somehow affected by theory and can never be an 'objective fact'. For instance, you might record a gesture as 'sudden' and a request as 'impolite', where I might call the former 'threatening' and the latter 'curt'. Nevertheless, a basic and important ground rule in reporting qualitative data is to distinguish very clearly between what actually happened and what is a matter of interpretation by the researcher. In quantitative work, as we shall see, this is like the difference between reporting 'descriptive results' and carrying on with data analysis or 'treatment'. The distinction between these two must be made clear to the reader of the research report and it is a good habit for the writer to deliberately consider and use language which makes it obvious when discussion is going beyond the information obtained. Phrases like 'could be' and 'possibly' serve as such indicators as does 'we formed the speculation that . . . .'

Categorisation

The results of interview sessions on what makes people anxious about computers will inevitably fall into several repetitive categories, with some factors unique and mentioned only briefly by one person. Common categories emerging might be:

1 general technophobia
2 fear of losing data
3 fear of destroying the computer
4 fear of looking stupid
5 feeling the computer will take over our thinking

One might be tempted to simply *count* the number of times each of these appears in all the participants' talk but a qualitative approach will be interested in the different *ways* in which each category is mentioned and the links participants see between them if any.

Respondents' and researchers' categories

It is important for the research report to distinguish clearly between categories freely appearing in the participants' talk and those categories which the researcher can justify as emerging from a study of all the interview material together. For instance, it might emerge, from the researcher's point of view, that an overriding category difference is the comparison between personal fears of not being competent and more general fears of a computer-led society, as expressed in items 1 and 5 above respectively. This partly repeats the point made above, that where the categories invented are the researcher's own, this must be made clear.

Quotations

A technique common in the interpretation of qualitative data is to include actual comments made by participants. Often these are 'illuminative' and stand out from others because they 'tell it like it is'; they are the ones we tend to keep recalling and use when we want to relate a typical finding to others. An example for me would be the student who said 'But Gross says it so much better than I can' when interviewed about why he had copied pages of Gross' textbook into his essay assignment (i.e. *plagiarised*).

Reliability – participant consultation

Quotations included in this way must be the *exact* statement made by participants and not adulterated in order to tell a better story. In some research, such comments are taken back to the participant who made them so that they can comment further and for these comments, in turn, to be included in the discussion of results. In this way researchers claim they are supporting *reliability* in their studies – an important feature since standard quantitative methods for achieving reliability, explained briefly in Chapter 3, are not available.

Reliability – triangulation

This term is borrowed from the techniques of surveying and refers to researchers' attempts to compare two different views of the same thing. We might, for instance, seek reasons for aggression through interviews with children and compare these with what occurs in observation of their play activities.

Changing qualitative data to quantitative data

Much originally qualitative data can be reduced to numerical form, for purposes of quantitative analysis. It is true that something of the richness obtained will now be lost but, on the other hand, we are then able to make specific contrasts and even test for significance of observed differences or to correlate one assessment with another and tease out possible relationships.

To achieve this aim, 'raters' or 'coders' would be trained in the use of a categorisation system or may even be given a numerical scale on which to assess strengths of, say, exhibited aggression or 'dependency behaviour'. The same procedures to operationalise measures, train coders and establish reliability would be used as are described briefly on page 75. Data obtained in this fashion can now be subjected to the statistical tests of significance outlined in Chapters 10 and 11. *Categories* would normally be analysed using the chi-square test, whilst assessments on a *rating scale* would usually be ordered and analysed for significance using one of the rank difference tests or rank correlation.

Content analysis

A popular method by which to reduce qualitative data to quantified form is that of *content analysis* which originated in attempts to analyse media messages. It was stimulated in particular during the 1930s and 1940s by the increasing use of propaganda and by the recognition that radio and television media could no longer be considered an extension of the press.

Examples of content analysis

Bruner & Kelso (1980) reviewed studies of toilet graffiti spanning 30 years. They found that, in general, men's graffiti content was power-oriented, ego-centric and competitive whereas women's messages were more co-operative, relationship-oriented and reflected themes of mutual help.

Cumberbatch (1990) analysed over 500 prime-time television advertisements over a two-week period. Interesting results were that men outnumbered women by 2:1 and 75% of them were over 30 compared with 25% of women. Most voice-overs were male, especially those for technical or expert information, whilst the majority of women's voice-overs were categorised as 'sexy/sensuous'.

These studies were conducted on already existing materials but some researchers *ask* participants to provide materials and then analyse these. Children for instance, might be asked to produce drawings, adults might keep diaries or write essays. Some examples of material which could be gathered in a psychology practical assignment and subjected to content analysis are provided in Box 7.1.

Box 7.1: *Materials which could be content analysed in psychology projects*

children's books for	• aggressive content • sex, class or racial stereotypes • messages of cultural morality • dealing with emotional issues – death, love, jealousy etc.
television ads, soap or drama for	• sex roles • violent themes • dealing with current moral dilemmas • political views
children's drawings for	• inclusion of significant people (mother, brother, teacher) • size of significant objects (e.g. Santa's sack before/after Christmas)
personal advertisements for	• reasons for desiring a partner • use of humour, pity, financial or material lure

Conducting a content analysis

SAMPLING: The research must include a reasonable sample of the material to be analysed, depending on the aim. If children's books are analysed for stereotyping, then the decision must concern the period of years to be covered, whether to include only fiction, what age range to cover, and so on. From within such categories the selection should be random, as far as possible, unless a specific target is identified (such as all the *Famous Five* books, for instance). Television sampling must pay attention to time of day and target audiences, links of advertising to certain programme types and so on.

CODING: A crucial aspect of content analysis is the development of an appropriate coding system. Such systems have already been mentioned as used in analysing observation or interview material. The analysis starts with a rigorously defined set of 'units' to be counted or rated on a scale. For example, the Cumberbatch raters were asked to identify technical and non-technical voice-overs and to specify whether they were male or female voices. Other sorts of item which might get coded might be:

words:	count sex-typing words in various magazines
themes:	rate incidents of aggression on 1–20 scale
items:	number of articles on Northern Ireland in media
time/space:	amount devoted to Northern Ireland in one newspaper or several

It became common in the 1980s to investigate children's literature and both children and adult television programmes for evidence of stereotyping, negative images or sheer omission of women or members of minority ethnic groups. Try the following exercise:

> Imagine that you are going to conduct a practical exercise in which the aim is to investigate cultural stereotyping in children's books, old and new. We are interested in the extent to which, and ways in which, black people are portrayed. What units (words, themes, characters) might you ask your coders to look out for?

Here are some possible units:

black person in picture
black person in leading role
black person in subsidiary role
European features; face made darker
disappearance from story pictures of black person who appeared earlier
success/failure/trouble – black and white characters compared
inappropriate words: 'coloured', 'immigrant'
portrayed as foreign/savage/'primitive' etc.
portrayed as comic, troublesome or problematic

Note: content analysis can highlight the *omission* of items, themes and characters.

PROCEDURE: To avoid accusations of coding bias, a researcher would traditionally hand a coding system and the material to be coded to assistants who are unaware of the research hypothesis. Their codings can be *correlated* in order to check that their codings have good *reliability* (see Chapters 3 and 12). This means that the researcher will have had to spend quite some time immersed in similar material in order to develop and pilot the coding system.

ANALYSIS: Quantitative analysis can be carried out on the coded results. If these are in the form of *categories* then the *chi-squared* test will be appropriate. Where items have been *ranked* (e.g. strength of self-image) or given values on a *scale* (e.g. children's drawings rated for originality), then the ordinal level tests – Mann-Whitney and Wilcoxon signed ranks – would be appropriate. These tests are introduced in Chapter 11.

GLOSSARY

In-depth study of one individual or group, usually qualitative in nature	____ _____	case-study
Analysis of content of media sources. Now also often used to quantify content of diaries, descriptions, verbal reports, etc. through coding, categorisation and rating	_____ _____	content analysis
The scientific belief that hard facts in the world can be established only through measurement of what is observable	_____	positivism
Research conducted by those who hold strong reservations about the conventional scientific model in psychology. The use of qualitative, action research, and participative methods to generate non-numerical data that focuses on meanings and real world intervention and change	__ _____ _____	new paradigm research

FURTHER READING

Burgess, R.G. and Bryman, A. (eds.) (1993) *Analysing Qualitative Data.* London: Routledge.

Edwards, D. and Potter, J. (1992) *Discursive Psychology.* London: Sage.

Hayes, N.J. (in press) *Introduction to Qualitative Research,* Hove: Lawrence Erlbaum Associates.

Henwood, K. and Pidgeon, N. (1992) Qualitative research and psychological theorising. *British Journal of Psychology,* 83, 97–111.

Patton, M.Q. (1980) *Qualitative Evaluation Methods.* London: Sage.

Reason, P. and Rowan, J. (eds.) (1981) *Human Enquiry: A Sourcebook in New Paradigm Research.* Chichester: Wiley.

Robson, C.R. (1993) *Real World Research.* Oxford: Blackwell.

Wilkinson, S. (1986) *Feminist Social Psychology.* Buckingham: Open University Press.

Organising quantitative data

How data arrive – various levels of measurement

Why do we have to learn about levels of measurement?

The *general* reasons are to do with getting more familiar with what numbers can do for you, what power different measurement methods possess. Thinking about your measurement method helps you organise a project successfully and ensures you will not gather useless and meaningless data. However, at the level of psychology which you're probably studying, the *main* reason you need to become skilled at spotting three different methods (or levels) of measurement is in order to be able to select the correct statistical test to analyse your data. That is, if you want to know whether your male group differed *significantly* from your female group on assertiveness, for instance, you must apply a statistical test and to choose it, you must decide *at what level* you measured assertiveness.

Can you give it to us in a nutshell?

Yes! Though the concept is sometimes tricky in operation, a simple demonstration should bring out the essence of the differences in about 5 minutes. Suppose it's a snowy day and only eight people have turned up for your psychology class. 'Blow it!' says the tutor, 'I was going to do a class experiment requiring at least 15 people. Tell you what, we'll do a quick demonstration of levels of measurement instead. Divide yourselves into two groups – shorter and taller'. After some shuffling around we get two groups – let's call them short and tall for now. Let's suppose you're in the tall group. As a measure of height in the class then, for the moment, all we know about you (we can't see into the classroom) is that you have the value 'tall', and we can't separate you from the other three people in your group. All four get the value 'tall'. this is our first level of measurement then, known as NOMINAL, for reasons I hope to make clear. The measurement system used on this occasion has just two values, 'short' and 'tall' and everyone must get one of these two values.

Now your tutor says 'Right, I'd like you, this time, to get into a line in order of your height'. This causes some more shuffling and a couple of back-to-back contests before the line is finally formed. Your position in this line is 7th, next to the tallest person. I hope it's fairly clear why we call this an ORDINAL level of measurement.

When we were using only the nominal level for information we had no way to separate members of the 'tall' group but now we know what *position* you occupy in the group, relative to the rest. However, notice that we still haven't a clue how far below the tallest person you are or how far above the 6th person in the line. The ordinal scale gives us more information but not the most.

To get the most subtle measure of class height we need a tape measure or wall chart. Of course the tutor has one and we now produce the familiar measurement of height in feet and inches which is an example of an **INTERVAL** scale (and also a **RATIO** scale – to be explained). Now we can say whether the tallest person is a smidgin above you or tends to gather snow on top. We can also compare you to the *general* measure of height used everywhere else. We can tell whether you are tall relative to the general population.

Psychologists very often find themselves needing to tackle the measurement, *somehow*, of differences between people, such as in attractiveness or creativity. Many people balk at reducing such qualities to numbers yet, if you say 'Jean is more creative than Natasha' you must be making *some* sort of comparison which you could justify, otherwise your statement is meaningless. Perhaps Jean does creative things more often or gets quicker or more practical results (leaving open the question of how we measure 'practical'). Reserving some doubt, this is the idea we'll proceed with for now as we consider ways of measuring psychological variables.

NOMINAL LEVEL – CATEGORICAL VARIABLES AND FREQUENCIES

Some differences are **QUALITATIVE** and some are **QUANTITATIVE**. The difference between spaghetti and pasta shells is qualitative but the difference in lengths of the same spaghetti is quantitative – we have to *measure* the difference. We do not need to measure, however, in order to sort people into *categories* of male/female or brown-eyed/blue-eyed. If I asked you to conduct a survey of voting behaviour, without further advice you would almost certainly categorise everyone into the party they intend to vote for, or have voted for. You would be unlikely to start measuring *how* Conservative or Labour people were.

How do I recognise categorical (nominal) data?

Ask: Do we have *categories* in which there are **FREQUENCIES** of people (or sometimes things) where we can't separate the people within each category because we know no more about them?

This type of data appears in examples 1 to 4 of Table 8.1. Look at the categories in example 1. The numbers given to the categories are *nominal* because they are 'in name only'. Number 1 (students) is not half of number 2 (staff) in any way. The numbers can stand in any order. The numbers are simply convenient but arbitrary *labels* – we could have used A, B, C, etc. The numbers do not stand for quantities or *distance* on a scale. In the same way, door numbers don't stand for quantity but indicate where to find people.

The numbers *within* each category *do* stand for quantities. These are *frequencies*. It is important not to confuse the nominal category headings with the frequencies *within* each category. In other words, *if you are assessed on it, the value you get is the label of the category*. Example 4 is tricky because you *can*, in this case, say that the categories have a particular order. However, the essential point of so-called nominal data, for the purposes of statistics in this book, is that data are in frequency form, in separate, exclusive categories, and that, while the data stay in this form, there is no distinction given between individuals *within* the same category. If we are not *categorising* people but *separating them out along a scale* which at least puts individuals in a definite *order*, then we are using a MEASURED VARIABLE.

Table 8.1   *Examples of measures at a nominal level*

Example 1 Number of people using the canteen				
Category	**1**	**2**	**3**	**4**	**5**
	Students	Teaching staff	Non-teaching staff	Visitors	Other
	650	34	43	17	2

Example 2 Type of play engaged in by children (mean age 4.5 years)				
Category	**A**	**B**	**C**	**D**	**E**
	Non-play	Solitary	Associative	Parallel	Cooperative
	8	5	17	23	6

Example 3 Voting intention				
Category	**I**	**II**	**III**	**IV**	**V**
	Communist	Conservative	Labour	Lib Dem	Other
	243	14,678	15,671	4371	567

Example 4 Number of people smoking *n* cigarettes per day						
Category	**None**	**1–5**	**6–10**	**11–20**	**21–30**	**31–40**	**41+**
	65	45	78	32	11	4	3

ORDINAL LEVEL OF MEASUREMENT

Ordinal numbers tell us the *position* of an item in a group. We knew you were 7th tallest but we still had no idea of the distance between you and the tallest person in the class. Ordinal data tells us nothing about distance between positions. It may be annoying to be beaten by one tenth of a second in a cycle race when you and the leader were ten kilometres ahead of the 'bunch', but what goes on your record is just 'second'.

Reducing data to ranks

Ordinal data appear as a set of ranks, as in the right-hand column of Table 8.2. In student reports it is often written that 'the data were ordinal' when in fact the data were scores (the middle column of the table) but it was decided to *reduce them to* ordinal level in order to conduct a non-parametric test (see Chapter 11). It is important to remember this in case you are asked in an exam to state which column contains the ordinal level data. In Table 8.2, 14 is the lowest score and gets the rank '1'. In statistics the 'best' person does not always get rank '1' – *this value is always given to the lowest score*. Persons E, F, and G 'share' the next three ranks (of second, third, and fourth). If the set of ranks shared is odd we give each person the middle value of the set. Here, then, 'third' is the middle value of the set and each person gets rank '3'. If the number of shared ranks is even, we take the mid-point of the two middle shared ranks. Persons A and D share ranks 5 and 6 so they each get the mid-point, 5.5. Four people sharing 6, 7, 8, and 9 would get 7.5 each.

Table 8.2 *Reduction of interval level data to ordinal level*

Person	Score	Rank of score
A	18	5.5
B	25	7
C	14	1
D	18	5.5
E	15	3
F	15	3
G	15	3
H	29	8

COMPARISON OF ORDINAL LEVEL WITH OTHER LEVELS

Suppose you were sensitive about your height and that the actual heights of the eight people in your class were shown in Figure 8.1. At the nominal level all we'd know is that you were in the 'tall' group. You'd be keen, then for us to know a bit more about the situation, since, relative to everyone else in the class you're not really *that* tall. The ordinal scale hasn't helped much however. Ordinal scales, in a sense, take frequencies out of their nominal box and onto a dimension, so we know the *positions* of people, but they don't give us the vital information about *distance between* positions.

INTERVAL LEVEL OF MEASUREMENT

At the interval level we can do justice to your feelings about being of not much more than average height for your group. We measure using a scale which has *equal units* on it. The distance from 160–165 cm is the same as that between 170–175 cm, for

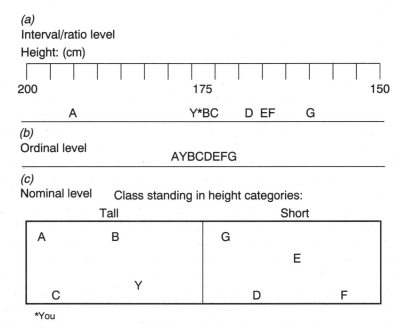

Figure 8.1 *Levels of measurement and information obtained*

instance. But what about *psychological* scales? If these were interval scales then it ought to be true that Jane, whose IQ is 100, is as far ahead of John (IQ 80) in intelligence as Jackie (IQ 120) is ahead of Jane. Is IQ an interval scale? Many scales *appear* to be interval but aren't. Your essay may get 68%. Can you take seriously the notion that it's as much better than Mark's (62) as Mark's is better than Alison's (56)? In higher education 40 is often a pass mark yet 40–70 contains all the grades from pass to first class!

In psychology it is common to use a scale which *appears* to be interval level. For example, in examples 2, 4, and 6 of Box 1.1 we are going to use some form of invented measuring instrument. In example 2 this will be a simple assessment scale for aggression shown in a film (say 0–40); in example 4 we'll devise a questionnaire on which our participant will get a score for aggression level; in example 6 we'll ask people to state how many years in prison they would give a fictitious criminal. In each case we might obtain a set of scores like those in Table 8.2. It would be unwise to treat these as interval level data because we have invented the scale and can't assume that intervals along all its length are equivalent (even for years in prison – my sense of 'long' may not be the same as yours). A general rule of thumb is that *it is always safer to treat invented scales, such as those involving human judgment* (e.g. student questionnaires and scales), *as ordinal* – that is, to *convert data* from the actual numbers obtained to ranks as in Table 8.2 and to carry out a 'non-parametric' test (Chapter 11).

So what about IQ? Research psychologists deal with this issue by attempting to *standardise* any created measure. In standardising a scale, PSYCHOMETRISTS are attempting to *calibrate* – just as one might calibrate a new measure of breath strength for people with asthma. In so doing they try to obtain standards for the test such that statements like the one about Jane's IQ, above, are at least roughly true for large numbers. Generally speaking, *psychologists treat standardised scales of intelligence, anxiety, and the like as being on a scale with equal intervals* and assume that the researcher will be able to recognise when this assumption of equal intervals is having a serious and distorting effect on results.

RATIO LEVEL OF MEASUREMENT

It certainly would seem odd to claim that your essay (68%) was *twice* as good as Hannah's, which got 34%. It would also be odd to say that it was twice as hot today, at 30 °C, as it was last Wednesday at 15 °C. In Fahrenheit the ratio just wouldn't be the same (86° and 59°). The *numbers* in centigrade are double but the proportions of heat measured aren't. This is because neither temperature scale has an absolute zero – you can go below zero on them. The zero is in a convenient, not a necessary, position. Likewise, 100 is a convenient, quite arbitrary, and not necessary position for average IQ. It would make no sense to say that anyone scoring zero on a test had anything like zero intelligence.

Ratio scales are interval scales with a necessary and absolute zero. No one in the world will ever do 100 metres in a *minus* number of seconds. Timing starts from zero, and if Jill takes 3 minutes and John takes 6, it makes sense to say that Jill was twice as fast. Examples of ratio scales would be reaction times or distance. As a psychology student, you will almost certainly only ever need to be able to state what the difference between ratio and non-ratio interval scales is. For choosing which test to use in the analysis of data it is enough to know that the data will be treated as *at least interval level* so, from now on, the term is 'interval/ratio'.

COMPARISON OF INTERVAL/RATIO LEVEL WITH OTHER LEVELS

As I said earlier, now we can do justice to your claim to be only a bit above average height for your group. We have the fullest information on class height with the interval (ratio) scale of (vertical) length in centimetres. I hope Figure 8.1 makes clear the transition from people in boxes (categories), through people in order, to people spread out on a proportional scale.

REDUCING INTERVAL/RATIO LEVEL DATA TO NOMINAL LEVEL

Table 8.3 *Reducing interval/ratio level data to nominal level*

Number of aggressive acts observed:				
Males	**Females**		**Males**	**Females**
14	10	**Above mean**	4	1
21	6			
7	13	**Below mean**	1	4
13	5			
18	11			
Mean 14.6	9.0			
Mean for whole group = 11.8				

It is common to reduce data like that in Table 8.3 to nominal level by grouping together those above the mean (or median) for the whole sample, and those below it.

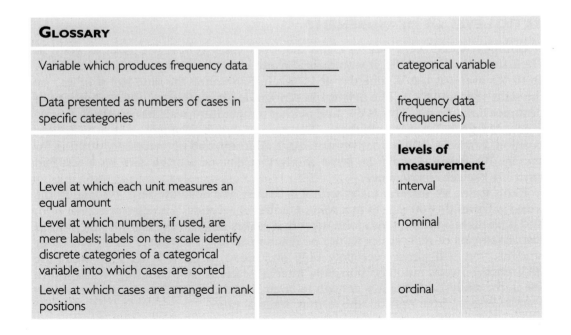

GLOSSARY		
Variable which produces frequency data	_____ _____	categorical variable
Data presented as numbers of cases in specific categories	_____ ____	frequency data (frequencies)
		levels of measurement
Level at which each unit measures an equal amount	_____	interval
Level at which numbers, if used, are mere labels; labels on the scale identify discrete categories of a categorical variable into which cases are sorted	_____	nominal
Level at which cases are arranged in rank positions	_____	ordinal

Level at which each unit measures an equal amount and proportions on the scale are meaningful; a real zero exists	_____	ratio
Variable producing data which gives a discrete value for each individual case, even if only a rank	_____ _____	measured variable
Person who develops psychological measures and attempts to standardise the scales up to an interval level of measurement	_____	psychometrist
Difference between cases in *kind*, which is not numerically measurable, though *being different* can be counted	_____ _____	qualitative difference
Difference between cases measurable by number	_____ _____	quantitative difference

EXERCISES

1 Find one example of each level of measurement from any text books (on psychology) you have available.

2 When judges give their marks in an ice-skating contest for style and presentation, what level of measurement is it safest to treat their data as?

3 A set of surgical records classifies patients as 'chronic', 'acute' or 'not yet classified'. What level of measurement is being used?

4 At what level are the measurements in Table 8.4 being made?

5 Which of the boxes, **a** to **d**, in Table 8.4, contains the most sensitive or informative level of measurement?

Table 8.4 *Exercise 4*

a) Placings of top five riders in Tour de France, 8 July, 1994		b) Time taken so far on whole race	c) Popularity rating (max. 20) (fictitious)	d) Riders still in race	Riders so far dropped out (fictitious)
Yates	1	28 h 44 m 22 s	18	121	77
Bortolami	2	28 h 44 m 23 s	15		
Museuw	3	28 h 44 m 26 s	12		
Andreu	4	28 h 44 m 27 s	10		
Vanzella	5	28 h 44 m 28 s	13		

6 Your daughter argues that, since she came top in each of the three maths tests held in her class this year, she must be *far* better than all the other pupils. What might you point out to her? (Would you dare?)

7 Think of three ways to measure driving ability, one using nominal level data, one ordinal and one interval/ratio.

8 Can you change the data in Table 8.5 first to ordinal level, then to nominal level? The blank tables are for you to fill in. For ordinal level, treat all the scores as *one* group.

Table 8.5 *Exercise 8*

a) Time taken to read (seconds)		b) Ordinal level		c) Nominal level
Consistent story	Inconsistent story	Consistent story	Inconsistent story	
127	138			
136	154			
104	138			
111	117			
152	167			
111	117			
127	135			
138	149			
145	151			
Mean of all times: $(\bar{x}) = 134.3$				

9 Below are several methods for measuring dependent variables. For each method decide what level of measurement is being used. Choose from:

1 Nominal   **2** Ordinal   **3** Interval/Ratio

a) People are interviewed in the street and, on the basis of their replies, are recorded as either: pro-hanging, undecided, or anti-hanging
b) Stress questionnaire for which various occupational norms have been established
c) Photographs organised by participants according to level of attractiveness as follows:

Photos: F C B G E A H D
Most attractive ←   → Least attractive

d) Participants' estimates of various line lengths
e) Time taken to sort cards into categories
f) Number of people who read: *The Sun*, *The Times*, or *The Guardian*
g) Participants' sense of self-worth, estimated on a scale of 1–10
h) Participants' scores on Cattell's 16PF questionnaire
i) Distance two participants stand apart when asked to take part in an intimate conversation, measured from photos
j) Critical life events given positions 1–10 according to their perceived importance to each participant

DESCRIPTIVE STATISTICS

STATISTICS ARE A SELECTION

In this section, we are looking simply at the ways in which statistical information can be presented. Statistical information follows from organising the numerical data gathered during quantitative research. Most research gathers far too much information for every little bit of it to be presented. When a survey of voting preference is conducted, or an experiment is run on 35 participants, it is not useful to be given just the RAW DATA, that is, every individual's answers or scores. We expect to be given a *summary* of the data which highlights major trends and differences. However, it is important to note that the very act of summarising introduces distortions. We will be given what the researcher decides is the most important information and this will be presented in what is believed to be the most appropriate manner. Politicians and companies, among others, are renowned for presenting data in the best possible light. A psychologist should be looking at the best way to present data *only* in terms of what gives the clearest, least ambiguous picture of what was found in a research study.

BUT I CAN'T DO SUMS!

As with many ideas in this book, the things we will study are based on everyday common-sense notions you have undoubtedly used before. Even if you hate maths, dread statistics and have never done any formal work in this area, you have undoubtedly made statistical descriptions many times in your life without necessarily being aware of it. You may believe that only clever, numerically minded people do this sort of thing, but consider this. Imagine you have just come home from your first day on a new college course and I ask you what your class is like. You would not proceed to tell me the exact age of each class member. This could take far too long. You'd be likely to say something like 'Well, most people in the class are around 25 years old but there are a couple of teenagers and one or two are over 40.' You have in fact summarised the class ages statistically, albeit rather loosely too. First you gave me a rough AVERAGE, the typical age in the group, then you gave me an idea of the actual *variation* from this typical age present in the group. Let's look at these aspects of description in a little more detail. Have a look at the data in Table 9.1.

Before looking at the comments, see what conclusions you can come to about the talking of girls and boys.

Table 9.1 *Number of seconds 5-year-old nursery class children spent talking in a 10-minute observation period, by sex*

Child	Male	Child	Female
1	132	6	332
2	34	7	345
3	5	8	289
4	237	9	503
5	450	10	367

Overall, the girls speak just about twice the amount that boys do. We could see this by looking at the *average* for each group. But not only this, the boys' times vary *very* widely compared with the girls', from as little as 5 seconds to nearly the highest girl's time.

We shall now introduce two formal terms which are used to describe these two aspects of group data description.

1 CENTRAL TENDENCY. This is the value in a group of values which is the most *typical* for the group, or the score which all other scores are evenly clustered around. In normal language, this is better and more loosely known as 'the average'. In statistical description, though, we have to be more precise about just what sort of average we mean.

2 DISPERSION. This is a measure of how much or how little the rest of the values tend to *vary* around this central or typical value.

MEASURES OF CENTRAL TENDENCY

THE MEAN

In normal language we use the term 'average' for what is technically known as the ARITHMETIC MEAN. This is what we get when we add up all the values in a group and then divide by the number of values there are. Hence, if five people took 135, 109, 95, 121, and 140 seconds to solve an anagram, the mean time taken is:

$$\frac{135 + 109 + 95 + 121 + 140}{5} = \frac{600}{5} = 120 \text{ seconds}$$

Calculation of the mean:
Term used: ($\bar{x}$)   Formula: $\bar{x} = \dfrac{\Sigma x}{N}$

Procedure: 1 Add up all values. Each value is an 'x', so the sum is Σx
            2 Divide by total number of values (denoted as N)

This is our first use of a 'formula', which is simply a set of instructions. You just have to follow them faithfully to get the desired result, rather like following a recipe or instructions for Dr Jekyll's magic potion. The formula above tells you to add up all the scores (Σx) and divide by the number of scores in the sample (N). There is a section at the end of this chapter on notation (e.g. Σ) and the rules for following a formula. I hope this will help you if it's some time since you did any 'sums' or hated them (or thought they were pointless). Rest assured that the *only* mathematical operations you need to perform, in going through this book, are the four junior school operations (+ − × ÷) and squares (which are multiplication anyway – the square of 6 is 6 × 6 = 36) and square roots (which can be found at the touch of a button – square root of 36 = 6). All work *can* be done on the simplest of calculators but, of course, and certainly towards the end of the book, computer programmes can make life a lot easier.

Advantages and disadvantages of the mean

ADVANTAGES

The mean is the statistic used in estimating population parameters (see page 125) and this estimation is the basis for PARAMETRIC TESTS(Chapter 11).

Very often the mean is not the same value as any of the values in the group. It acts like the fulcrum of a balanced pair of scales sitting exactly at the centre of all the DEVIATIONS from itself, as I hope Figure 9.1 illustrates, using the anagram time scores from the previous example. A DEVIATION is the *distance of a score from its group mean.*

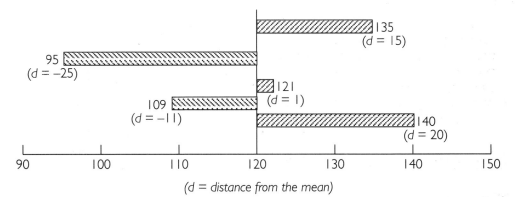

(d = distance from the mean)

Figure 9.1 *Position of the mean*

The positive and negative distances of the individual scores to the mean exactly cancel out ([−25] + [−11] + 1 + 15 + 20 = 0). This can only happen because the mean takes an exactly central position on an interval scale. This makes it the most sensitive of the measures of central tendency covered here.

DISADVANTAGES

This very sensitivity, however, can also be something of a disadvantage in certain circumstances. Suppose we add a sixth person's value to our set of anagram-solving times. This person had a bad night's sleep and doesn't particularly like doing word games, having had an exceptionally competitive sister who always won at Scrabble. This person sits and stares at the anagram for exactly 8 minutes before getting the answer. Our mean for the six values now becomes:

$$\frac{600 + 480}{6} = \frac{1080}{6} = 180 \text{ seconds}$$

180 seconds is just not representative of the group in general. It is a highly misleading figure to describe what most of the group did. Five out of six people took a lot less time than this to solve the anagram. A single extreme score in one direction (an

Figure 9.2 *One rogue value can distort the mean*

'outlier') can distort the mean (see Figure 9.2) whereas extremes in both directions tend to cancel each other out. The mean should only be used on interval level data.

THE MEDIAN

Using the median gets us around the difficulty for the mean outlined just above. The median is the *central* value of a set. If we have an odd number of values in our set then this couldn't be easier to find. The central value of our first five anagram solution times above is the third one. *To find this we must first put all five values in numerical order.* This gives:

95, 109, 121, 135, 140   The median is 121   (1)

If there is an even number of values, as with our sixth person's time added, we take the mean of the two central values, thus:

95, 109, 121, 135, 140, 480   The median is $\dfrac{121+135}{2} = 128$ (2)

Notice that this value is still reasonably representative of the group of values.

Calculation of the median

PROCEDURE

1 Find the **MEDIAN POSITION** or **LOCATION**. This is the *place* where we will find the median value. This is at:

$$\frac{N+1}{2}$$

2 If N is odd this will be a whole number. In (1), above, we would get:

$$\frac{5+1}{2} = 3$$

The median is at the third position *when the data are ordered.*

3 If N is even the position will be midway between two of the values in the set. In (2), above, we get:

$$\frac{6+1}{2} = 3.5$$

The median is midway between the third and fourth values when the data are ordered.

If the median falls among a set of the same value (as in: 2, 3, 5, 5, 5, 5, 8, 8, 9) then, technically speaking, one should apply a formula to find the exact value. In most practical circumstances, however, this is not necessary. '5' is a perfectly reasonable and useful result for the example just given. The exact method is given in Coolican (1994).

Advantages and disadvantages of the median

ADVANTAGES
1 Can be used on interval or ordinal level data.
2 Easier to calculate than the mean (with small groups and no ties).
3 Unaffected by extreme values in one direction, therefore better with skewed data than the mean (see later this chapter).
4 Can be obtained when extreme values are unknown.

DISADVANTAGES
1 Doesn't take into account the exact values of each item.
2 Can't be used in estimates of population parameters.
3 If values are few it can be unrepresentative; for instance, with 2, 3, 5, 98, 112 the median would be 5.

THE MODE

If we have data on a nominal scale, as with categories of play in Table 8.1, we cannot calculate a mean or a median. We can, however, say which type of play was engaged in most, i.e. which category had the highest frequency count. This is what is known as the MODE or MODAL VALUE. It is the most frequently occurring value and therefore even easier to find than the mean or median.

The mode of the set of numbers:

$$1, 2, 3, 3, 3, 4, 4, 4, 5, 5, 5, 5, 5, 5, 6, 6, 7, 7, 7, 8$$

is therefore **5**, as this value occurs most often. For the set of anagram-solving times there is no single modal value because each time occurs once only. For the set of numbers 7, 7, 7, 8, 8, 9, 9, 9, 10, 10 there are two modes, 7 and 9, and the set is said to be BI-MODAL. For the table of play categories, the modal value is 'parallel play'. Be careful here to note that the mode is not the number of times the most frequent value occurs but that value itself. Parallel play occurred most often.

Advantages and disadvantages of the mode

ADVANTAGES
1 Can be used on interval, ordinal, or nominal data.
2 Shows the most important value of a set.
3 Unaffected by extreme values in one direction.
4 Can be obtained when extreme values are unknown.

DISADVANTAGES
1 Doesn't take into account the exact value of each item.
2 Can't be used in estimates of population parameters.
3 Not useful for relatively small sets of data where several values occur equally frequently (e.g. 1, 1, 2, 3, 4, 4).
4 Can't be estimated accurately when data are grouped into class intervals. We can have a modal interval – like 6–10 cigarettes in example 4 in Table 8.1 – but this may change if the data are categorised differently.

MEASURES OF DISPERSION

THE RANGE

Think back to the description of new college classmates. The central tendency of age was given as 25 but some 'guesstimate' was also given of the way people spread around this central point. Without knowledge of spread (or more technically, **DISPERSION**) a mean can be very misleading. Take a look at the bowling performance of two cricketers shown in Figure 9.3. Both average around the middle stump but (a)

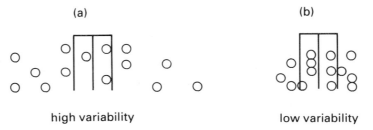

Figure 9.3 *Dispersion in bowlers' deliveries*

varies much more than (b). The attempts of (a) are far more widely *dispersed*. Average wages in two companies may be the same but distribution of wages may be very different. Now let's see how we can summarise the dispersion of times spent talking by children in Table 9.1. There, we saw that, as well as talking less overall, the boys *varied* amongst themselves far more than did the girls. The simplest way to measure the variation among a set of values is to use what is called the **RANGE**. This is simply the distance between the top and bottom values of a set.

Calculation of the range
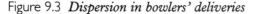
FORMULA
$(X_{top} - X_{bottom}) + 1$
PROCEDURE
1 Find top value of the set
2 Find bottom value of the set
3 Subtract bottom value from top value and add 1

For Table 9.1 this gives: Boys $(450 - 5) + 1 = 446$
Girls $(503 - 289) + 1 = 215$

Why add 1?
The addition of 1 may seem a little strange. Surely the distance between 5 and 450 is, straightforwardly, 445? The addition of 1 allows for possible measurement error.

When we say that a child spoke for 5 seconds, if our lowest unit of measurement is 1 second, then we can only claim that the child spoke for something between 4.5 and 5.5 seconds, the limits of our lowest measurement interval. If we had measured to *tenths* of a second then 4.3 seconds represents a value between 4.25 and 4.35. Hence, the range is measured from the lowest possible limit of the lowest value to the highest limit of the highest value, in the case of boys' talking times, 4.5 to 450.5.

VARIATION RATIO

This measure of dispersion is appropriate for data where the central tendency used is the *mode*. 5 was the mode of the set of data given on p. 121. Suppose these were the ages of children at a party. We could ask the question 'Well, how many of the children are *not* aged 5 (the modal age)?' There are 20 children altogether and six of these are 5. Hence, 14 children are *not* at the modal age of 5. 14 out of 20 values are not modal. The VARIATION RATIO is this proportion and can be defined generally as: *the proportion of the total number of values which are not at the modal value.* That is:

$$\frac{\text{number of non-modal values}}{\text{total number of values}} = \frac{14}{20} = 0.7$$

DEALING WITH DEVIATIONS

In Figure 9.1 we encountered the concept of a 'deviation' score. From the scores on an IQ test given below you'll see that the mean IQ score is 100. You scored 115 so therefore your *deviation* is 15 and mine, at 90, would be −10 (note the minus sign). The deviations for this group are listed in Table 9.2, column 3.

Helga	Hugh	Harry	Helena	You
85	90	100	110	115

We want some measure of how much dispersion there is in such a group. Are scores closely spaced round the mean (are the deviations generally small)? Or are the scores widely spread (are the deviations generally large)? Well, why not just find the (mean) average of all the deviations? One problem with this would be that we'd have to first add up all the deviations and, as I hope figure 9.1 makes clear, the sum of all the deviations would come to zero. There *is* a statistic called the *mean deviation* which simply finds the (mean) average of all the *absolute* deviations – that's the average of the *size* of each deviation, ignoring its *sign*. However, this is little used in statistical work in psychology.

THE STANDARD DEVIATION AND VARIANCE

A statistic which is of *very great* importance in the social sciences, and very widely used indeed, is the STANDARD DEVIATION. This also has a very close relation known as the VARIANCE. The calculation of variance is really quite simple. We *square* all the deviations (see column 4 of Table 9.2) and then find the mean average of all these squared deviations. The standard deviation is simply *the square root of the variance*. You will see below that there are two versions of the equation for standard deviation. The value S is for the standard deviation of *just* the group of scores you are dealing with. In fact it is not often used. The value s is usually calculated because it is appropriate when making estimates from a *sample* to the underlying *population*, as occurs in the powerful 'parametric' tests to be introduced later on. The only

Table 9.2 *Deviations of IQ scores and calculation of variance using formula 3*

1 Score	2 Mean	3 Deviation $(\bar{x} - x)$	4 Squared deviation	5 Square of each score
(x)	$(\bar{x}r)$	(d)	(d^2)	(x^2)
85	100	−15	225	7225
90	100	−10	100	8100
100	100	0	0	10000
110	100	10	100	12100
115	100	15	225	13225

$$\Sigma x = 500 \qquad\qquad\qquad \Sigma d^2 = 650 \qquad \Sigma x^2 = 50650$$
$$\bar{x} = 100$$

Alternative calculation without deviations: (see equation (3)

$$(\Sigma x)^2 = 250\,000 \qquad\qquad\qquad (\Sigma x)^2 / N = 50\,000$$

$$\Sigma x^2 - \frac{(\Sigma x)^2}{N} = 50\,650 - 50\,000 = 650$$

$$s^2 = \frac{\Sigma x^2 - \dfrac{(\Sigma x)^2}{N}}{N - 1} = \frac{650}{4} = 162.5 \qquad s = \sqrt{162.5} = 12.75$$

difference between the two equations is that for s we divide by $N - 1$ rather than by N in the fraction within the square root bracket. Where s is used, later in this book, always assume it is the 'unbiased population estimate' version. Note also that S^2 and s^2 are the equivalent symbols for variance and that they are each the *square* of the appropriate standard deviation (i.e. the value you obtain *before* finding the square root in the equations below).

Equations for standard deviation

For a group of scores treated solely as a group ('uncorrected'):	For a sample used for an estimate of the population standard deviation ('unbiased'):
$S = \sqrt{\dfrac{\Sigma d^2}{N}}$　　(1)	$s = \sqrt{\dfrac{\Sigma d^2}{(N - 1)}}$　　(2)

There is a version of equation (2) which avoids the calculation of deviations and for which you only need columns 1 and 5 of Table 9.2:

$$s = \sqrt{\left(\frac{\Sigma x^2 - (\Sigma x)^2 / N}{N - 1}\right)} \qquad (3)$$

If you use this version, *do* beware the difference between Σx^2 and $(\Sigma x)^2$

Procedure for calculation of standard deviation and variance

Refer to the IQ data in Table 9.2.

1 Calculate the sample mean $(\bar{x})$ $\qquad\qquad\qquad\qquad = 100$

2 Subtract the mean from each value $(x - \bar{x})$ $\quad$ to obtain a set of deviations (d)
$\qquad\qquad\qquad\qquad\qquad\qquad\qquad\qquad\qquad$ see Table 9.2, column 3

3 Square each deviation (d^2) $\qquad\qquad\qquad\qquad$ see Table 9.2, column 4

4 Find the sum of the squared deviations $\qquad$ see Table 9.2 $\Sigma d^2 = 650$

5 Divide the result of step 4 by $N - 1$★ $\qquad$ (N for just the group variance)

$$s^2 = \frac{650}{4} = \mathbf{162.5}$$

You have now found the *variance*. The standard deviation is found by taking the square root:

6 Find the square root of step 5 $\qquad\qquad\qquad\qquad s = \sqrt{162.5} = 12.75$

★ Note: This is using the common $N - 1$ population estimate version. The values for *just* the group ('uncorrected') would be $S^2 = 130$, $S = 11.4$.

POPULATION PARAMETERS AND SAMPLE STATISTICS

Equation 2, above, introduces a central notion in statistical work. Measures of a *sample*, known as STATISTICS, are very frequently used to *estimate* the same measures of a *population*, known as PARAMETERS. The measures concerned are most often the *mean* and *variance* (which is just the square of the standard deviation). These estimates are used in conducting PARAMETRIC TESTS (to be met in Chapter 11) which are very powerful tests and give us an accurate assessment of whether or not we should accept differences as significant, given certain assumptions about our data.

When these estimates are made it is assumed that the population mean is the same as our sample mean. Since the sample mean will always be a little different from the true population mean, the difference is known as SAMPLING ERROR. To compensate for this, the estimate from the sample is made larger by reducing the bottom of the equation by 1. For large N this difference will become trivial.

RELATIVE ADVANTAGES AND DISADVANTAGES OF MEASURES OF DISPERSION

	Range	Variation ratio	Standard deviation/ variance
Affected by extreme scores in one direction	yes	no	yes
Takes account of grouping round mean	no	no	yes
Takes account of all values in set	no	yes	yes
Can be used in population parameter estimates	no	no	yes

DISTRIBUTIONS

When we wish to communicate the nature of our results to others, be it to our tutor, class colleagues, or for official publication, we would usually present at least the central tendency and dispersion of any set of numerical data. We might wish, for instance, to report that the mean age at which 'telegraphic' utterances were first noticed by parents was 18.3 months but that there was a wide variation from this shown by a standard deviation of 5.02 months.

Where possible, we'd usually like to go further than this and present a table of our results, such as Table 9.3.

Table 9.3 *Result table for small sample*

Child	Mean age at which telegraphic utterances first noticed (in months)
A	18
B	21
C	26
D	13
E	11
F	19
G	20
	$\Sigma x = 128$
	$\bar{x} = 18.3$
	$s = 5.02$

Now we can refer to individual variations and oddities, such as the child who doesn't produce until 26 months and the rather suspicious report of 11 months.

This method of displaying results is useful when the sample taken is relatively small. Had we questioned about 300 parents, however, this approach would be inappropriate and would consume too much space. The RAW DATA – would be kept safe by the researcher but, for public display, they would be collated into a table known as a FREQUENCY DISTRIBUTION, like that shown in Table 9.4.

Table 9.4 *Frequency distribution showing ages at which parents report first noticeable telegraphic utterances*

Age (months)	13	14	15	16	17	18	19	20	21	22	23	24	25	26	27	Total
No. of children reported	1	0	5	12	37	64	59	83	17	41	12	0	4	5	0	340

CLASS INTERVALS AND CUMULATIVE FREQUENCY

Some types of data are on a scale too large to produce a frequency distribution like Table 9.4. Table 9.5 would have 80 categories but these have been reduced to eight by grouping numbers of telegraphic utterances into 'class intervals'. The third column shows the CUMULATIVE FREQUENCY, which is the number of cases *altogether* in that interval or below it. For instance, 61 children produced 39 or less telegraphic utterances per day. The awkward looking figures in the right-hand column take into account the point made earlier that the upper class limit is, for instance, 9.5 not 9 (a rather pedantic point here though, as a child can't make half an utterance!).

Table 9.5 *Number of children and number of daily telegraphic utterances*

No. of telegraphic utterances	No. of children	Cumulative frequency	Utterances less than:	
0– 9	3	3	9.5	(These are the
10–19	0	3	19.5	upper limits of
20–29	15	18	29.5	each class
30–39	43	61	39.5	interval)
40–49	69	130	49.5	
50–59	17	147	59.5	
60–69	24	171	69.5	
70–79	4	175	79.5	
	$N = \Sigma = 175$			

GRAPHICAL REPRESENTATION

To demonstrate to our readers the characteristics of this distribution more clearly, we could draw up a pictorial representation of the data. One of the advantages of doing this is that the mode will be immediately apparent, as will other features, such as the rate at which numbers fall off to either side and any specially interesting clusters of data.

Graphs are summaries – avoid drawing the raw data!

It is important to remember that graphs, like statistics, are intended to *summarise* a set of data. Having tested 12 people on, say, extroversion, many people like to present a chart, like that in Figure 9.4, *with every participants' score given as a column*. This *isn't* a useful chart. Why? Because the order of participants' scores is arbitrary so we usually end up with an unruly set of mountain peaks and valleys. Second, it isn't a *summary*. It shows everything in a way which tells us nothing general. What we want is an overall picture of what *pattern* occurred in the data.

   This would happen if we *grouped* the data into class intervals, as happens with the *histogram* in Figure 9.5. Another common form of chart is to plot, as columns, just the *means* of two groups. The data in Figure 9.4, transformed to the mean of the whole group, would then become just *one* column. This might usefully be put alongside the mean of a second group to produce a conventional *bar chart*.

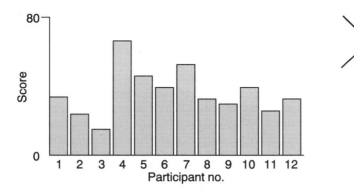

Figure 9.4 *Inappropriate chart of individual participants' scores*

The histogram

A histogram of the distribution in Table 9.5 would look like Figure 9.5. The width of each column is the same and represents one class interval. Class intervals are represented by their mid-point at the centre of each column. Again, the measurement interval point gives rather odd numbers, but 24.5, for instance, is the exact mid-point of the 19.5 to 29.5 interval and we know exactly who should go in there. If class intervals are combined – it might have been desirable to start with 0–19.5 as there are so few in this bracket – the interval must be of appropriate width. Hence, 0–19.5 would be two columns wide. In a histogram, unlike a bar chart, all intervals are represented, even if empty, as for the 9.5–19.5 interval.

The height of each column represents the number of values found in that interval – the frequency of occurrence. Frequency is usually shown on the y- (vertical) axis and the scale or class intervals on the x-axis, although some statistical programmes (like Minitab™) present the categories on the vertical axis and the frequencies increasing from left to right, horizontally. As columns are equal in width, it follows that the area of each column is proportional to the number of cases it represents throughout the histogram. It also follows that the total of all column areas represents the whole sample. If we call the whole area one unit (which is the convention), then a column which represents 10% of the sample will occupy 10% of the total area, that is 0.1 units. The column representing 59.5–69.5 utterances represents 24 of the 175 cases. Therefore its area will be 24/175 = 0.137 of the total area (or 13.7%).

FEATURES OF THE HISTOGRAM
1 All categories represented.
2 Columns are equal width per equal category interval.
3 No category is omitted even if it is empty.
4 Column areas proportional to frequency represented and these sum to the total area of one unit.
5 Columns can *only* represent frequencies.

Frequency polygon

If we redraw the histogram in Figure 9.5 with only a dot at the top of the centre of each column, then join the dots, we get what is called a FREQUENCY POLYGON – Figure 9.6. Where there is an empty category at either side of the distribution it is conventional to start the drawing from the centre of that category's column, as happens for the empty category '79.9'.

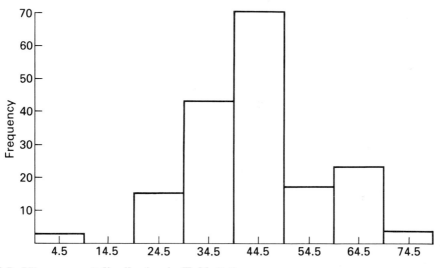

Figure 9.5 *Histogram of distribution in Table 9.5*

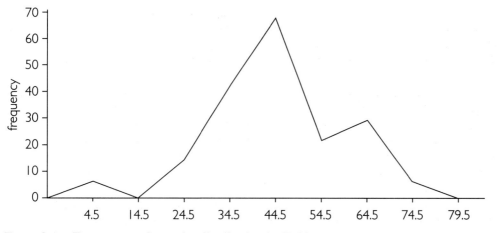

Figure 9.6 *Frequency polygon for distribution in Table 9.5*

The bar chart

The horizontal (bottom) axis of a histogram is a complete scale (no gaps). A bar chart often displays a nominal type variable where the things represented are in discrete categories, such as male and female mean scores. Because of this:

- The columns of a bar chart should be separated.
- Not *all* the values of the discrete variable need be shown on the horizontal axis. We may only show, for instance, by way of contrast, the number of psychological articles published on Aids in France and the UK, and not all other countries.

The columns of a bar chart can represent frequencies or single statistics, such as the mean of a sample, or a percentage, or another proportion.

The chart in Figure 9.7 shows the results of Duncan's (1976) experiment in which White participants were asked to categorise the behaviour of a person who pushed

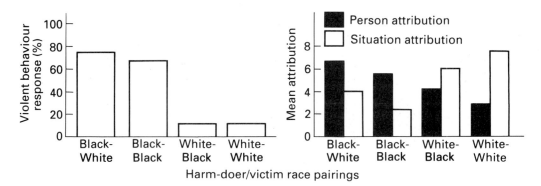

Figure 9.7 and Figure 9.8 *Description and attribution in intraracial and interacial behaviour (based on Duncan, 1976)*

another after a heated argument. The pusher could be Black or White, as could the person pushed, thus producing four experimental conditions. The height of each column represents the percentage of participants calling the behaviour 'violent' rather than alternatives such as 'playing around'.

COMBINED BAR CHARTS

A bar chart can display two values together. Duncan also asked participants to explain the pusher's behaviour as either caused by the person's enduring personality characteristics or more likely to have been induced by the particular situation – what is known as 'internal or external attribution'. The 'legend' or key to the combined bar chart in Figure 9.8 tells us, for each pusher/pushed condition, the mean attribution score to person or situation.

MISLEADING BAR CHARTS

It is very easy to mislead with unfairly displayed bar charts. Newspapers do it very frequently. Take a look at the charts in Figure 9.9 representing numbers of violent crimes in London for 1987 and 1988. The left-hand chart is correct. The right-hand one, by chopping off the scale from 0 to about 18,000, for convenience, makes the rise in one year look far steeper than it really is. It's the chart to present if you want to scare Londoners into paying more for their police force – it's what Huff (1954) called a 'gee-whizz graph' and shouldn't be used at all. The convention for avoiding this possible misrepresentation, when you need to economise on space in your diagram, is

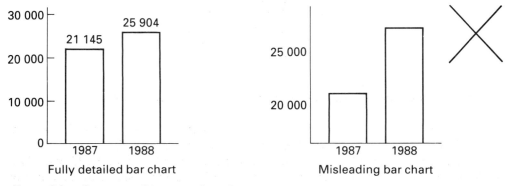

Figure 9.9 *Correct and incorrect bar charts*

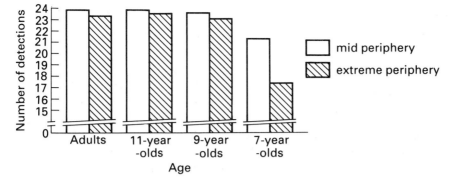

Figure 9.10 *Mean number of apparent movement detections made by the four age groups in the mid- and extreme periphery (from David et al., 1986)*

shown in the chart produced by David et al. (1986) – Figure 9.10. Notice that the vertical scale has been chopped between 0 and 15 but this is made obvious to the reader.

THE NORMAL DISTRIBUTION

Earlier in this chapter, I pointed out that a measurement value, such as a person's height of, say, 163 cm, is really a statement that the value falls within a class interval. We are saying that the person, for instance, is closer to 163 cm than 162 or 164 cm, rather than that they measure 163 cm exactly. They are in the interval between 162.5 and 163.5 cm. In effect, if we measure to the nearest cm we are placing individuals in class intervals 1 cm wide. It happens that if we take a large enough random sample of individuals from a population and measure physical qualities such as height (or weight, or length of finger), especially if we use a fine scale of measurement (such as to the nearest millimetre), we get a distribution looking like Figure 9.11.

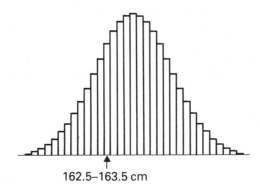

162.5–163.5 cm

Figure 9.11 *Distribution of height approximating to a normal distribution*

The curve which typically results from such measurements *closely approximates* to a very well-known 'bell-shaped' mathematical curve, produced from a shockingly complicated formula (which you or I need not bother with) devised by Gauss. The curve is therefore known as 'Gaussian' but in statistical work we more commonly refer to it as a **NORMAL DISTRIBUTION CURVE** (Figure 9.12).

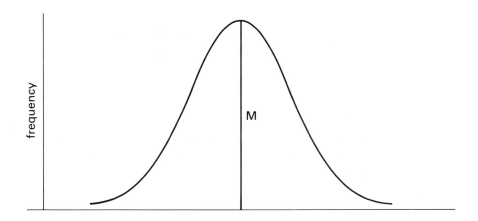

Figure 9.12   *A normal distribution curve*

Characteristics of a normal distribution curve

1 It is symmetrical about the mid-point of the horizontal axis.
2 The point about which it is symmetrical (the line marked 'M' in Figure 9.12) is the point at which the mean, median, and mode all fall.
3 The 'asymptotes' (tail ends) of the perfect curve never quite meet the horizontal axis. Although for distributions of real large samples there are existing real limits, we can always hypothesise a more extreme score.

Approximations to the normal curve

It's very important to note that when psychological variables are said to be normally distributed, or standardised to fit a normal distribution, that we are *always* talking about approximations to a pure normal curve. This matters, because, when we come on to testing significance, for some tests, the statistical theory assumes a normal distribution and if there isn't really anything like a normal distribution in the population, for the variable measured, then the conclusions from the test may be seriously in error.

If a distribution has a lot more extreme scores in one direction it is said to be SKEWED in that direction (see Figure 9.13). If the skew is very great then the median or mode are more appropriate measures of central tendency because the mean, as you can see from the figure, will be distorted by the longer 'tail'.

Normal curves and normal people

It is also important not to be morally outraged by the use of the term 'normal'. The curve is called 'normal' for purely *mathematical* reasons (you may remember the use of the term 'normal' as meaning 'perpendicular' in geometry).

AREA UNDER THE NORMAL DISTRIBUTION CURVE

Suppose we devise a reading test for 8-year-olds and the maximum score possible in the test is 80. The test is standardised to a normal distribution such that the mean score, for a large, representative sample of 8-year-olds, is 40 and the standard deviation is 10. I hope it is obvious, for starters, that 50% of 8-year-olds will therefore be above 40 and 50% below. The area for the top 50% is *all* the shaded area in Figure 9.14.

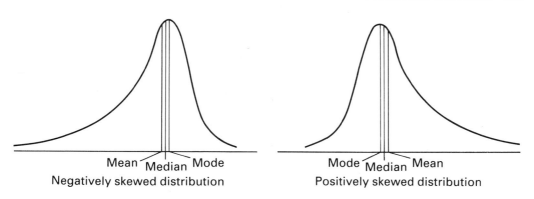

Figure 9.13   *Positive and negative skews*

What we know, from the theory of the normal curve, is that one standard deviation, on any normal distribution curve, falls at the position shown by the line above 50 on Figure 9.14. We also know that the area trapped between the mean and this point is 0.3413 of the whole, shown cross-hatched. Hence we know that 34.13% of children score between 40 and 50 points on this test, because the standard deviation is 10 points. Figures worth noting are that:

34.13% of all values fall between ($\bar{x}$) and +1 (or −1) standard deviations (area = 0.3413)
47.72% of all values fall between ($\bar{x}$) and +2 (or −2) standard deviations (area = 0.4772)
49.87% of all values fall between ($\bar{x}$) and +3 (or −3) standard deviations (area = 0.4987)

The positions of these standard deviations are shown in Figure 9.15. Note the values above are doubled for areas between −n and +n standard deviations.

We have just talked of the percentage of people between the mean and 1 or 2 or even 3 standard deviations from the mean, in either direction. A person whose score falls one standard deviation above the mean is said to have a **STANDARD** (or *z* score)

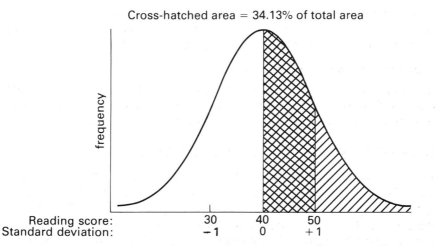

Figure 9.14   *Reading and distribution curve*

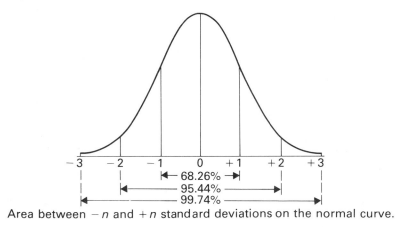

Area between $-n$ and $+n$ standard deviations on the normal curve.

Figure 9.15   *Positions of standard deviations on the normal distribution*

of $+1$. In general, *a standard (z) score is the number of standard deviations a particular score falls above or below the mean.* For instance, a child with a score of 25 on our reading test has a deviation score (*d*) of -15 and is 1.5 standard deviations *below* the mean. Hence their standard (*z*) score is -1.5. The negative sign tells us that the score is below, not above the mean. In general:

$$z = \frac{d}{s} = \frac{\text{deviation of score from mean}}{\text{standard deviation}}$$

From Table 2 in Appendix 2, you can see that a *z* score of 1.5 cuts off 0.43 (43%) of the area under the normal curve between it and the mean. Note that whatever is true to the *right*, positive side, of the mean, shown in the diagram at the top of this table, is also true to the left, negative side. Hence, 43% of children score between a *z* of -1.5 and the mean, that is, between 25 and 40. A person can, of course, be a difficult number of standard deviations from the mean, such as 1.63 or 2.91. It is possible, using Table 2 in Appendix 2, to calculate the percentage of people between the mean and any *z* score, so long as the distribution concerned is normal.

It is important to note that when psychologists 'standardise' a test to create a normal distribution, they then have a powerful instrument for assessing where any child is, say, on a reading ability or numeracy test, relative to other children who have taken that test. It is also important to note that intelligence, as measured by IQ test, was not *discovered* to be normally distributed in the population, like so many human biological qualities. The originators of the IQ test *created* a normal distribution by modifying and standardising their pilot tests, mainly for research and practical purposes. IQ tests are usually *standardised* at 100 for the mean and 15 points for the standard deviation.

Glossary

Value of a number, ignoring its sign; a number treated as positive even if it is originally negative	_____ _____	absolute value
Common language term for central tendency	_____	average
Chart in which one axis (usually the horizontal) represents a categorical or at least discrete variable	___ _____	bar chart
Formal term for any measure of the typical or middle value in a group	_____ _____	central tendency
Categories into which a continuous data scale is divided in order to summarise frequencies	_____ _____	class interval
Amount by which a particular score is different from the mean of its set	_____ _____	deviation value/score
Technical term for any measure of the spread of a sample of data or a population	_____	dispersion

		distributions
Distribution showing total numbers above or below each class interval	_____	cumulative frequency
Distribution showing how often certain values occurred	_____	frequency
Distribution which is not symmetrical about the vertical centre and which contains a lot more lower than higher values	_____ ____	negatively skewed
Continuous distribution, bell-shaped, symmetrical about its mid-point and the result of a variable affected by many random influences	_____	normal
Distribution which is not symmetrical about the vertical centre and which contains a lot more higher than lower values	_____ ____	positively skewed

Chart showing only the peaks of class intervals in a frequency distribution	_____-____	frequency polygon
Chart containing whole of continuous data set divided into proportional intervals	_____	histogram
Measure central tendency – sum of scores divided by number of scores	____	mean

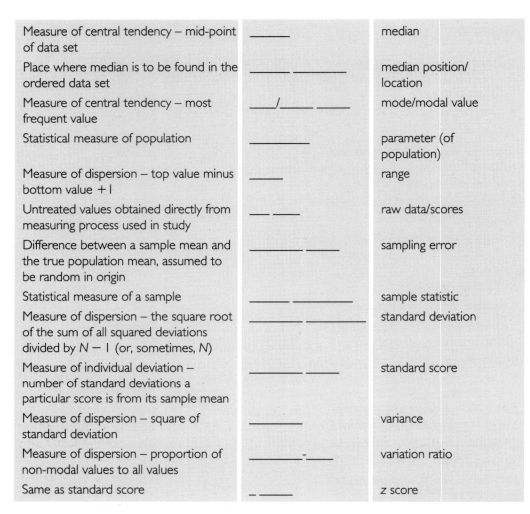

Measure of central tendency – mid-point of data set	_____	median
Place where median is to be found in the ordered data set	_____ _____	median position/ location
Measure of central tendency – most frequent value	____/_____ _____	mode/modal value
Statistical measure of population	_____	parameter (of population)
Measure of dispersion – top value minus bottom value +1	_____	range
Untreated values obtained directly from measuring process used in study	____ _____	raw data/scores
Difference between a sample mean and the true population mean, assumed to be random in origin	_____ _____	sampling error
Statistical measure of a sample	_____ _____	sample statistic
Measure of dispersion – the square root of the sum of all squared deviations divided by $N - 1$ (or, sometimes, N)	_____ _____	standard deviation
Measure of individual deviation – number of standard deviations a particular score is from its sample mean	_____ _____	standard score
Measure of dispersion – square of standard deviation	_____	variance
Measure of dispersion – proportion of non-modal values to all values	_____-_____	variation ratio
Same as standard score	__ _____	z score

EXERCISES

1 Find the mean and median of the two sets of talking times in Table 9.1.

2 What are the standard deviations of the two sets of talking times in Table 9.1?

3 Consider the following set of times, measured in 1/100ths of a second:

62 65 71 72 73 75 76 77 79 80 82 83 92 100 106 117 127

65 70 72 72 74 75 76 77 79 80 82 88 93 102 110 121 128

65 70 72 73 74 76 76 78 80 81 83 90 95 103 112 122 135

  a) Sketch a distribution for the data and decide which would be the most appropriate measure of central tendency for it. Calculate this measure and also a measure of dispersion.

  b) What is the range for this data?

4 Draw a histogram for the data in Table 9.4. Calculate the mean for this data.

5 Sketch two roughly normal distributions which have the same mean but quite different

standard deviations. Also sketch two normal distributions with the same standard deviation but different means.

6 You are told that a set of data includes one score which is 0.8. The standard deviation for the set is 0. Can you give the mean of the set and say anything else about the six other scores in the set?

7 In an IQ distribution, where the mean is 100 and standard deviation 15,
   a) what IQ score are 16% of people above?
   b) what percentage of people would score less than 70?
   c) what percentage of people would score less than someone with a z-score of − 1
   d) what is the IQ score of someone with a z-score of 2?

8 Participants were asked to assess the trustworthiness of a fictitious person on a scale of 1 to 10. Find the mode and variation ratio of the following set of assessment values:

1 2 2 2 3 3 3 3 4 4 4 4 4 5 5 5 6 7 7 7 7 7 9

NOTATION

N	is the number in a sample
N_A	is the number in sample A
X	is a value from the sample, such as Jane's score
Y	is also a value where there are two measured variables
Σ	Greek letter S ('sigma') – means 'add up each of what follows'. For instance:
ΣX	means 'add up all the Xs in the sample'
ΣXY	means 'multiply all the Xs by their paired Ys and add up all the results'. Notice that XY means 'multiply X by Y'. Always do what's directly *after* the Σ before proceeding to add up, for instance:
ΣX^2	means 'square all the Xs, *then* add them all up'. *Be careful* to distinguish this from:
$(\Sigma X)^2$	which means find the total of all the Xs and square the result

STATISTICAL SYMBOLS

	Sample		Population
	Sample		**Population**
mean	*standard deviation*	*mean*	*standard deviation*
$\bar{x}$	unbiased estimate of population – s	μ	σ
	'uncorrected' – S		
d	is a deviation score – distance of a particular score from the mean of the sample $= x - \bar{x}$		

SOME RULES

1 In mathematical formulae it is confusing, especially in statistics, to use the multiplication sign ('×') because there are also many 'X's or 'x's dotted around which mean a particular score or value. Therefore, when one value is next to another, always assume you have to multiply. For instance, rN means multiply r by N.

2 Always complete what is *inside* brackets before going on to do the operations *outside* them. Do the same thing with the Σ or $\sqrt{}$ (square root) symbols. Here are some examples using these two rules:

$\Sigma X \Sigma Y$ — Multiply the sum of all Xs by the sum of all Ys. Notice this is *not* the same as multiplying each X by each Y and *then* adding results – which would be ΣXY as given above

$\Sigma(x - \bar{x})^2$ — Take the mean from each x and square each result. Finally, add all the results

$(N - 1)(N - 2)$ — Find $N - 1$. Find $N - 2$. Multiply the results

$r \sqrt{\left(\dfrac{(N - 2)}{(1 - r^2)}\right)}$

1 Find r^2

2 Find $1 - r^2$

3 Find $N - 2$

4 Divide step **3** by step **2**

5 Find the square root of step **4**

6 Multiply r by result of step **5**

Analysing quantitative data

IS IT A REAL EFFECT? TESTING FOR STATISTICAL SIGNIFICANCE

Suppose one of our proposed research studies in Box 1.1 was successful. That is, we find that people in a hot room *do* report a higher level of aggression in a film which they've been asked to view. Would you accept my report just like that? Wouldn't your very next question be 'Well, but how *much* higher were the hot room group's ratings?' There will always be *some* difference between the scores of two groups but the question here is: 'Are the two groups' scores *significantly* different?' That is, can we reject the *null hypothesis* that no difference exists between hot and cold conditions, or must we accept that the differences were so slight that we can't seriously use them as evidence. Is it pretty well beyond doubt that the differences are real and not just expected random variation? I hope that sets the scene for the only focus of this chapter. We shall investigate how psychologists and other social scientists make SIGNIFICANCE DECISIONS.

OF MARROWS AND MEMORY

In order to bring out more clearly the ideas of hypothesis and significance testing let me take you through a fictitious but, I hope, illuminating example of how we reason when deciding whether differences found in psychological research are significant or not. Of course, this example will have little to do with psychology but is a *physical* example (and therefore more easily 'grabbed') with which I shall then compare our memory experiment example which was introduced on page 10. In fact, we are entering into the world of competitive allotment gardening!

Suppose that my neighbour Bill grows marrows and so do I. I suspect that, contrary to marrow growers' club rules, he is putting artificial fertiliser on his marrows (my theory). I form the hypothesis from this theory that his marrows are bigger than mine. My partner first asks me to be precise and *operationalise* what I mean by 'bigger'. I specify *length in centimetres*. She then tells me not to be paranoid and of course there's no difference between the length of his marrows and the length of mine. She is holding the *null hypothesis*.

Note two things. First, we are hypothesising about the *whole field* <u>not</u> any particular sample *from* that field. The field is a 'population'. Second, the mean lengths for the two fields of marrows, if it were at all possible to calculate them, will not be *exactly* equal. The null hypothesis is an *ideal* state of affairs, a 'thought experiment' against which to test the variation of particular (sets of) marrows. In reality I can't measure *all* the marrows. I must estimate from *samples*. At dead of night I nip over the fence and take a dozen, *selected randomly* as are an equivalent sample from my own field. I measure the difference between the average length of the marrows in each sample and find (lo and behold, I told you so) that his sample average is longer than mine! My partner, however, says what psychology students should *always* say about any difference between people they may hear about: 'Ah, but is it a *significant* difference?' There will always be *some* difference between randomly drawn samples from the same population but is the difference *I've* found large enough to say 'Well that's an unlikely difference to occur if the fields don't actually differ'. As we shall see in the next three chapters, we can calculate the probability that I would obtain a difference as large as I have obtained, *given the assumption that the null hypothesis is true*. If this probability is very low we say we have a *significant difference* between the two samples and we go on to *reject* the idea that they are drawn from the same or identical populations. In other words, we *reject* the null hypothesis and *accept* our *alternative hypothesis*.

Now let's relate this example back to the world of psychological research and our memory experiment in particular. Instead of fields or 'populations' of marrows we must think of two populations of memory recall scores which, unlike the marrows, are infinite. However, as with my nipping over Bill's hedge, when we conduct a psychology experiment, we effectively take *samples* of these scores. Our null hypothesis is that the means of the *populations* of rehearsal and image-linking scores are equal (*or* that both sets of scores are randomly sampled from the *same* population). Our *alternative is that they differ*. We estimate the probability of obtaining the difference we *did* obtain between our samples *if* the null hypothesis is true. To do this we employ a statistical test. If the outcome is a decision of significant difference (the probability was low) then we have supported our hypothesis and consequently the general theory. If we get no significant difference we must think again. If the marrow means

Box 10.1 *The language of hypothesis testing*

	Marrows	**Memory hypothesis test**
Theory	Bill uses fertiliser	Humans make information meaningful in order to store it
Hypothesis	His marrows are longer	People recall more items if they form images than when they simply rehearse
Test of hypothesis	Take samples from both fields of marrows	Take samples of scores under two conditions – image-linking and rehearsal
Research outcomes if null hypothesis to be rejected	Significant difference between sample marrow means	Significant difference between means for words recalled under image-linking and under rehearsal conditions

Test significance of difference between samples

Samples are significantly different	**Samples are quite similar**
support for hypothesis and theory	theory not supported; may need modification
reject null hypothesis	retain null hypothesis

are not significantly different this could be because I took biased samples – perhaps Bill's came from a poor growing patch and mine from a good patch, hence I unfortunately discover no difference between samples even though his marrows *are* longer overall (he *is* using fertiliser!). When we fail to confirm a hypothesis we might modify our theory, question the data-gathering method, reconsider the sampling method, re-run the experiment again under modified conditions and so on.

To relate this horticultural example directly to the situation in psychological research have a look at Box 10.1 which outlines theory and hypothesis in each case.

THE CONCEPT OF PROBABILITY

What we need to engage in now are the specific means by which we calculate the probability of events occurring by chance, that is, the probability of things occurring at random when a null hypothesis is true. Beware! This *may* make you a little less optimistic about the National Lottery where the null hypothesis (every ticket has an equal chance) gives you about a 1 in 14 million chance of winning!

Let's set out with a practical problem:

Suppose a friend said she could reliably forecast the sex of unborn babies by swinging a stone pendulum above the mother's womb. Let's assume she guesses your baby's sex correctly. Would you be impressed? Your personal involvement might well cause you to react with 'amazing!' or at least, 'well it is interesting; there *might* be something in it.' Stepping back coolly from the situation you realise she had a 50–50 chance of being correct. Nevertheless most people would begin to think she had something going if she managed to go on to predict correctly the sex of two or three more friends' babies. Suppose she has 10 babies' sexes to guess. How many would you expect her to predict correctly in order for you to be impressed that she's not just guessing and being lucky? For instance, would 7 out of 10 convince you? Or would you want more or would less do?

When teaching research methods and statistics in psychology, I always tell my students that they already have many of the important concepts framed in their heads, perhaps somewhat vaguely, developed through years of worldly experience. My job is to illuminate, clarify, and name these concepts. This is particularly true of the concept of probability and yet it is the area which causes a relatively higher degree of anxiety and confusion. Most people do have a very good sense of how probable various events are and yet many people are also loath to get involved in giving such probabilities a numerical value, either because it seems complicated or because one then seems committed to mysterious 'laws of chance'. A recent conversation with my friend's 11-year-old son, whilst giving him and his family a lift to the airport, is a good example:

'But planes do crash.' 'Yes, but you only hear about the accidents. Thousands of flights run safely and the odds of you crashing are hundreds of thousands to one.' 'I know but it still *could* be our plane.'

. . . and so on, as if this were an argument when, really, we are both saying the same thing but with different emphasis and personal involvement.

Box 10.2 *Percentage to decimal conversion*

From percentage to decimal
5% to $p = 0.05$

1 Remove the '%' sign (= 5)
2 Put decimal point after the whole number (= 5.)*
3 Move the decimal point *two* places to the left, inserting zeros as you go where necessary (i.e. first move 0.5, second move 0.05)

*If there already *is* a decimal point, leave it where it is, and go straight to step **3**, e.g.
$2.5\% \rightarrow 2.5 \rightarrow 0.25 \rightarrow 0.025$

From decimal to percentage
$p = 0.05$ to 5%

1 Move the decimal point *two* places to the right (005.)
2 Lose any zeros to the left of the first left hand whole digit (= 5.)
3 Lose the decimal point if there is nothing to the right of it (= 5)
4 Add the '%' sign (= 5%)

e.g. for 0.025:
$0.025 \rightarrow 00.25 \rightarrow 002.5 \rightarrow 2.5 \rightarrow 2.5\%$

GIVING PROBABILITY A VALUE

Have a look at the statements below. For most of them, you'll find you have some idea of how likely or not it is that these events will occur. Try to give a value between zero (not at all likely) and 100 (highly likely) to each statement, depending on how likely you think it is to occur:

1 It will rain on Wednesday of next week
2 You will eat breakfast on the first day of next month
3 Your psychology tutor will sneeze in the next lesson
4 The sun will rise tomorrow morning
5 You will think about elephants later today
6 A coin tossed fairly will come down showing tails
7 Two coins tossed fairly will both come down tails

For number 1, if you live in the UK, whatever the time of year, you may have answered with 50, whereas if you live in Bombay, and the month is October, you'd say about 3. Number 2 depends on your habits. I would be interested in what happens with number 5, now I've said it!

Now divide all the values you gave by 100. So, if you answered 20 to number seven, for instance, then divide 20 by 100 and you get 0.2.

Probability is always measured on a scale of:

$$0 \longleftarrow \qquad\qquad\qquad \text{to} \qquad\qquad\qquad \longrightarrow 1$$

NOT possible   MUST happen

. . . usually in decimal values, like 0.3, 0.5 and so on.

The work in the statistics part of your course will require you to switch quite frequently between percentage and equivalent decimals so, if this is all a bit hazy to you, take a look at Box 10.2 and refer to it whenever necessary. Next, I hope to explain why it makes sense to have probability measured between 0 and 1.

THE LOGIC OF PROBABILITY

Although we are about to look at the purely *logical* calculation of probability this doesn't always reassure us. As for my 11-year-old friend, it's hard to be convinced when entering a big metal tube that is about to hurtle through the sky 6 miles up at 550 miles an hour! Take a look at Box 10.3 for a light-hearted account of testing 'subjective probability'.

Box 10.3 *Sod's law*

Do you ever get the feeling that fate has it in for you? At the supermarket, for instance, do you always pick the wrong queue, the one looking shorter but which contains someone with five unpriced items and several redemption coupons? Do you take the outside lane only to find there's a hidden right-turner? Sod's law (known as Murphy's law in the USA), in its simplest form states that whatever can go wrong, will. Have you ever returned an item to a shop, or taken a car to the garage with a problem, only to find it working perfectly for the assistant? This is Sod's law working in reverse but still against you. A colleague of mine holds the extension of Sod's law that things will go wrong even if they can't.

An amusing *QED* TV programme tested this perspective of subjective probability. The particular hypothesis, following from the law, was that celebrated kitchen occurrence where toast always falls butter side down – doesn't it? First attempts engaged a University Physics professor in developing machines for tossing the toast without bias. These included modified toasters and an electric typewriter. Results from this were not encouraging. The null hypothesis doggedly retained itself, buttered sides not making significantly more contact with the floor. It was decided that the human element was missing. Sod's law might only work for human toast droppers.

The attempt at greater ecological validity was made using students and a stately home. Benches and tables were laid out in the grounds and dozens of students asked to butter one side of bread then throw it in a specially trained fashion to avoid toss bias. In a cunning variation of the experiment a new independent variable was introduced. Students were asked to pull out their slice of bread and, just before they were about to butter a side, to change their decision and butter the other side instead. This should produce a bias away from butter on grass if sides to fall on the floor are decided by fate early on in the buttering process. Sadly neither this nor the first experiment produced verification of Sod's law. I don't recall the exact figures but results were out of 300 tosses each time and were around 154 butter side, 146 plain, and 148–152. Now the scientists had one of those flashes of creative insight. A corollary of Sod's law is that when things go wrong (as they surely will – general rule) they will go wrong in the worst possible manner. The researchers now placed expensive carpet over the large lawns. Surely this would tempt fate into a reaction? Do things fall butter side down more often on the living room carpet? (*I'm* sure they do!)

I'm afraid this was the extent of the research. Results were yet again around the 148–152 mark. (Incidentally what test would be done on these frequencies? see page 161.) Murphy, it turned out, was a United States services officer testing for space flight by sending service men on a horizontally jet propelled chair across a mid-Western desert to produce many Gs of gravitational pressure. I'm still not convinced about his law. The psychologists suggest the explanation might lie in selective memory – we tend to remember the annoying incidents and ignore all the unnotable dry sides down or whizzes through the supermarket tills. But I still see looks on customer's faces as they wait patiently – they seem to *know* something about my queue . . .

LOGICAL PROBABILITY

Your answer to number 6 in the exercise above should have been exactly 50 which converts to 0.5. If you answered 25 (converts to 0.25) to number 7, you can already calculate probability (probably!).

Statements 6 and 7 are quite different from the rest. We can calculate the probability involved from *logical* principles. The reasoning for statement 6 runs as follows:

There are two possible outcomes – a head or a tail. (We discount occasions when it falls on its edge!)

One of these is the outcome we want.

There is therefore one chance in two that tails will come up.

The formula for logical probability is:

$$p = \frac{\text{number of ways desired outcome can occur}}{\text{total number of outcomes possible}}$$

where p stands for 'probability' when all events are equally likely.

When we toss one coin then, using the above formula and what we just said about outcomes:

$$p = \frac{1}{2}$$

(or 0.5) for the probability of getting a tail (or a head). Notice that the probability of getting a tail (0.5) *added* to the probability of getting a head (0.5) = 1. This makes sense because we know the predictability of what *must* happen is 1 and either a tail *or* a head must happen.

For statement 7 in the last exercise the answer was 0.25. Where did that answer come from? Well, if you look at Table 10.1 you'll see that if we toss two coins and look at the first and second tosses separately, there are four possible outcomes. We want the odds of just *one* of these occurring so, using the equation for p above, we get just 1 on the top (only one of the possible outcomes in Table 10.1 is two tails) and 4 on the bottom (the four *possible* outcomes shown in Table 10.1). Hence the probability is $\frac{1}{4}$ and this is 0.25. The outcomes and probabilities for tossing three coins are shown in Table 10.2 – notice that, for instance, the probability of getting two tails and one head, *in any order*, is $\frac{3}{8}$, or 0.375, as there are three ways of getting two tails and eight possible results altogether.

Table 10.1 *The possible outcomes that could have occurred in tossing two coins*

1st toss	2nd toss
H	H
H	T
T	H
T	T

H = head   T = tail

IS OUR SEX-GUESSER TOSSING COINS?

If you think about it, if our sex-predicting friend is actually a bit of a con artist (well, not *just* a bit if she's only guessing!) she may as well toss a coin as use her magic stone pendulum. Suppose she does just guess? What might happen? Subjectively, every one who got the predicted result would be 'over the moon' and broadcast her 'success' quite loudly, whereas the disappointed ones might just forget about it. This sort of thing happens with the Radio 1 DJ who can 'tell people's star signs' – the successes are noted but I suspect few people keep a good tally of the (very many) misses.

If our friend is just guessing what *should* happen? How many would she get right each time she guessed a set of ten babies? On average she should get five right. This is what the *null hypothesis* would predict. Don't be duped into thinking that five is better than zero and 'at least she got *some* right' (honestly, people say this). None right would be as special a coincidence as ten right. If getting none right wasn't just a fluke coincidence, then she might have had her stone the wrong way round!

Notice that, if she *does* get ten right, as you'll see, we can reject the null hypothesis and accept that the results were *not* a chance occurrence. This doesn't mean, however, that her system works. We have not automatically 'proved her theory correct'. She may have access to the local hospital's scanner records or she may guess from tummy shape!

How are we to work out the probability of her predicting ten right, nine right and so on? If only we could list them as we did for tossing three coins. Well, we can.

Table 10.2 *Tossing a coin outcomes*

		$p =$
TTT	one way to get three tails	0.125
(TTH) (THT) (HTT)	three ways to get two tails + one head	0.375
(THH) (HTH) (HHT)	three ways to get two heads + one tail	0.375
HHH	one way to get three heads	0.125
Total possible outcomes = 8		

Although it would be tedious to proceed with all possible combinations, as we did for two and three coins, we can skip some donkey work and just look at Table 10.3. Here we see that if you tossed ten coins, or had to guess the sex of ten babies, the total possible number of outcomes is 1024 (ten tails; nine tails + 1 head, with the head in any of the ten possible positions; and so on . . .). The number of combinations, within that 1024 total, which have ten tails in them is just the one (as there was only one way of getting three tails out of eight possible combinations – see Table 10.2). So, the probability that our friend is guessing, if she gets all ten babies' sex correct, is just $\frac{1}{1024}$, which is a little less than 0.001.[1] That is, the chance of her doing this by accident is a little under 1 in a 1000. Pretty impressive, huh?

Table 10.3 *Probabilities of obtaining* N *tails when ten coins are tossed together*

No. of tails – N (or no. of correct guesses)	No. of combinations with N tails in them	Probability of N tails occurring when 10 coins thrown together	Probability of N tails occurring – as decimal
0	1	$\frac{1}{1024}$	0.001
1	10	$\frac{10}{1024}$	0.01
2	45	$\frac{45}{1024}$	0.044
3	120	$\frac{120}{1024}$	0.117
4	210	$\frac{210}{1024}$	0.205
5	252	$\frac{252}{1024}$	0.246
6	210	$\frac{210}{1024}$	0.205
7	120	$\frac{120}{1024}$	0.117
8	45	$\frac{45}{1024}$	0.044
9	10	$\frac{10}{1024}$	0.01
10	1	$\frac{1}{1024}$	0.001
Total possible combinations = 1024			

SIGNIFICANCE IS THE PROBLEM NOW

There is always some cynical person in a class who doesn't even accept that $\frac{1}{1000}$ ($p = 0.001$) is good enough to rule out chance. Like my 11-year-old friend, they say 'ah but it *could* happen by chance still', with which I am forced to agree. To this I add, 'Yes, but we have to think *forwards*. If I *predict* that X will happen, as a result of a theory, and it does, with less than $\frac{1}{1000}$ probability of it happening by chance, in everyday life we usually accept that I have some sort of control or understanding. For instance, imagine I ask a member of the audience to select a number between 1 and 1 000. I then ask *you* to pick a number from 1 000 raffle tickets, already checked and shuffled in a bag. If I "get" you to pick the same number as the audience member selected you'd think I was a pretty good conjuror, *not* just lucky!' We can rely on

---

[1] For those familiar with simple probability calculations, another way to get this result is to take p for the first correct guess ($\frac{1}{2}$) and multiply by p for the second correct guess ($\frac{1}{2}$) and so on, ten times. This is $\frac{1}{2} \times \frac{1}{2} \times \frac{1}{2} \times \frac{1}{2} \times \frac{1}{2} \times \frac{1}{2} \times \frac{1}{2} \times \frac{1}{2} \times \frac{1}{2} \times \frac{1}{2} = \frac{1}{2^{10}} = \frac{1}{1024}$.

extremes of probability so much that, at a recent village fete, a local garage safely offered a free new car if anyone threw seven 6s with seven dice.

SIGNIFICANCE

We are often faced with informal significance decisions in everyday life. Suppose you received 62% for your last essay and 60% for the one you've just had marked. Are you doing worse or is this just forgettable fluctuation in your tutor's grading? If you got 45% next time, you'd know there was a difference which mattered. The current difference, however, is unlikely to bother you. So, we are often certain that a difference indicates a real change and often certain that it doesn't. That's the easy part. When do we change from one decision to the other? How far below 62% indicates a real drop in your standard? What we are looking for now is a system for making a decision of **STATISTICAL SIGNIFICANCE**.

In TV commercials we often see just one person successfully choosing the promoted margarine rather than its anonymous rival. How many people would you want to see making this rather fortunate choice before you were convinced that the result you see is not a fluke? For situations like these we need a formal test.

There will always be some difference between the results of two conditions in an experiment or investigation. It is not enough to show that a difference occurred in the direction we wanted or predicted, which is all the television advertisements do. We have to show that the difference is *significant*. Have a look at the results of the two memory experiments in Table 10.4.

Table 10.4 *Significant and non-significant memory experiment results*

Pt	No. of words recalled out of 20: Common words	Uncommon words	Pt	No. of words recalled out of 20: 6-letter words	7-letter words
1	15	10	1	14	13
2	14	7	2	13	14
3	10	6	3	10	12
4	18	11	4	15	13
5	16	4	5	9	7
6	12	7	6	11	15
7	9	2	7	12	13
8	16	9	8	16	15
	Mean = 13.75	Mean = 7		Mean = 12.5	Mean = 12.75
	Difference between means = 6.75			Difference between means = 0.25	

THE 'EYEBALL TEST'

An **EYEBALL TEST** is an inspection of results prior to formal testing. Without yet knowing the formal rules of significance decisions we can come to some pretty safe conclusions about the results in Table 10.4. On the right, we can see that the difference between means is quite unimpressive. On the left, it seems equally obvious that something has happened. Surely these differences could not be caused by chance fluctuation alone?

*One can never rely **only** on an eyeball test.* A formal statistical test must always be applied to the main data. It is useful, though, where several differences have been hypothesised, and some of these can be ruled out as unworthy of testing because obviously insignificant.

What we are seeking now, however, is a formal cut-off level. How unlikely does a difference have to be before we can call it a 'significant' one?

As I said earlier, if you said five correct guesses by our sex-predictor was quite convincing you would actually be accepting the number she is most likely to get if she's only guessing. The number we are looking for in this exercise, then must lie somewhere between six and ten. Six would obviously be generous and ten is the strictest we can be. Beyond ten lie the real cynics. The issue of where to draw the line is the process of SIGNIFICANCE TESTING in which we make a significance decision, based on conventional statistical principles, as to whether we should reject the null hypothesis or not.

SIGNIFICANCE LEVELS

To reject a null hypothesis social scientists must calculate the probability that their samples would differ as much as they do if they were, in fact, drawn randomly from two equal populations or from the same population. We ask what is the probability of obtaining this set of rehearsal scores and this set of image-linking scores if rehearsal and image-linking produce identical populations of scores? We want the probability to be low but *how* low? Social scientists use several levels of probability as criteria for rejecting the null hypothesis but there is, however, one level of probability which is a standard. If the probability of a difference occurring were higher than this value then, by convention, no researcher would claim significance for the result. Now what is this level? Should probability for a difference always be below 0.001 ($\frac{1}{1000}$), 0.01, 0.05 or what?

> Let's see if you already have a sense of where this limit might lie. Suppose I hand you a pack of cards. There are only two possibilities: *either* all the red cards are on top *or* the pack is randomly shuffled. The second alternative is equivalent to the null hypothesis. Your job is to decide which of these two alternatives is the truth by turning over one card at a time from the top. There is a catch. You start with £1000. Every time you turn over a card this amount halves. If you take a guess after turning over two cards, then, you stand to win £250. After turning over how many red cards would you decide, fairly confidently, that the reds are all on top? If you wait till 17 reds are turned over, you'll win just 1p! Even after ten reds you'll only get £1. Make your choice now.

Well, the exact probability of drawing four red cards in succession off the top of a properly shuffled pack is 0.055. My experience in classes has been that very many people would be confident in claiming the pack was *not* shuffled if *five* successive reds were drawn ($p = 0.025$). At four reds fewer people are confident and, on the other side, several people would prefer to see six or seven, with a tiny minority above this. Only those who have not yet got the point of probability want to see the first 26 cards come up red!

The 5% significance level

The vast majority of people, then, confidently reject the notion that the pack is shuffled somewhere between $p = 0.055$ and 0.025. Why is this interesting? Well, they almost certainly don't calculate the odds or fully appreciate significance testing. Yet, the level of probability at which social scientists reject *their* null hypotheses is 0.05. When the probability that differences found would occur *if the null hypothesis is* true is 0.05 or less, they claim a significant result. That is, when a psychologist tells you that group A differed from group B on such and such a test they are assuring you that the probability of the differences between groups A and B occurring coincidentally was less than 0.05. Another way of saying this is that *if* the null hypothesis is true, and there is no real difference between groups under these conditions, then you'd get a difference as extreme as this one only once in every 20 times the testing was run ($0.05 = \frac{1}{20}$).

SIGNIFICANCE DECISIONS

We have come to an absolutely fundamental principle underpinning much social science research – the notion of rejecting the null hypothesis at a certain level of significance. In a sense, the level of $p \leqslant 0.05$ is the golden standard by which differences or relationships are counted as significant or not:

- If a result is significant ($p \leqslant 0.05$) the null hypothesis is rejected
- If a result is not significant ($p > 0.05$) the null hypothesis is retained

It is usually said that, if analysis of your results produces significance at this level, you qualify for publication. However, there are times when *support for a null hypothesis* is what our theory predicts – the finding of *no* difference can be very important. But in that case, the level used to make the decision would still be $p \leqslant 0.05$, except under special circumstances.

But couldn't it still be a fluke?

About one time in 20 you *will* deal four red cards off the top of a shuffled pack. I can hear students going home, playing snap with their younger sister or brother and saying, 'There! Four reds! . . . and that Coolican says it's rare.' Well, we *expect* you to get this result around one time in 20, remember. So now you can hear a little voice (like my 11-year-old friend) saying, 'Well that means, if social scientists accept results less likely than 0.05 by chance, that one time in 20 they're accepting fluke results!' And the voice is right! (In a way.) Let's think about this:

> What steps can be taken to ensure that, when a researcher finds results significant at $p \leqslant 0.05$, the pattern of results is not a fluke occurrence?

What researchers do is to *replicate* studies. If an effect is taken as significant, and therefore published, someone else would try to obtain the same results in a repeat of the original study. The chances of two significant differences occurring together by chance are smaller than just one occurring.

CRITICAL VALUE

We just need to compare then, what our sex-predicter did with what the convention says. Was the probability of her result less than 0.05? Well, this seems obvious. The probability of her getting ten sexes right is 0.001. That's well under 0.05. True, but hold on just a second. Things are not *quite* that simple, but they're very nearly that simple.

First, let's start talking about how many babies' sexes she guessed wrong. This will make things easier for the first statistical test in the next chapter. The figures are just the same. The probability of her getting none wrong (by chance) is the same as the probability of her getting them all right (0.001). Let's now suppose she gets two wrong out of ten. Many people would feel this isn't a bad performance. It does seem convincing. One might say 'The probability of her getting only two wrong is 0.044 (see Table 10.3). You said if she gets under $p = 0.05$ for the likelihood that her result is a fluke then we can count this as significant.'

The slight problem here is that we didn't predict she'd get *exactly* eight right and two wrong. We said she'd 'do well', or she'd have to do well to convince us. What she has done is get *more than seven right* or, *less than three wrong*. What's the probability of *this* happening? This still isn't hard to work out. It's the probabilities of her getting none wrong and one wrong and two wrong added together. Consulting Table 10.3, that's 0.001 plus 0.01 plus 0.044. This comes to 0.055 and is just outside the limit where we'd accept her result as significant. If she gets only *one* wrong (nine right) the probability is just 0.011 (0.001 + 0.01) and her result *is* counted as significant (we reject the null hypothesis that her predictions are just guesses – there *is* something going on here we assume). In this case, then *before we start the test*, if ten predictions are to be made, we know there is a CRITICAL VALUE of wrong predictions which our friend must not exceed (if she wants to be believed) and here that value is just 1.

ONE-TAILED AND TWO-TAILED TESTS

In Figure 10.1 you can see the probability values from Table 10.3 plotted as a histogram. This is known as a 'probability distribution'. You can see here how unlikely it is, just by guessing ten babies' sexes, that our result will fall at the extreme ends. It is *highly* likely that our result will fall in the middle, say between 3 and 7. If you try the exercise of tossing ten coins many times this is the sort of distribution you'll get. You'll very rarely get 10 heads or 10 tails – about once in every 1024 times in fact. The ends of the distribution are known as its 'tails'. Note that our sex-guesser had to achieve a result in the shaded right hand 'tail' in order for us to take her seriously (for her result to be 'significant').

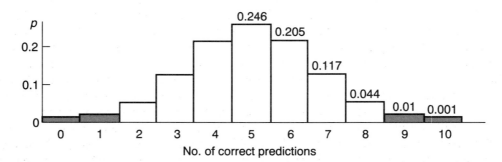

Figure 10.1 *Probability distribution for ten predictions of two equally likely outcomes*

A DIRECTIONAL HYPOTHESIS

Very often, as with the sex-predicter, we state *before* we test a hypothesis in which direction the results will fall. Here we say she will do *better* than the null hypothesis prediction of five right. Our ALTERNATIVE HYPOTHESIS, then, is that she will get significantly *more* than five right. The hypothesis is *directional* and the appropriate statistical test of this hypothesis is called ONE-TAILED.

A NON-DIRECTIONAL HYPOTHESIS

This will occur when we do *not* state the direction in which we think the results will go. We might investigate whether males and females differ in their attitude to male homosexuality, but we might leave open the question of which sex will be more positive. This hypothesis, being *non-directional*, requires a TWO-TAILED test.

Suppose we switch now from the situation where there are just ten events with equally likely outcomes (ten coin tosses or ten baby sex guesses) to those where there are very many possible outcomes – for instance, if we were daft enough to want to toss 80 coins and work out all the possible combinations that could result and their relative frequency of occurrence. In such cases the probability distribution which would occur is like that in Figure 10.2, which is a rather generalised version of Figure

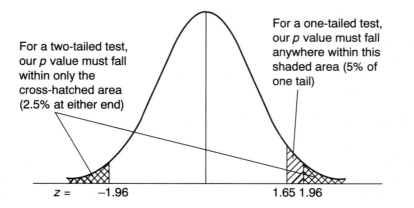

For a two-tailed test, our *p* value must fall within only the cross-hatched area (2.5% at either end)

For a one-tailed test, our *p* value must fall anywhere within this shaded area (5% of one tail)

$z =$ -1.96 1.65 1.96

Figure 10.2 *Tails of a distribution for one- and two-tailed tests*

10.1 but for many, not just ten, events. If we are making a directional prediction we are saying, *before we test*, that the probability of occurrence of our results *by chance alone* should be in the extreme right-hand of this distribution. As we have put our eggs in the one (directional) basket we take into account the whole of the right-hand 5% of the distribution and, so long as our result falls anywhere in the right-hand shaded portion, we get significance. We have considered one-tail of the distribution only. If, however, we made a non-directional prediction we want a result *anywhere in the extreme 5% of the distribution*, which is the top and bottom (cross-hatched) 2.5%. I hope you can see that now our result must fall at an even more extreme point of the distribution but, of course, a result in either direction will count as significant.

So why not always conduct one-tailed tests then? It seems that a 'weaker' result will be counted as significant if we do. However, there is a price to be paid for this relative ease of obtaining significance with a one-tailed test. Remember, a one-tailed test implies you have committed yourself to a result in one of the two possible directions. If we conduct a one-tailed test and the result then goes in the opposite direction to that predicted, *no matter how extreme*, you can't then claim this as significant. You can't have your cake and eat it too, as they say.

All right then, why not always do two-tailed tests? At least we can claim the result as significant whatever direction it's in so long as our probability is that little bit more extreme. Well, it doesn't make sense to make a two-tailed prediction when the hypothesis we are testing comes from a tightly argued theory. Suppose our theory concerns the effects of stimulants on motor performance. Stimulants generally speed up simple reactions. Amphetamine is a stimulant. It makes no sense here to predict that tasks performed with amphetamine will be performed significantly faster *or* slower than those performed without it. Our theory dictates a directional hypothesis and a one-tailed test of it. A summary is shown in Table 10.5.

Table 10.5 *Summary of one and two-tailed tests*

Is the direction of difference predicted? →	Yes	No
Hypothesis	*Directional* (or one-tailed)	*Non-directional* (or 'two-tailed')
Statistical test	*One-tailed*	*Two-tailed*
Where p must fall in area of probability distribution	Extreme 5% in predicted direction	Extreme 2.5% at either end
Comment	If results go past critical value in opposite direction significance cannot be claimed	Critical value less likely to be exceeded by chance if null hypothesis is true

OTHER LEVELS OF SIGNIFICANCE

If the baby sexer had got all ten predictions correct it would seem necessary to say that she didn't produce a result which was *just* significant at 5%. Her result was less likely than $p = 0.001$, which is 0.1%. When this happens, psychologists point out the level obtained in their final report. There is a tendency to use the following language in reporting results:

Significant at 5%   'The difference was significant'
Significant at 1%   'The difference was highly significant'

The 10% level ($p \leqslant 0.1$)

A researcher cannot be confident of results, or publish them as an effect, if the level achieved is only 10%. But if the level is in fact close to 5% (like the sex guesser's results if she gets eight predictions correct) it may well be decided that the research is worth pursuing. Procedure would be tightened or altered, the design may be slightly changed and sampling might be scrutinised.

The 1% level (p ≤ 0.01)

Sometimes it is necessary to be more certain of our results. If we are about to challenge a well-established theory or research finding by publishing results which contradict it, the convention is to achieve 1% significance before publication. A further reason for requiring 1% significance would be when the researcher only has a one-off chance to demonstrate an effect. Replication may be impossible in many field studies or 'natural experiments'. In any case, significance at 1% gives researchers greater confidence in rejecting the null hypothesis.

Lower than 1% (p < 0.01)

In research which may produce applications affecting human health or life changes, such as the testing of drugs for unwanted psychological or behavioural effects, we'd want to be even more certain that no chance effects were being recorded.

Above 5% (p > 0.05)

Yes, it seems we covered this with the 10% level. But the emphasis here is different. A researcher may be replicating a study which was a challenge to their work. It may be that showing there *isn't* a difference is the research aim. This would be the case with a lot of modern studies aimed at demonstrating a *lack* of difference between men and women on various tests and tasks. In this case the prediction is that the null hypothesis will be retained. The probability associated with results must now fall in the less extreme 95% area under the probability curve.

TYPE I AND TYPE II ERROR

When we have finished analysing research results, and we have tested for significance, we make a statement that we must accept or reject the null hypothesis at the set level of significance, usually $p < 0.05$.

We may be right or wrong. We can never be *absolutely* certain that an apparent effect is not a fluke. Sometimes it seems crazy to challenge. Say, for instance, we ran an experiment in which there were two conditions: recall of common words, like 'cat', and recall of uncommon words, like 'otiose'. A significant difference at $p < 0.001$ would appear unassailable. However, within psychological research, results are rarely as unambiguous as this, though high levels of significance are what good research aims at.

If a researcher claims support for the research hypothesis with a significant result when, in fact, variations in results are caused by random variables alone, then a TYPE ONE ERROR would be said to have occurred.

Through poor design or faulty sampling, researchers may fail to achieve significance, *even though the effect they were attempting to demonstrate actually does exist*. In this case it would be said that they had made a TYPE TWO ERROR. These outcomes are summarised in Table 10.6.

Obviously, if we set a stringent (low) significance level, such as 1%, we may well make a type two error. At 10%, a type one error is much more likely.

Table 10.6 *Type* I *and type* II *errors*

Null hypothesis is actually:	Null hypothesis is:	
	Accepted	Rejected
True	√	Type I error
False	Type II error	√

GLOSSARY

Value with which a statistic, calculated from sample data, can be compared in order to decide whether a null hypothesis should be rejected; the value is related to the particular level of probability chosen	_____ _____	critical value
Prediction which states in which direction differences (or correlation) will occur	_____ _____	directional hypothesis
Informal test of data made simply by inspection and mental calculation plus experience of values	_____ ____	eyeball test
Prediction which does not state in which direction differences (or correlation) will occur	___-_____ _____	non-directional hypothesis
Test made if the research hypothesis is directional	___-_____ ___	one-tailed test
A numerical measure of pure 'chance'	_____	**probability**
A measure of probability calculated from analytical formulae and first principles	_____	logical
A histogram or table showing the probabilities associated with a complete range of possible events	_____ _____	probability distribution
Levels of probability at which it is agreed that the null hypothesis will be rejected	_____ ____	**significance levels**
Significance level generally considered too high for rejection of the null hypothesis but which might merit further investigation	___	10% ($p < 0.1$)
Conventional significance level	___	5% ($p < 0.05$)

Significance level preferred for greater confidence than the conventional one and which should be set where research is controversial or unique	___	1% (p<0.01)
Test performed in order to decide whether the null hypothesis should be retained or rejected	_____ ____	significance test/ decision
Test made if the research hypothesis is non-directional	___-_____ ____	two-tailed test
Mistake made in rejecting the null hypothesis when it is true	_____ __ _____	type I error
Mistake made in retaining the null hypothesis when it is false	_____ __ _____	type II error

EXERCISES

1 State whether tests of the following hypotheses would permit one- or two-tailed tests:
   a) Diabetics will be more health conscious than other people
   b) Extroverts and introverts will differ in their ability to learn people's names
   c) Job satisfaction will correlate negatively (see Chapter 12) with absenteeism
   d) Self-esteem will correlate with outward confidence

2 A student sets out to show that attitude change will be greater if people are paid more to make a speech which contradicts their present attitude. Her tutor tells her that this runs directly counter to research findings on 'cognitive dissonance'.
   a) What would be the appropriate significance level for her to set?
   b) If she had originally intended to use the 5% level, is she now more or less likely to make a type II error?

3 This question is for those 'rusty' or insecure with decimal – per cent – fraction conversions. Just complete the gaps in the table:
   (If you're happy with this sort of arithmetic then leave this exercise and press on!)

Decimal	Per cent	Fraction
0.01		
		$\frac{1}{1000}$
	0.05%	
0.1		
		$\frac{1}{100}$
	0.1%	
0.005		

IS THERE A REAL DIFFERENCE? TESTS OF SIGNIFICANT DIFFERENCE

Significance tests are used when you've collected and organised your relevant data and you want to know if it (the independent variable) 'worked', i.e. was there a real difference (or, for correlation, were the two variables really related)? The tests to follow are organised in the following manner (Table 11.1). First we deal with tests of *difference*, followed by *correlation*. The tests of difference are organised according to measurement level, first *nominal*, then *ordinal* and finally *interval*. Within each level we look at two tests, one for *related* data and one for *unrelated* data. The asterisked tests are *parametric* tests.

Table 11.1 *Arrangement of all statistical significance tests covered*

		Related design	**Unrelated design**
Tests of difference (Chapter 11)	**Nominal level**	Binomial sign test – s	Chi square – χ^2
	Ordinal level	Wilcoxon T for signed ranks	Mann-Whitney U
	*Interval level	Related t	Unrelated t
Correlations (Chapter 12)	**Ordinal level**	Spearman's r_s	
	*Interval level	Pearson's r	

*These are *parametric* tests

In the last chapter, in order to explain the concept and workings of significance and probability, we actually went through the basics of what amounts to a 'sign test' – the first test which we'll cover formally in this section. Without further ado, I'd like to go through this test using some fictitious data shown in Table 11.2.

Table 11.2 *Therapy data*

Client No. (N = 10)	A Self-image rating Pre-therapy	B After 3 months' therapy	C Difference (B − A)	D Sign of difference
1	3	7	4	+
2	12	18	6	+
3	9	5	−4	−
4	7	7	0	
5	8	12	4	+
6	1	5	4	+
7	15	16	1	+
8	10	12	2	+
9	11	15	4	+
10	10	17	7	+

TESTS AT THE NOMINAL LEVEL OF MEASUREMENT

RELATED DATA – THE BINOMIAL SIGN TEST (USUALLY SHORTENED TO 'SIGN TEST')

CONDITIONS FOR USE

- Differences or correlation   Differences
- Level of data   Nominal
- Type of design   Related

DATA

A psychotherapist wishes to assess a therapeutic method. Clients are asked whether, after 3 months of therapy, they feel better about themselves. They are asked to rate their self-image by giving a score out of 20, before and after the 3 months of therapy (see Table 11.2). We test whether the second ratings are generally higher.

+		−
8		1

Figure 11.1 *The sign test gives the probability of drawing plusses and minuses at random*

Procedure	*Calculation on our data*
1 Calculate the difference between A and B, always subtracting in the same direction. If a one-tailed hypothesis has been made, it makes sense to subtract the score expected to be lower from that expected to be higher. Enter difference in column C.	See column C.
2 Enter sign of difference in column D. Ignore any zero values (i.e. cases where there is no difference in score pairs).	See column D. N becomes 9 because one result is zero.
3 Add up the number of times the less frequent sign occurs. Call this 's'.	Negative signs occur less frequently, so $s = 1$.
4 Find the relevant line of critical values from Appendix 2, Table 3 where N = total number of positive and negative signs (not zeros). Decide whether to pay attention to one- or two-tailed 'p' values.	Consult table and look at the horizontal line next to $N = 9$. Since therapy was intended to *improve* people's self-image, we are conducting a one-tailed test.
5 Compare s with the critical value shown for the significance level set. s must be equal to or lower than the critical value for results to be considered significant.	Our s is 1. The critical value under the column headed '$p < 0.05$' (one-tailed) is 1. Therefore, our result matches the conditions required for significance.
6 Make statement of significance.	We reject the null hypothesis. The probability of our results, if it is true is $p < 0.05$.

SUMMARY

The test looks only at the *direction* of differences. The critical value tells us the maximum number of differences in the unwanted direction we can have and still call our results significant at a particular level.

EXPLANATORY NOTES

The level is nominal because, for each result, all we know is whether there was a difference and the direction of that difference. We started with numbers looking like interval level data but we reduced these to just sign of difference, thereby losing any information about *sizes* of difference. For each result we have just three possible categories: '+', '−' or '0'. In our test we use only two of these, ignoring any zeros. The null hypothesis is that in the theoretical population, pluses and minuses are equal. Underlying this is the interpreted view that our ten clients rate themselves no differently from any other ten similar people asked to rate their self-image either side of a 3-month interval and with no therapy. We reject this view because we are rejecting the statistical null hypothesis. Another, purely statistical way to look at the reasoning is that, drawing samples of nine at random (we ignored zeros), and with replacement, from a barrel containing equal numbers of pluses and minuses, we would get a distribution this extreme (8:1) less times than 1 in 20.

USING TESTS OF SIGNIFICANCE – THE GENERAL PROCEDURE

Reporting the analysis of results (the section where you tell your reader what you tested and with what significance result) is the hardest task for students new to the subject, probably because this is done well before the logical process of significance testing has been fully absorbed. Often, given syllabus and timetable requirements this can't be helped. What I strongly suggest is that you turn to this section every time you have a test result to report and follow the steps in the procedure shown here. *All* the steps in Table 11.3 should appear in your results section in the order shown, for each hypothesis tested.

Table 11.3 *Procedure in conducting and reporting a statistical test of significance*

Choose appropriate statistical test	When we've covered all the tests, Chapter 13 will help you through this step. In a report, *justify* your choice.
Calculate test statistic	In the example just worked this was $s = 1$, the number of clients apparently worse. In all cases the statistic will be denoted by a letter, for instance t or U. Report this statistic but not all the calculations.
Compare test statistic with critical value in tables. Take account of:	Tables are provided at the back of the book for all the tests introduced. In calculating our critical value, we took account of:
1 Number of non-zero cases in sample (Sign test and Wilcoxon); df for χ^2 and parametric tests; N_A and N_B for Mann–Whitney; N for Spearman 2 Whether one- or two-tailed test 3 Maximum probability level acceptable (usually 0.05)	1 $N = 9$ 2 one-tailed test 3 $p \leqslant 0.05$ and we used Table 3 in Appendix 2 to obtain a critical value of 1. Our value ($s = 1$) is less than or equal to this value.
Decide which side of the critical value your result is on. Pay attention to instructions accompanying the table	Our result was on the significant side of the critical value for $p < 0.05$.
Report the decision. Whether to retain or reject the null hypothesis and at what level of confidence	We rejected the null hypothesis. We found a probability $\leqslant 0.05$ that our results could occur if it were true. Hence we had sufficient confidence to reject it.

UNRELATED DATA – THE χ^2 TEST (ALSO WRITTEN AS 'CHI-SQUARE' AND PRONOUNCED 'KY SQUARE')

CONDITIONS FOR USE

- Differences or correlation   Differences (tested by 'association')
- Level of data   Nominal
- Type of design   Unrelated
- Special note   Data must be in the form of frequencies. Although we are usually looking for differences in the effect of the IV, the test actually looks at the *association* between row categories and column categories.

There are other limitations on the use of χ^2, outlined at the end of this chapter.

DATA

The results in Table 11.4a were actually obtained at a psychology workshop. Students observed whether male and female drivers stopped at a pedestrian traffic light or not if it turned to amber as they approached it. The data in cells A, B, C and D are *frequencies* (see Chapter 8).

Table 11.4a *Observed frequencies*

	Sex of driver		Total
	Female	Male	
Driver stopped	90 a	b 88	178
Driver didn't stop	56 c	d 89	145
Total:	146	177	323

Table 11.4b *Expected frequencies*

	Sex of driver		Total
	Female	Male	
Driver stopped	80.46 a	b 97.54	178
Driver didn't stop	65.54 c	d 79.46	145
Total:	146	177	323

Procedure	*Calculation on our data*
1 Give the raw data (OBSERVED FREQUENCIES) a letter for each cell	See Table 11.4a

2 Calculated corresponding EX-PECTED FREQUENCIES as follows:

Formula: $E = \dfrac{RC}{T}$ where:

R = total of row cells
(a + b) or (c + d)

C = total of column cells
(a + c) or (b + d)

T = total of all cells
(a + b + c + d)

Cell A: $E = \dfrac{178 \times 146}{323} = 80.46$

Cell B: $E = \dfrac{178 \times 177}{323} = 97.54$

Cell C: $E = \dfrac{145 \times 146}{323} = 65.54$

Cell D: $E = \dfrac{145 \times 177}{323} = 79.46$

3 Call data in observed cells 'O' and expected cells 'E' and put values into the following equation:

$$\chi^2 = \sum \frac{(O-E)^2}{E}$$ by operating as follows:

i) Subtract E from O

ii) Square the result of step **i**

iii) Divide the result of step **ii** by E

Cell	Step i $(O-E)$	Step ii $(O-E)^2$	Step iii $(O-E)^2/E$
A	90 − 80.46 = **9.54**	9.54^2 = **91.01**	91.01 ÷ 80.46 = **1.13**
B	88 − 97.54 = **−9.54**	$−9.54^2$ = **91.01**	91.01 ÷ 97.54 = **0.93**
C	56 − 65.54 = **−9.54**	$−9.54^2$ = **91.01**	91.01 ÷ 65.54 = **1.39**
D	89 − 79.46 = **9.54**	9.54^2 = **91.01**	91.01 ÷ 79.46 = **1.15**

$\chi^2 = 1.13 + 0.93 + 1.39 + 1.15 = $ **4.6**

iv) Add the results of step **iii**

4 Find DEGREES OF FREEDOM as follows:
$df = (R - 1)(C - 1)$
where R is number of rows and C is number of columns

$df = 1 \times 1 = $ **1**

5 Using the df found, consult Appendix 2, Table 4 and find the relevant critical value

Using $df = 1$ we find that a value of 3.84 is required for significance with $p < 0.05$.

6 Make significance decision

Our obtained value is higher than the critical value required. Note that, with χ^2, obtained values must be *higher* than the critical value. Always check the instructions with the tables. Note, also, that we could not have reported significance at any higher level. We did not 'beat' the critical value for $p < 0.01$, which is 5.41.

NOTE 1: ONE- AND TWO-TAILED TESTS WITH χ^2 – Always use two-tailed values except in one special case to be discussed later. Don't worry! χ^2 is the only test which doesn't follow the usual pattern of one- and two-tailed tests. It doesn't matter in which direction we predicted here, we still use two-tailed values.

NOTE 2: **DEGREES OF FREEDOM** (*df*) – This is a complicated notion but it needn't worry you much here. For χ^2 and all parametric tests you need to calculate *df* before checking for the critical values in tables. For χ^2 it is calculated as shown above.

NOTE 3 – In line with modern practice this text does *not* recommend the use of 'Yates' correction' when *df* = 1. You may find this recommended in some texts.

Quick 2 × 2 formula

This can be used only where there are two columns and two rows, as in the example above. It saves the labour of calculating expected frequencies and, if you're handy with a calculator, you'll find this can be done in one move from the cell totals:

$$\chi^2 = \frac{N(ad-bc)^2}{(a+b)(c+d)(a+c)(b+d)}$$

where *N* is the total sample size.

SUMMARY

The test looks at the variation between observed frequencies and expected frequencies – those expected if, given row and column totals, there was absolutely no association between the vertical and horizontal variables, i.e. no systematic relationship between the DV and levels of the IV.

EXPLANATORY NOTES

If you consider our data, it is obvious that, of the 177 males observed, just 50% of them stopped on amber, whereas 62% of females (90 out of 146) stopped. The χ^2 test looks at these relative proportions. Let's consider a convenient but fictitious example.

Assume 50 high extroverts and 50 high introverts were asked whether they would feel comfortable on a nudist beach. The results might run like those in Table 11.5a.

Table 11.5a *Observed frequencies*

Would feel:	Extroverts	Introverts	Total
comfortable	40	10	**50**
uncomfortable	10	40	**50**
Total	**50**	**50**	**100**

Note that, of all 100 people asked, 50 said they would be comfortable and 50 said they wouldn't. But these 50 aren't evenly spread between the two types of person. A large proportion of extroverts would feel comfortable. Statistically, because 50 out of 100 people *in all* said they'd feel comfortable, we'd expect half the introverts, as well as half the extroverts, to say this *if* there is no relationship between extroversion/introversion and feeling comfortable on a nudist beach. If you agree with that point then, in your head, you actually performed a version of the expected cells formula:

$$E = \frac{RC}{T}$$

You agreed that 1/2 (50/100) of each 50 should appear in each cell, i.e.:

$$\frac{50}{100} \times 50$$

Table 11.5b gives us the relationship that *should* occur if the null hypothesis is true – that is, if there is absolutely no relationship between extroversion and nudism comfort. χ^2 tells us the likelihood of obtaining the results we *did* get (Table 11.5a) *if* this null hypothesis is true.

Table 11.5b *Expected frequencies*

Would feel:	Extroverts	Introverts
comfortable	25	25
uncomfortable	25	25

In fact, the calculation of χ^2 on the extrovert/introvert data shows a very large deviation of the observed from the expected data. χ^2 is 33.64 and the probability of this value occurring by chance was: $p < 0.0001$. Hence, we could safely assume, if these results were real, that the null hypothesis can be rejected and this therefore would support (*not* prove!) the theory that feeling comfortable with nudists *is associated with* extroversion. The χ^2 test is, in fact, often called a *test of association* between two variables.

Returning to our original real data then, the expected frequencies show that, as 178 drivers in all stopped, out of a total of 323, then we'd expect 178/323 of the 146 female drivers to stop *if* sex is not associated with stopping on amber. This expected value is 80.46. In fact, 90 females stopped. Male drivers stopped *less* frequently than the expected totals would predict on the null hypothesis. The χ^2 being significant at $p < 0.05$, we assume that (female) sex *is* associated with stopping on amber.

Warning for tests and exams!

It is very easy to get the idea of expected frequencies wrong. When asked what they are, many people answer that they are 'what the researcher expects' or similar. I hope you see that they are the *opposite* of what the researcher (usually) wants to happen. *The expected frequencies are what is expected to occur (most often) under the null hypothesis* (i.e. if 'nothing's going on').

THE $R \times C \, \chi^2$ TEST

We can extend this test to situations where either of the two variables being tested for association has more than two values. There can be R rows and C columns. For instance, four different colleges might be compared for their students' performances in a psychology A level exam (Table 11.6).

Table 11.6 *A 4 × 2 frequency table*

	College A	**College B**	**College C**	**College D**	Total
Passed	32	46	34	23	135
Failed	5	12	18	1	36
Total	37	58	52	24	171

The test will tell us whether these ratios of pass and fail are significantly different among the four colleges. Degrees of freedom here are $(R-1)(C-1) = (2-1)(4-1) = 3$. I haven't included the calculation because it follows the earlier method exactly. The χ^2 result is 11.14 and $p < 0.02$ (usually published as < 0.05).

χ^2 'GOODNESS OF FIT' TEST

A special use of χ^2 occurs when we want to investigate a set of data measured on only one variable. For instance, suppose we weren't interested in sex differences for stopping at an amber light. However, we are interested in how all drivers behave at a variety of traffic stopping points. Consider Table 11.7.

Table 11.7 *'Failure-to-halt' offences for county of Undershire*

a	b	c	d	e	
	Junction	Traffic	Pedestrian	Police controlled	
Roundabout	stop sign	light	crossing	junction	Total
47	17	19	12	3	98

An 'eyeball test' of this data surely leads us to suspect that drivers are far more careless or disrespectful of driving laws at roundabouts than elsewhere (and, of course, obedient with police officers!). We can treat this as a $R \times C$ test with just one row but five columns. Degrees of freedom for a 'goodness of fit' test are given by $C-1$.

Calculation

1 Calculate expected frequencies on the basis of the null hypothesis that all cells should be equal $\qquad 98 \div 5 = \mathbf{19.6}$

2 Using the observed values from Table 11.7 and the expected frequency calculated, use the χ^2 equation as before:

O: 47   17   19   12   3
E: 19.6   19.6   19.6   19.6   19.6

3 **a** $(O-E)$ $\qquad$ **b** $(O-E)^2$ $\qquad$ **c** $(O-E)^2/E$

Cell a $47 - 19.6 = 27.4$	$27.4^2 = 750.76$	$750.76/19.6 = 38.30$
Cell b $17 - 19.6 = -2.6$	$-2.6^2 = 6.76$	$6.76/19.6 = 0.34$
Cell c $19 - 19.6 = -0.6$	$-0.6^2 = 0.36$	$0.36/19.6 = 0.02$
Cell d $12 - 19.6 = -7.6$	$-7.6^2 = 57.76$	$57.76/19.6 = 2.95$
Cell e $3 - 19.6 = -16.6$	$-16.6^2 = 275.56$	$275.56/19.6 = 14.06$

$$\chi^2 = \mathbf{55.67}$$

4	Find critical value using $df (C - 1)$ and two-tailed values	$df = 5 - 1 = 4$ critical value for $p < 0.001$ is 18.46
5	Make significance decision	Assume we can reject null hypothesis of no difference with $p < 0.001$

Our result is far higher than the maximum table value given so there is an extremely significant 'lump' in the distribution of scores. Notice that the calculation of cell E contributes quite a lot to the overall χ^2 value, but nothing like that contributed by cell A. Roundabout misbehaviour is far *further* from the average number of mis-demeanours per category than is obedience at police-controlled crossings.

This **GOODNESS OF FIT** test can be used to decide whether a large sample closely approximates to a normal distribution or not.

GOODNESS OF FIT WITH ONLY TWO CATEGORIES

This is a special case of the 'goodness of fit' χ^2 where we have data measured on just one variable and have only split it into two cells. Suppose, for instance, we told people that a fictitious person was 'warm' and asked them to decide whether the person would also be happy or unhappy. We might ask them to rate several such 'bi-polar opposites' but let's just deal with one result shown in Table 11.8.

If people are choosing at random (the null hypothesis) then we should get about half the total in each cell, that is, 25. So expected frequencies are 25 for each cell. The calculation then proceeds as normal.

Table 11.8 *'Warm' ratings*

	Happy	**Unhappy**	Total
No. of participants choosing	42	8	50

The χ^2 value in this case would be 23.12. I hope you'll find this very highly significant.

This is the 'special case' referred to earlier when we can take the test to be one-tailed, if our hypothesis correctly predicted the direction of any difference.

LIMITATIONS ON THE USE OF χ^2

Observations must appear in one cell only. For instance, if we looked at male and female swimmers and hurdlers, one person could appear in both the swimmers *and* the hurdlers category if they enjoyed both sports. This would make use of χ^2 invalid.

Actual frequencies must appear in the cells, not percentages, proportions or numbers which do anything other than count. For instance, the mean of an interval scale variable cannot appear.

Low expected frequencies are a problem

A general, if conservative, rule of thumb is to discount the results of a χ^2 test when *more than 20% of expected cell frequencies fall below 5*. Note that this refers to *expected*, not observed cell frequencies. So long as you gather a large enough sample, say 50 people, 25 per group, for a 2 × 2 design like that for the male and female drivers, you should be all right and it won't matter if there are very few in one observed cell – in fact, that's usually what you're looking for! The *expected* cells should still all be well above 5 *or* it will be clear that people in each group have varied in the same direction and that there's obviously no association.

The low expected frequency rule given above is argued about in respected journals and generally now treated as a bit restrictive. A bit more detail is given in Coolican (1994), but the best approach is to ensure you include enough people to start with. Typically, some student projects fail to study enough participants in, say, a classroom test of children's conservation or in a study of babies' actions or language. This will be because it is hard to find enough participants or sufficient time for testing. *If in doubt, **please** consult your tutor before starting on such a project, otherwise you may end up with untestable data.*

Tests at the ordinal level of measurement

RELATED DATA – THE WILCOXON (*T*) SIGNED RANKS TEST

CONDITIONS FOR USE

- Differences or correlation   Differences
- Level of data   Ordinal
- Type of design   Related
- Special notes   Don't confuse this with the little *t* test to be met later in this chapter.
  Where *N* is large (>) see 'When *N* is large', p. 166

DATA

Students were asked to assess two teaching/learning methods, experienced for one term each, using a specially devised attitude questionnaire (Table 11.9).

Procedure

1 Calculate the difference between the pairs of scores (in columns A and B), always subtracting in the same direction. As with the sign test, with a one-tailed hypothesis it makes sense to subtract in the direction differences are predicted to go, i.e. predicted smaller from predicted larger value.

2 Rank the differences in the usual way (see page 107). Ignore the sign of the difference. For instance, Laver's difference (−5) is given rank

Calculation on our data

See Table 11.9

See Table 11.9. Note that Higgs' results are dropped from the analysis

Table 11.9 *Student assessment data*

Student (N = 15)	Rating of traditional lecture A	Rating of assignment based method B	Difference (B − A) C	Rank of difference D
Abassi	23	33	10	12
Bennett	14	22	8	9.5
Berridge	35	38	3	3
Chapman	26	30	4	5
Collins	28	31	3	3
Gentry	19	17	−2	1
Higgs	42	42	0	
Laver	30	25	−5	6
Montgomery	26	34	8	9.5
Parrott	31	24	−7	8
Peart	18	21	3	3
Ramakrishnan	25	46	21	14
Spencer	23	29	6	7
Turner	31	40	9	11
Williams	30	41	11	13

6 because it is the next largest, in absolute size, after the value (+)4. Also ignore any zero values. These results are omitted from the analysis.

3 Find the sum of the ranks of positive differences, and the sum of ranks of negative differences. The *smaller* of these is T. If the sum of one set of ranks is obviously smaller, you need only add these.

Sum of ranks of negative signed differences (−2, −5, and −7) will obviously be smaller. Therefore add their ranks: $1 + 6 + 8$. Hence, $T = 15$

4 Find relevant line (using N which doesn't include zero differences) in Appendix 2, Table 6 and decide whether to pay attention to one- or two-tailed values.

Relevant line is $N = 14$ (remember one result has been dropped). Assume preferred teaching method not predicted. Therefore two-tailed test is appropriate.

5 Find lowest critical value which T does not exceed. If T exceeds all critical values, results are not significant.

T does not exceed 25 or 21 or 15, but it does exceed 6. 15 is therefore the relevant critical value. It is under $p < 0.02$.

6 Make statement of significance.

Differences are significant ($p < 0.02$).

SUMMARY

The Wilcoxon test looks at the differences between related pairs of values. It ranks these according to absolute size, ignoring the direction of the difference. Statistic T is calculated by adding the ranks of the positive and negative differences and taking the smaller sum. Critical values are the maximum value T can be for the particular significance level. In a sense it asks 'How likely is it that differences this size, relative to all other differences, would occur in the 'wrong' direction?'

EXPLANATORY NOTES

Like the sign test, the Wilcoxon looks at differences between paired values. The sign test looked only at the probability of the *number* of differences in the less frequent direction being so low. The Wilcoxon also looks at the rank of these differences relative to the other differences. If we've made a one-tailed prediction that scores in one condition will be higher than scores in the other, we can say, loosely, that the smaller sum of (negative) differences is 'unwanted'. The test asks, in effect, 'what positions in the whole set do these unwanted differences take relative to the wanted ones?' We can have *very few* relatively large differences in the wrong direction, or we can have rather more relatively small differences in the wrong direction.

UNRELATED DATA – THE MANN–WHITNEY (U) TEST

CONDITIONS OF USE

• Differences or correlation   Differences
• Level of data   Ordinal
• Type of design   Unrelated
• Special notes   Where N is large (>20) see 'When N is large', p. 172

DATA

Children's tendency to stereotype according to traditional sex roles was observed. They were asked questions about several stories. The maximum score was 100, indicating extreme stereotyping. Two groups were used, one with mothers who had full time paid employment and one whose mothers did not work outside the home (Table 11.10).

Table 11.10 *Sex-role stereotyping*

	Scores of children whose mothers:		
had full-time jobs		had no job outside home	
$N = 7$	Rank	$N = 9$	Rank
17	1	19	2
32	7	63	12
39	9	78	15
27	4	29	5
58	10	35	8
25	3	59	11
31	6	77	14
		81	16
		68	13
Rank totals	40		96
	(R_A)		(R_B)

Note that, since the design is independent samples, there is no requirement for samples to be equal in size.

Procedure	*Calculation on our data*
1 If one group is smaller call this group A	The full-time job mothers are group A
2 Rank all the scores as one group	See Table 11.10
3 Find the sum of the ranks in group A (R_A) and group B (R_B)	See Table 11.10 $R_A = 40$; $R_B = 96$

4 Use the following formula to calculate U_A:

$$U_A = N_A N_B + \frac{N_A(N_A + 1)}{2} - R_A$$

$$U_A = 7 \times 9 + \frac{7 \times (7 + 1)}{2} - 40$$

$$= 63 + \frac{56}{2} - 40 = 63 + 28 - 40$$

$$= \mathbf{51}$$

5 Then calculate U_B from:

$$U_B = N_A N_B + \frac{N_B(N_B + 1)}{2} - R_B$$

$$U_B = 7 \times 9 + \frac{9 \times (9 + 1)}{2} - 96$$

$$= 63 + \frac{90}{2} - 96 = 63 + 45 - 96$$

$$= \mathbf{12}$$

6 Select the smaller of U_A and U_B and call it U

As $12 < 51$ then $U = 12$

7 Check the value of U against critical values in Appendix 2, Table 5

Our two sample sizes are 7 and 9. We'll treat the test as one-tailed. For $p < 0.01$ the U has to be equal to or less than ($\leq$)9. Our value is not this low. The $p < 0.05$ critical value is 12 so our U just reaches this level.

8 Make statement of significance

We would report the result as significant with $p < 0.05$. If the test had been two-tailed we could also report $p < 0.05$.

If there are many tied ranks you should use the formula given under the heading 'When N is large' further on.

SUMMARY

The test looks at differences between the sums of two sets of ranks. The value U is calculated from the two rank sums. The critical value gives the value of U, for the particular numbers in each group, below which less than 5% (or 1% etc.) of Us would fall if members of each group acquired their rank on a random basis.

EXPLANATORY NOTES

This test can be related to a very familiar situation in which we look at the performance of two teams. Suppose you were in a five-person school cross-country

Figure 11.2 *The B team position looks good! – the logic of the Mann–Whitney test*

team, competing against a local school (Figure 11.2). You would have to be impressed if the other school took, say, the first four places with the last of their team coming seventh. The sum of their places is $1 + 2 + 3 + 4 + 7 = 17$. The total sum of places (1 to 10) is 55. Our rank sum must be $55 - 17 = 38$.

Imagine, instead, that members of the two teams each drew from the numbers one to ten placed in a hat. The Mann–Whitney, in a sense, looks at all the combinations of rank sums which are possible when doing this. By comparing our result (for U) with tables, we know whether our split in rank sums (17 against 38) is one which would occur less than 5% of the time, if we repeated the number drawing many times. In other words, the critical value is the point below which we start saying 'The other school's apparent superiority was not a fluke!', something which of course we would rush to admit!

WEAKNESS OF RANK TESTS

The rank tests are relatively easy to perform and are generally as powerful as the parametric tests which we'll look at in the next chapter. Whenever you could use a parametric test you could, instead, use a rank test. The reverse of this is not true. Parametric tests must use interval/ratio level data. There are occasions, however, when a rank test result would lead us to reject the null hypothesis where a parametric test wouldn't (or to accept a null hypothesis when we could reject it). Parametric tests are said to be more **POWER EFFICIENT**, a concept we shall tackle later in this chapter.

WHEN N IS LARGE

Non-parametric rank tests use tables in which N, for either group, only goes up to a modest value of 20 or 25. For larger values we need to use a conversion formula. Suppose we drew two sets of related or unrelated ranks *at random* very many times and, each time, obtained U or T as appropriate. The distributions of U or T would form normal-like distributions and we can find where any particular U or T would fall on that distribution. We want *our* U or T to fall in the extreme tail(s) of the distribution. The relevant formulae are:

Mann–Whitney

$$z = \frac{U - \dfrac{N_A N_B}{2}}{\sqrt{\left(\left[\dfrac{N_A N_B}{N(N-1)}\right] \times \left[\dfrac{N^3 - N}{12} - \Sigma T\right]\right)}}$$

where N = the sum of N_A and N_B and

$$T = \frac{t^3 - t}{12}$$

each time a number of values are tied at a particular rank and t is the number of times the value occurs. For instance, for the data in Table 11.12, the score 8 appears three times. $t = 3$ and $T = (3^3 - 3)/12 = 2$. This would then be repeated for 9, which occurs twice. This time $T = (2^3 - 2)/12 = 0.5$. This would be repeated for 10, 12, and so on. ΣT is then the addition of all these results.

Wilcoxon signed ranks

$$z = \frac{N(N+1) - 4T}{\sqrt{\left(\dfrac{2N(N+1)(2N+1)}{3}\right)}}$$

where T is Wilcoxon's T calculated in the usual way.

z is a 'standard score'. As you may recall from page 130, a z score is expressed in standard deviations and cuts off a proportion of the normal distribution curve. We want the values cutting off 5% or 1%, at one end or both, depending on whether our test is one- or two-tailed. The values your z must exceed for significance are:

1.645	one-tailed 5%	1.96	two-tailed 5%
2.33	one-tailed 1%	2.575	two-tailed 1%

Other significance levels can be calculated from Table 2 in Appendix 2.

Tests at the interval/ratio level of measurement

PARAMETRIC TESTS

Some way back we discussed 'parameters'. Perhaps you'd like to try and remember what these are before reading any further, or to remind yourself by looking back to page 125. Here, anyway, is a redefinition. Parameters are measures of populations, in particular the mean and variance. Remember that the variance is the square of the standard deviation. Parametric tests are so called because *their calculation involves an estimate of population parameters made on the basis of sample statistics*. The larger the sample, the more accurate the estimate will be. The smaller the sample, the more distorted the sample mean will be by the odd, extreme value – see p. 119.

POWER

Parametric tests are said to have more **POWER**. Power is defined as *the likelihood of the test detecting a significant difference when the null hypothesis is false*, i.e. when there really *is* a difference associated with the independent variable. Put another way, it is the probability of *not* making a type II error. Non-parametric tests generally require more data (more sets of scores, so more participants in the study) to reach the same power as parametric tests.

The comparison of the power of, say, a parametric and non-parametric test is known as **POWER EFFICIENCY** and is expressed as a ratio. You would encounter the mathematics behind this in a more advanced text. Non-mathematically speaking, efficiency is, in a sense, the savings made by the more powerful test in terms of finding more differences that are non-random differences and in, therefore, helping to dismiss 'no difference' assumptions, that is, to avoid type II errors.

It is important to remember, however, that parametric tests can't undo damage already done. If data have been collected poorly and/or there are just too few data (*N* is very low) then the greater sensitivity of the parametric test will not compensate for this. Very often the slight advantage of the parametric test can be neutralised, by using a rank type test with just a few more participants. Non-parametric tests also have the advantages of being easier to calculate and being usable on data that parametric tests cannot use, as we shall see.

The greater power of parametric tests comes from their greater sensitivity to the data. This in turn is because they use *all* the information available. They look at *size* of differences and values involved, not just ranks (order of sizes). They are more subtle, then, in their analysis of data.

This power and accuracy, however, has to be paid for. The tests make estimates of underlying population parameters. These estimates are made on the assumption that the underlying population has certain characteristics.

ASSUMPTIONS FOR PARAMETRIC TESTS IN THIS BOOK

1 The level of measurement must be at least interval.
2 The sample data are drawn from a normally distributed population.
3 The variances of the two samples are not significantly different – this is known as the principle of **HOMOGENEITY OF VARIANCE** (but see note 3).

Notes on assumption number:

1 We must make a decision about our dependent variable. Is it truly interval level? If it is an unstandardised scale, or if it is based on human estimation or rating, would it be safer to make it ordinal? Remember, data don't often get collected *as* ordinal. They often appear interval-like but we *reduce* them to ordinal by ranking them.

2 This principle is often written in error as 'the sample must be normally distributed'. This is not so. Most samples are too small to look anything like a normal distribution, which only gets its characteristic bell-like shape from the accumulation of very many scores. A largish sample can be tested for the

likelihood that it came from a normal distribution using the χ^2 'goodness of fit' test covered earlier.

In practice, for small samples, we have to assume that the population they were drawn from is a normal distribution on grounds of past experience or theory. It may be known, from other research, that the variable tested is normally distributed, or it may be possible to argue that, given what we do know, the assumption is reasonable.

3 Statisticians have further investigated this requirement, which used to demand very similar variances. Fortunately, we can now largely ignore it when dealing with *related* samples, without any great risk of distortion in our result. For *unrelated* samples we need to be more careful *where sample sizes are quite different.*

More advanced texts give you information on how to check that variances aren't significantly different. The best thing to do, however, if you want to use a parametric test with an unrelated design, is to ensure you get similar size samples.

PARAMETRIC TESTS ARE ROBUST

The principles above are not set in concrete. One can do a parametric test on data which don't fit the assumptions exactly. The fact that the tests, under such conditions, still give fairly accurate probability estimates has led to them being called ROBUST. They do not break down, or produce many errors in significance decisions, unless the assumptions are quite poorly met.

COMPARISON OF PARAMETRIC AND NON-PARAMETRIC TESTS

Parametric	*Non-parametric*
More power; higher power-efficiency compared with non-parametric tests	Power often not far from parametric equivalent
	May need higher N to match power of parametric test
More sensitive to features of data collected	Simpler and quicker to calculate
Robust – data can depart somewhat from assumptions	No need to meet data requirements of parametric tests at all

THE *t*-TEST FOR RELATED DATA

CONDITIONS FOR USE

- Differences or correlation   Differences
- Level of data   Interval or ratio
- Type of design   Related (repeated measures or matched pairs)
- Special note   Data must satisfy parametric assumptions

Sometimes called a correlated '*t*-test'; *do not confuse this with correlation* (see Chapter 12).

DATA

Participants were given two equivalent sets of 15 words to memorise under two conditions. In condition A they were instructed to form visual imagery links between each item and the next. In condition B they were instructed only to rehearse the words as they heard them. Participants had two minutes immediately after list presentation, to 'free recall' the words (recall in any order).

JUSTIFICATION OF USE OF t-TEST

- The data are of interval level status
- It is commonly assumed that recall totals in a free recall task such as this would form a normal-like distribution
- The standard deviations are quite different. However, this is a related design and therefore the homogeneity of variance requirement is not so important.

FORMULA

$$t = \frac{\Sigma d}{\sqrt{\left(\dfrac{N\Sigma d^2 - [\Sigma d]^2}{N-1}\right)}}$$

Note: There are several variations of this formula so don't get worried if you find another which looks different. This is the easiest to work with on a simple calculator. On page 178 there is a version which is even easier if your calculator gives standard deviations, or you have them already calculated.

Table 11.11 *Word recall data*

| Participant number | Number of words recalled in: | | Difference | |
	Imagery condition (A)	Rehearsal condition (B)	d	d^2
1	6	6	0	0
2	15	10	5	25
3	13	7	6	36
4	14	8	6	36
5	12	8	4	16
6	16	12	4	16
7	14	10	4	16
8	15	10	5	25
9	18	11	7	49
10	17	9	8	64
15	12	8	4	16
12	7	8	−1	1
13	15	8	7	49
	$\bar{x}_A = 13.38$	$\bar{x}_B = 8.85$	$\Sigma d = 59$	$\Sigma d^2 = 349$
	$s_A = 3.52$	$s_B = 1.68$	$(\Sigma d)^2 = 3481$	

Mean of differences ('difference mean') $\bar{d} = 4.54$

$s_d = 2.60$

Procedure	**Calculation on our data**
1 Calculate the mean of the scores in each condition	See Table 11.11
2 Arrange the final results table such that the first column has the higher mean and call this group (or column) A. Call its mean $\bar{x}_A$. Call the other mean $\bar{x}_B$ and the group (or column) B (see note below)	See Table 11.11
3 Subtract each participant's B score from their A score. Call this d	See Table 11.11
4 Square the d for each participant	See Table 11.11
5 Add up all the ds (Σd) and all the d^2s (Σd^2)	$\Sigma d = 59 \quad \Sigma d^2 = 349$
6 Square Σd. Note this is $(\Sigma d)^2$. *Be careful to distinguish between Σd^2 and $(\Sigma d)^2$!*	$(\Sigma d)^2 = 3481$
7 Multiply N (the number of pairs of scores there are) by Σd^2	$13 \times 349 = 4537$
8 Subtract $(\Sigma d)^2$ from the result of step **7**	$4537 - 3481 = 1056$
9 Divide the result of step **8** by $N - 1$	$1056 \div 12 = 88$
10 Find the square root of step **9**	$\sqrt{(88)} = 9.381$
11 Divide Σd by the result of step **10** to give t	$59 \div 9.381 = 6.289 \quad t = 6.289$
12 Find degrees of freedom (df). For a related design this is $N - 1$ where N is the number of *pairs of values*	$13 - 1 = 12$
13 Find the largest value of t in Appendix 2, Table 7, given the degrees of freedom and appropriate number of tails, which does not exceed our obtained value of t. Make significance statement	Critical value for $p < 0.01$ is 3.055, assuming a two-tailed test. The table goes no higher than this. Our value of 6.289 easily exceeds it. Therefore, the probability of our t value occurring by chance alone is at least as low as 0.01 and probably a lot lower. The difference is therefore highly significant.

Note on step 2: if your hypothesis is one-tailed (you already *expect* one mean to be higher than the other from your research theory and aims) then there is no need to arrange the columns this way. Just take the values you predict to be lower from the other values. If you're wrong, and the results, in fact, go the other way (the *other* mean is the higher) then your t value will arrive with a negative sign (and you can't, anyway, have a significant result; see page 152 on one-tailed tests)

PROCEDURE WITH AUTOMATIC CALCULATION OF STANDARD DEVIATION

If your calculator gives you the standard deviation of a set of values directly there is a far easier route to t. This is:

$$t = \frac{\bar{d}}{\sqrt{s_d^2/N}}$$

1 Find the standard deviation of the differences, using the population estimate $(N-1)$ version. In the example above $s_d = 2.60$

2 Find s_d^2 (This is the *variance* of the differences) ($= 6.76$)

3 Divide s_d^2 by N ($= 0.52$)

4 Find the square root of step 3 ($= 0.721$)

5 Divide the mean of the differences ($\bar{d}$) by the result of step 4 ($t = 6.297$) (the slightly different result occurs through rounding decimals).

EXPLANATORY NOTES

The idea tested here is that, *if the null hypothesis is true*, the average of the differences between each participants' two scores will not differ significantly from zero. Suppose we repeated a test over and over again, in which the independent variable has absolutely no effect. Each time there would be a set of differences like that in the 'd' column of Table 11.11. Each person's second score would differ from their first score in a completely random manner. There would always be a value for $\bar{d}$ but it would tend to be small, only rarely large and half the time negative. The distribution of $\bar{d}$s would look pretty much, but not exactly, like the normal distribution. If we wish to reject the null hypothesis then our result must fall to the extreme right (one-tailed). The t value tells us how far to the extreme right or left our obtained $\bar{d}$ actually does fall on this distribution. The larger the t the further towards one extreme end our obtained $\bar{d}$ falls and the more unlikely it was to occur by chance. The distribution is not conjured out of thin air but is based on statistical *estimates* using the parameters of the samples being tested. *This is why it is so important that the sample data must follow parametric assumptions. Otherwise all these estimations will be faulty.*

THE t-TEST FOR UNRELATED DATA

CONDITIONS FOR USE

- Differences or correlation   Differences
- Level of data   Interval or ratio
- Type of design   Unrelated
- Special note   Data must satisfy parametric assumptions

Also known as an 'independent t-test' and sometimes called an 'uncorrelated' t test; *do not confuse this with correlation*, which is covered in Chapter 12.

DATA

Twelve participants were asked to use visual image linking in memorising a list of 15 words. Thirteen participants were asked to use only rehearsal on the same list of words. Participants used free recall to demonstrate retention (Table 11.12).

Table 11.12 *Imagery/rehearsal recall data*

Number of words correctly recalled in:			
Group A (N = 12) (score = x_A)	x_A^2	Group B (N = 13) (score = x_B)	x_B^2
12	144	12	144
18	324	9	81
12	144	12	144
10	100	8	64
10	100	10	100
14	196	8	64
14	196	7	49
18	324	13	169
12	144	16	256
8	64	11	121
14	196	15	225
14	196	13	169
		9	81
$\Sigma x_A =$ 156	$\Sigma x_A^2 = 2128$	$\Sigma x_B = 143$	$\Sigma x_B^2 =$ 1667
$\bar{x}_A =$ 13		$\bar{x}_B =$ 11	
$(\Sigma x_A)^2 = 24336$		$(\Sigma x_B)^2 = 20449$	
$s_A =$ 3.015		$s_B =$ 2.799	

JUSTIFICATION OF USE OF *t*-TEST

- The data are of interval level status
- It is commonly assumed that recall totals in a free-recall task such as this would form a near normal distribution
- The standard deviations are not very different. Even if they were, sample numbers are very close and therefore the homogeneity of variance requirement is not so important.

FORMULA

$$\text{Unrelated } t = \frac{|\bar{x}_A - \bar{x}_B|}{\sqrt{\left[\frac{\left(\sum x_A^2 - \frac{(\Sigma x_A)^2}{N_A}\right) + \left(\sum x_B^2 - \frac{(\Sigma x_B)^2}{N_B}\right)}{(N_A + N_B - 2)}\right]\left[\frac{N_A + N_B}{(N_A)(N_B)}\right]}}$$

This is the most complex formula, with the greatest number of steps, in the book, so do try to be careful and patient!

Procedure	*Calculation on our data*
1 Add up all the scores (x_A) in group A to give Σx_A	See Table 11.12
2 Add up all the squares of group A scores (x_A^2) to give Σx_A^2	See Table 11.12
3 Square the result of step **1** to give $(\Sigma x_A)^2$. Again, be careful to distinguish this from Σx_A^2	See Table 11.12
4 Divide the result of step **3** by N_A (number of results in group A)	$24336 \div 12 = 2028$
5 Subtract result of step **4** from result of step **2**	$2128 - 2028 = 100$
6–8 Repeat steps **1** to **3** on the group B scores to give: Σx_B (step **6**), Σx_B^2 (step 7) and $(\Sigma x_B)^2$ (step **8**)	See Table 11.12
9 Divide the result of step **8** by N_B (number of results in group B)	$20449 \div 13 = 1573$
10 Subtract result of step **9** from result of step **7**	$1667 - 1573 = 94$
11 Add the results of steps **5** and **10**	$100 + 94 = 194$
12 Divide the result of step **11** by $(N_A + N_B - 2)$	$194 \div (12 + 13 - 2) = 194 \div 23 = 8.435$
13 Multiply the result of step **12** by $\dfrac{N_A + N_B}{N_A \times N_B}$	$8.435 \times \dfrac{(12+13)}{12 \times 13} = 8.435 \times \dfrac{25}{156}$ $= 8.435 \times 0.16 = 1.35$
14 Find the square root of the result of step **13**	$\sqrt{1.35} = 1.162$
15 Find the difference between the two means: $\bar{x}_A - \bar{x}_B$	$13 - 11 = 2$
16 Divide the result of step **15** by the result of step **14** to give t	$2 \div 1.162 = 1.721$ Therefore $t = 1.721$
17 Calculate degrees of freedom when $df = N_A + N_B - 2$	$12 + 13 - 2 = 23$
18 Consult Appendix 2, Table 7, and make significance statement as for related t	For a one-tailed test, with $df = 23$, the critical value of t is 1.714 for significance with $p < 0.05$. Hence, our result is significant (by the narrowest of margins!). Note, for a two-tailed test significance would not be achieved.

EXPLANATORY NOTES

Suppose we took two samples from just one barrel of 2 cm screws and calculated the means of these two samples. Screws are not always exactly the same length; manufacturing produces tiny variations from perfection. There will therefore be some difference between the two sample means but *we know* that this difference will mostly be trivial. If we did this many times we could draw up the distribution of differences between means. This, yet again, would resemble a normal distribution if we did this enough times. Again, the *t* value tells us how far along this hypothetical distribution our *obtained* difference between two means would fall, given the sample parameters, *if the null hypothesis is true*. If the distance is great, and likely to occur by chance with $p < 0.05$, we can reject this null hypothesis. Again, because population estimates are made, it is important that the gathered data satisfy the assumptions necessary for a parametric test.

GLOSSARY

Number of cells in frequency table which are free to vary if row and column totals are known. In parametric tests it defines the number of values free to vary when a group total is known	_____ __ _____	degrees of freedom
Frequencies theoretically expected in (χ^2) table if no relationship exists between variables	_____ _____	expected frequencies
Assumption to be satisfied by data before proceeding with a parametric test – this condition occurs when the two variances are not significantly different	_____ __ _____	homogeneity of variance
Frequencies actually obtained and submitted to a significance test using χ^2	_____ _____	observed frequencies
Relatively powerful significance test for data at interval level. The tests make estimations of population characteristics and the data tested must therefore satisfy certain assumptions	_____ ____	parametric test
Likelihood of a test detecting a significant difference when the null hypothesis is false	____	power (of test)
Comparison of the power of two different tests of significance	____ _____	power efficiency
Tendency of test to give satisfactory probability estimates even when data assumptions for the test vary somewhat from the ideal	_____	robustness
The figure calculated at the end of a statistical test which is then compared with critical values	____ _____	test statistic

		tests of difference
Test of association between two variables, using unrelated data at nominal level (but can show *difference* between results for different values of the IV)	_____	Chi-squared (χ^2)
Frequency level test used to decide whether a given distribution is close enough to a theoretical pattern	_____ __ ___	Goodness of fit (chi-squared)
Ordinal level test for differences between two sets of unrelated data – using U	____-_____	Mann–Whitney (U)
Parametric difference test for related data	_____ --____	Related (correlated) t-test
Nominal level test for differences between two sets of related data	____ ___	Sign test (binomial)
Parametric difference test for unrelated data	_____ --____	Unrelated (uncorrelated) t-test
Ordinal level test for differences between two related sets of data – using T	_____ _____ _____	Wilcoxon (T) signed ranks

EXERCISES

1 Carry out a χ^2 test on the following data:

	pro-hanging	anti-hanging
politics		
left	17	48
right	33	16

2 Should a χ^2 test be carried out on the following data?
$$\begin{matrix} 7 & 1 \\ 2 & 7 \end{matrix}$$

3 A (fictitious) survey shows that, in a sample of 100, 91 people are against the privatisation of health services, whereas nine support the idea.
  a) What test of significance can be performed on this data?
  b) Calculate the χ^2 value and check it for significance.
  c) Could this test be one-tailed?
  d) If, for a large sample, we knew *only* that 87% of people were against the idea and 13% were for it, could we carry out the same test to see whether this split is significant?

4 Nine people are sent on an interpersonal skills training course. They are asked to rate their opinion of the need for this type of course both before and after attendance. Seven people rated the need lower having attended, one rated it higher and one didn't change in opinion. Using a sign test, decide whether this apparent negative effect of the course is significant.

5 Find out whether the following test statistics are significant, and at what level, for the one- or two-tailed tests indicated. You can put the probability value (p) achieved in the blank columns under 'sig'.

	No. in each group		Mann–Whitney $U=$	Sig.			$N=$	Wilcoxon signed ranks $T=$	Sig.	
	$N_A=$	$N_B=$		One-tail	Two-tail				One-tail	Two-sail
a)	14	15	49			**c)**	18	35		
b)	8	12	5			**d)**	30	48		

6 Carry out the appropriate test (either Mann–Whitney or Wilcoxon signed ranks) on the data in:
a) Table 11.11
b) Table 11.12
and test the results for significance using one-tailed values.

7 Comment on the wisdom of carrying out a t-test on the following two sets of data:

a) 17   23
    18   9   (unrelated data)
    18   31
    16   45
        16
        18
        17
         6

b) 17   23
    18   11   (related data)
    18   24
    16   29
    12   19
    15   16

For each of **a)** and **b)**, what is an appropriate non-parametric test?

8 A report claims that a t-value of 2.85 is significant ($p < 0.01$) when the number of people in a repeated measures design was 11. Could the hypothesis tested have been two-tailed?

9 At what level, if any, are the following values of t significant? The last three columns are for you to fill in. Don't forget to think about degrees of freedom.

	$t=$	N	Design of study	One- or two-tailed	$p\leqslant$	Significant at (%)	Reject null hypothesis?
a)	1.750	16	related	1			
b)	2.88	20	unrelated	2			
c)	1.70	26	unrelated	1			
d)	5.1	10	unrelated	1			
e)	2.09	16	related	2			
f)	3.7	30	related	2			

10 Two groups of children are observed for the number of times they make a generous response during one day. The researcher wishes to conduct a parametric test for differences between the two groups and their 'generosity response score'. A rough grouping of the data shows this distribution of scores:

	| Number of generous responses						
	0–3	4–6	7–9	10–12	13–15	16–19	20–22
Group							
A	2	16	24	8	3	0	1
B	5	18	19	10	5	1	3

Why does the researcher's colleague advise that a t-test would be an inappropriate test to use on this occasion?

12

Is there a real relationship? Testing for correlation between pairs of data

The nature of correlation

POSITIVE AND NEGATIVE CORRELATIONS

Have a look at the following statements:

1 The older I get, the worse my memory becomes.
2 The more you give kids, the more they expect.
3 Taller people tend to be more successful in their careers.
4 The more physical punishment children receive, the more aggressive they become when they're older.
5 Good musicians are usually good at maths.
6 People who are good at maths tend to be poor at literature.
7 The more you practise guitar playing, the less mistakes you make.

These are all examples of relationships known as CORRELATION. In each statement it is proposed that two variables are correlated, i.e. they go together in the sense that either:

• as one variable increases so does the other. For instance:

   The further you walk, the more money you collect for charity.
   The more papers you have to deliver, the longer it takes you.
   or

• as one variable *increases* the other variable *decreases*. For instance:

   As temperature increases, sales of woolly jumpers decrease.
   The more papers you have to carry, the slower you walk.

The correlations of the type stated first are known as POSITIVE; those stated second are NEGATIVE (someone once suggested the following memory 'hook' for negative correlation: 'as rain comes down so umbrellas go up', a common enough *negative* experience for British people!). There is a more graphic example in Figure 12.1 – but the seesaw will only be a negative experience for some readers.

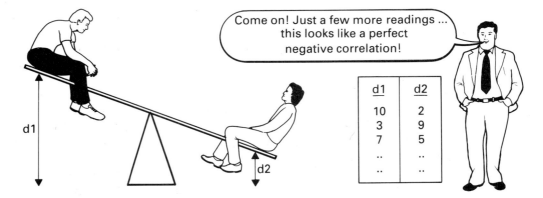

Figure 12.1 *A perfect negative correlation between d1and d2 . . . but is it a negative experience?*

Decide which of the proposed correlations (1–7) above are positive and which are negative.

Think of other examples of positive and negative correlation, in particular, two of each from the research you have studied so far.

SETTING UP A CORRELATIONAL STUDY

It is fairly easy to see how we could check out the validity of statement **6** above. We could have a look at school class-test grades or exam results for people who have taken both subjects. To test statement **3** we have a straightforward measure of variable one (height) but how do we go about measuring the second variable, 'career success'? Do we measure only salary or should we include a factor of 'job satisfaction' – and with what sort of weighting? We would need to *operationalise* our variables.

Describe *specifically* the two variables to be compared in each of statements **1** to **7** above, and how exactly you would *operationalise* them for precise measurement.

MEASUREMENT OF A CORRELATION

Statements like 'there is a correlation between severe punishment and later delinquency in young boys' or 'severe punishment and delinquency in young boys tend to correlate' are often made in theoretical literature. Actually the golden word 'significant' is missing from the first statement and 'significantly' from the second. Also, both fail to report the *strength* of the relationship. We can actually calculate the strength of correlation between any two measurable variables under the sun so long as there is some way of pairing values. Values may be paired because they belong to the same individual (for instance, maths and literature mark in class), or to larger or more abstract units (for instance, resources of school and exam passes, average temperature for the week and number of suicides in that week). When a correlation is announced in the loose manner above, however, it is assumed that the relationship is not coincidental or likely by chance alone.

The *calculation* of correlation between two variables is a *descriptive* measure. We measure the 'togetherness' of the two variables. Testing the correlation for significance is inferential.

The **STRENGTH** of relationship between two variables is the degree to which one variable *does* tend to be high if the other variable is high (or low, for negative correlation). This strength of relationship is expressed on a scale ranging from -1 (perfect negative) through zero (no relationship) to $+1$ (perfect positive). The figure arrived at to express the relationship is known as a **CORRELATION COEFFICIENT** or **COEFFICIENT OF CORRELATION**. This figure can be calculated for the relationship between any two variables and, as explained above, when it is stated that there *is* a correlation, what is meant is that the coefficient calculated is strong enough not to be considered likely by chance alone. Oddly enough, a fairly weak coefficient, as low as 0.3, can be counted as significant if the number of pairs of values is quite high, a point to be explained below.

It is not possible to obtain a coefficient less than -1 or greater than $+1$. If you do obtain such a value there is a mistake somewhere in your calculations (but this can't indicate an error in your raw data). The interpretation of the correlation coefficient scale is, in general, as shown in Figure 12.2.

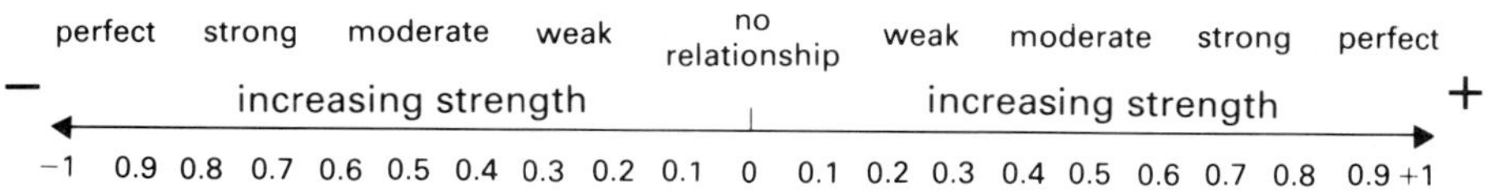

perfect	strong	moderate	weak	no relationship	weak	moderate	strong	perfect

$-$ ◄──────── increasing strength ────────   │   ──────── increasing strength ────────► $+$

-1 0.9 0.8 0.7 0.6 0.5 0.4 0.3 0.2 0.1   0   0.1 0.2 0.3 0.4 0.5 0.6 0.7 0.8 0.9 $+1$

Figure 12.2 *Scale of correlation*

Something might jar here. How can something getting more negative be described as getting stronger? Well it can. The sign simply tells us the *direction* of the relationship.

Warning for tests and exams!

It is very easy to call a *negative* correlation 'no correlation', probably because the two terms 'negative' and 'no' sometimes are equivalent. Here, beware! To assess strength of correlation *ignore the sign*. Negative correlation means the two variables are *inversely* related. *Zero* correlation means there is no relationship at all.

SCATTERGRAMS

One way to investigate the relationship between two variables is to plot pairs of values (one on variable A, the other on variable B) on a **SCATTERGRAM**, so named because it shows the scattering of pairs. The extent to which pairs of readings are not scattered randomly on the diagram, but do form a consistent pattern, is a sign of the strength of the relationship. I hope the scattergrams in Figures 12.3–12.9 will demonstrate this. The first three represent data from one person taken after each trial on a simulated driving task:

In the first example (Figure 12.3) you'll see that the cross for the pair of values 4 trials/105 points is placed on a vertical line up from 4 on the 'trials' axis and on a horizontal line from 105 on the 'points' axis. All points are plotted in this way. For trials/points we get a picture of a strong positive correlation, for trials/time taken

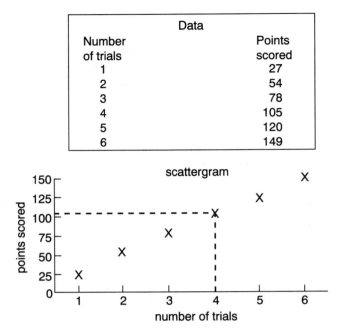

Data	
Number of trials	Points scored
1	27
2	54
3	78
4	105
5	120
6	149

Figure 12.3 *Driving task-points*

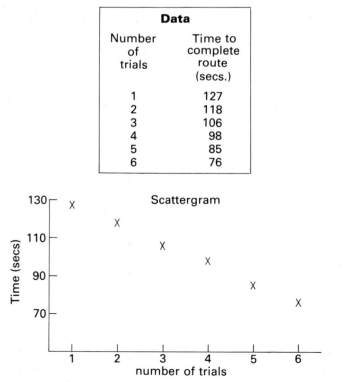

Data	
Number of trials	Time to complete route (secs.)
1	127
2	118
3	106
4	98
5	85
6	76

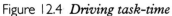

Figure 12.4 *Driving task-time*

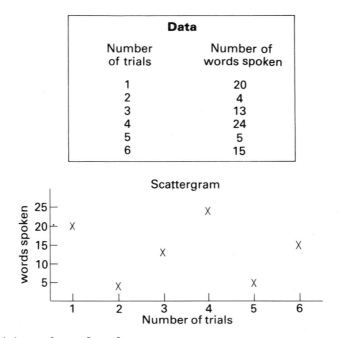

Data	
Number of trials	Number of words spoken
1	20
2	4
3	13
4	24
5	5
6	15

Figure 12.5 *Driving task-words spoken*

(Figure 12.4) a strong negative, and for trials/number of words spoken throughout the trial (Figure 12.5) we get no relationship at all. Perfect correlations would take the shapes shown in Figures 12.6 and 12.7.

If there were no relationship at all between two variables, we could end up with the scattergram shown in Figure 12.8.

In Figure 12.8 we have no relationship because variable Y does not change in any way that is related to changes in variable X. Another way of putting this is to say that changes in Y are not at all predictable from changes in X.

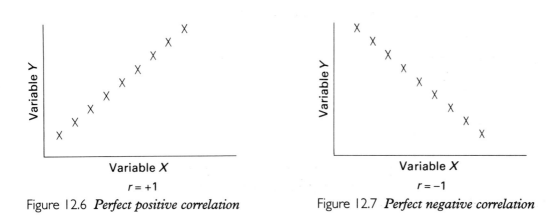

Figure 12.6 *Perfect positive correlation*

Figure 12.7 *Perfect negative correlation*

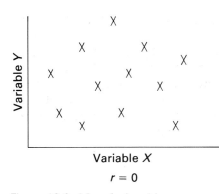

Figure 12.8 *No relationship*

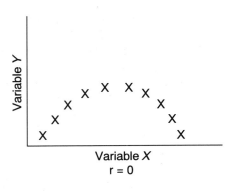

Figure 12.9 *Curvilinear relationship*

DOES $r = 0$ ALWAYS MEAN NO RELATIONSHIP?

Why bother to plot the values if the size of r tells us the strength of the relationship? There are several patterned relationships which might show up on a scattergram when our calculation of r gives us near zero. Look, for instance, at Figure 12.9. This is called a CURVILINEAR relationship for obvious reasons. What might show this relationship? What about temperatures and months of the year? Is there a good psychological example? People perform worse on memory tasks both when there has been extreme sensory deprivation and with sensory overload. One's interest in a task might increase then wane with increasing practice.

Draw the scattergrams for the data in Tables 12.1 (columns A and C) and 12.2 (columns C and D).

CALCULATING CORRELATION COEFFICIENTS

The two most frequently used coefficients are:

Name	Symbol	Level of data used with
Pearson	r	Interval/Ratio (PARAMETRIC test)
Spearman	$\rho\star$	Ordinal (NON-PARAMETRIC test)

$\star$pronounced 'ro', this is the Greek letter rho and is also often written as r_s.

PEARSON'S PRODUCT–MOMENT CORRELATION
COEFFICIENT

CONDITIONS FOR USE

- Differences or correlation   Correlation
- Level of data   Interval/ratio
- Type of design   Related (correlations are by definition)
- Special note   Data must be in the form of related pairs of scores

The grand title of this coefficient might make you feel that this could just be a little complicated . . . and you'd be right!

Suppose we were testing the validity of a new reading test by comparing it with an older version. We expect children to score roughly the same on both tests. Our sample data is in Table 12.1. Formula (a), below, may look ominous but at least it can be used straight away with just the table data and a calculator. If you've already calculated standard deviations however, formula (b) is easier. Note that s_x and s_y are the population estimate formula versions, i.e. formula (2) on page 123.

a)
$$r = \frac{N\Sigma(XY) - \Sigma X \Sigma Y}{\sqrt{[N\Sigma X^2 - (\Sigma X)^2][N\Sigma Y^2 - (\Sigma Y)^2]}}$$

b)
$$r = \frac{\Sigma(X - \bar{X})(Y - \bar{Y})}{(N-1)s_X s_Y}$$

Procedure using version **a**	*Calculation on our data*
1 Find ΣX and $(\Sigma X)^2$	See column A, Table 12.1
2 Add all X^2 to get ΣX^2	See column B, Table 12.1
3 Multiply ΣX^2 (step **2** result) by N	$23256 \times 7 = 162792$
4 Subtract $(\Sigma X)^2$ from step **3** result	$162792 - 156816 = 5976$
5 to **8** Repeat steps **1** to **4** on the Y data	See columns C and D, Table 12.1 $25771 \times 7 = 180397$ $180397 - 172225 = 8172$
9 Multiply step **4** result by step **8** result	$5976 \times 8172 = 48835872$
10 Take square root of step **9** result	$\sqrt{48835872} = 6988.27$
11 Multiply ΣX by ΣY	$396 \times 415 = 164340$
12 Find ΣXY (multiply *each* X by its Y and add the results)	See column E, Table 12.1
13 Multiply step **12** result by N	$24405 \times 7 = 170835$
14 Subtract step **11** result from step **13** result	$170835 - 164340 = 6495$
15 Divide step **14** result by step **10** result	$6495 \div 6988.27 = 0.929 = 0.93$
16 For the significance check, use Table 9, Appendix 2 with $df = N - 2$.	0.93 is greater than the CV of 0.875 with $df = 5$, $p < 0.005$, one-tailed

Note If we predict the *direction* of correlation (positive or negative) the test is one-tailed; otherwise (if we only look for a correlation) the test is two-tailed.

As an exercise, try checking that Formula b produces the same result.

Table 12.1 *Reading test values and calculation of correlation*

Column:	A	B	C	D	E
	Score on old test		Score on new test		
Child number	X	(Score X)^2	Y	(Score Y)^2	(X × Y)
1	67	4489	65	4225	4355
2	72	5184	84	7056	6048
3	45	2025	51	2601	2295
4	58	3364	56	3136	3248
5	63	3969	67	4489	4221
6	39	1521	42	1764	1638
7	52	2704	50	2500	2600

$\Sigma X = 396$ $\Sigma X^2 = 23256$ $\Sigma Y = 415$ $\Sigma Y^2 = 25771$ $\Sigma XY = 24405$

$\bar{X} = 56.6$ $\qquad\qquad \bar{Y} = 59.3$

$S_x = 11.9$ $\qquad\qquad S_y = 13.9$

$(\Sigma X)^2 = 156816$ $\qquad (\Sigma Y)^2 = 172225$

SUMMARY

Pearson's correlation coefficient (r) shows the degree of correlation, on a scale of $+1$ to -1, between two interval level variables where each value on one variable has a partner in the other set. The higher the value of r, the more positive the correlation. The lower the value (below zero) the more negative the correlation.

SPEARMAN'S RHO

CONDITIONS FOR USE

- Differences or correlation   Correlation
- Level of data   Ordinal
- Type of design   Related (correlations are by definition)
- Special note   Data must be in the form of related pairs of scores

DATA

The following fictitious data give students' maths and music class test grades (Table 12.2). Columns C and D give the results in rank order form.

Formula: $r_s = 1 - \dfrac{6\Sigma d^2}{N(N^2 - 1)}$

Table 12.2 *Class test results*

	A	B	C	D	E	F
	Maths	**Music**	**Maths**	**Music**	**Difference between ranks**	
Student	**mark**	**mark**	**rank**	**rank**	**(d)**	**d²**
John	53	34	5	2	3	9
Julia	91	43	7	3	4	16
Jerry	49	73	4	5	−1	1
Jean	45	75	3	6	−3	9
Jill	38	93	2	7	−5	25
Jonah	17	18	1	1	0	0
Jasmine	58	71	6	4	2	4
						$\Sigma d^2 = 64$

Before starting on the Spearman procedure take a look at the squared rank differences in column F above. If we are expecting people to score about the same on both tests, what size would we expect these values to be, large or small? What size would we expect Σd^2 to be then, if there is to be a strong positive correlation?

I hope you agree that, if there is to be a strong positive correlation between pairs of values, each of the differences (*d*) should be small or zero. This will indicate that students are scoring at about the same *position* on both tests. Σd^2 should therefore be small. Let's see how Spearman's approach incorporates this expectation.

Procedure

1 Give ranks to values of variable X

2 Give ranks to values of variable Y

3 Subtract each rank on Y from each paired rank on X

4 Square results of step **3**

5 Add the results of step **4**

6 Insert the result of step **5** into the formula:

$$r_s = 1 - \frac{6 \times \Sigma d^2}{N(N^2 - 1)}$$

where N is the number of pairs

Calculation on our data

See column C, Table 12.2

See column D, Table 12.2

See column E, Table 12.2

See column F, Table 12.2

Total of column F = 64 (= Σd^2)

$$r_s = 1 - \frac{6 \times 64}{7(7^2 - 1)} = 1 - \frac{384}{336} = -0.143$$

Note Do watch the figure 1 here. Students often report wonderfully 'successful' results, about which they are understandably pleased, only to find that their result of, say, 0.81 has yet to be subtracted from 1.

7 Calculate r_s and consult Appendix 2, Table 8

$r_s = -0.143$

8 r_s has to be equal to or greater than the table value for significance at the level consulted

Critical value for $p \leq 0.05$, where $N = 7$ and test is one-tailed is 0.714

9 Make significance statement

Coefficient is not significant

Note   In fact, with a *one-tailed* prediction that the correlation is *positive*, there is no point even consulting tables because the negative sign here tells us that, whatever the size, the relationship found is *inverse* (i.e. negative) and opposite to what we expected.

When there are tied ranks

The Spearman formula above is technically for use *only* when there are no tied ranks. If ties occur the statistic becomes a weaker estimate of what it is supposed to measure. In fact, the formula is just a special case of what is done generally to correlate ranked values. The general approach is to carry out a Pearson calculation on the pairs of ranks. This is what you should do, then, if any values are tied. In Table 12.2 we would calculate a Pearson correlation on columns C and D. The resulting coefficient is still referred to as Spearman's r. In fact, if you have only a few ties the error involved, using the formula above, will not be worth worrying about.

WHEN N IS GREATER THAN 30

The table of critical values for r_s stops at $N = 30$. If N is larger than 30, r_s (or Pearson's r) can be converted to a t value using:

$$t = r_s \sqrt{\left(\frac{(N-2)}{(1 - r_s^2)} \right)}$$

t is then checked for significance with $N - 2$ degrees of freedom.

SUMMARY

Spearman's Rho (r_s or ρ) shows the degree of correlation between two sets of paired ranks on a scale of $+1$ (perfect positive) to -1 (perfect negative).

EXPLANATORY NOTES

As with the Wilcoxon signed ranks test, we are looking here at differences between pairs of ranks, one recorded on each of two variables. With Spearman's correlation, however, we don't want positive differences to be large to show an effect. Here, we want *all* differences to be as small as possible if we wish to demonstrate a strong, positive correlation. Consequently, the sum of the *squared* differences will be small.

ADVANTAGES AND DISADVANTAGES OF SPEARMAN'S RHO

The advantages are that it is easy to calculate (with no or few ties) and can be used on ordinal, as well as interval data.

The disadvantages are that the test is *non-parametric* and therefore suffers the associated weaknesses of these tests outlined in Chapter 11.

SIGNIFICANCE AND STRENGTH OF CORRELATIONS

It is very important to remember the following two points:

1 Strong correlations are not necessarily significant.

2 Significant correlations are not necessarily strong.

We saw above that 0.85 indicates a strong relationship between two variables. This is *always* true. What is *not* always true is that such a correlation is *significant*. If you look at the Spearman tables for $N = 5$ you'll find that a value of at least 0.9 is required for significance (one-tailed). This is because, with only five pairs of scores, a correlation above 0.85 would occur fairly frequently if we were just drawing pairs at random. It would occur more often than five times in 100. However, if we randomly organised 30 pairs of scores, then any value for r_s over just 0.31 would occur less times than five in 100 and is significant if it occurs in a study where N is 30 or more. This does *not* mean that the correlation is *strong*, however. With 90 pairs of scores and a Pearson's r of just 0.19, we would have what is often reported as a 'weak but significant trend'. *If N is low, we need a relatively high correlation value for significance.*

CORRELATION DOESN'T INDICATE CAUSE AND EFFECT

See if you can detect flaws in the following statements:

Research has established a strong correlation between the use of physical punishment by parents and the development of aggression in their children. Parents should not use this form of discipline then, if they don't want their children to end up aggressive.

There is a significant correlation between early weaning and later irritability in the infant, so don't hurry weaning if you want a good-tempered child.

Poverty is correlated with crime, so, if you can achieve a higher income, your children are less likely to become law-breakers.

In each case above it is assumed that one variable is the cause of another.

With any significant correlation there are several possible interpretations:

1 Variable A has a causal effect on variable B.

2 Variable B has a causal effect on variable A.

3 A and B are both related to some other linking factor(s).

4 We have type one error (i.e. a fluke coincidence).

A good example of situation **3** would be the perfect correlation of two adjacent thermometers, one in °C and the other in °F. The common factor is of course heat, and one thermometer cannot affect the other. Similarly, physical punishment may be a method of control used to a greater extent by parents who are also those more likely to encourage or fail to control aggression *or* who tend to live in environments where aggression is more likely to flourish. There again, interpretation **2** is interesting. Perhaps aggression has a substantial hereditary base and children born with more aggressive dispositions *invoke* more physical methods of control from their parents – not an explanation I support, but simply a possibility which can't be dismissed.

When you are asked: 'A researcher concludes from a correlation result that . . . (A is the cause of B) . . . Could there be an alternative interpretation? – try B causes A as the alternative. Then try looking for common causes of both A and B. Visually, with the arrows representing causal direction:

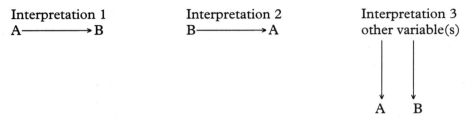

| Interpretation 1 | Interpretation 2 | Interpretation 3 |
| A——————→B | B——————→A | other variable(s) |

COMMON USES OF CORRELATION IN PSYCHOLOGY

1 *In lieu of experiments:* Correlations are used, especially in the field, where experiments would be impossible or unethical. They are used when we go out and measure 'what's already there'. We might compare: (1) amount smoked with (2) anxiety level, or (1) attitude on race with (2) attitude on poverty, or (1) perceived demands with (2) stress felt in one's job. These are sometimes known as '*ex post facto*' studies (investigating 'after the fact').

2 *Test-retest reliability:* (see page 51) This relies on correlation between scores on a test taken at one point, then at a later point, by the *same* group of people.

3 *Factor analysis:* This is used to develop psychological factors from batteries of tests (see Gross, 1992) and relies very heavily on correlational techniques.

4 *Twin studies:* Correlations are used to support the theory of inherited differences in intelligence or psychiatric disturbance by comparing measures of separated identical twins. Other kinship levels are also compared, such as siblings, uncle–nephew, and so on.

GLOSSARY

Relationship between two variables		**correlation**
Numerical value of relationship between two variables	_____	coefficient
Relationship between two variables which gives a low value for *r* because the relationship does not fit a straight line but a good curve	_____	curvilinear

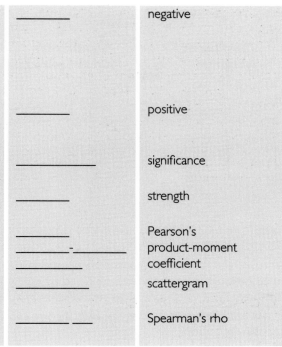

Relationship where, as values of one variable increase, related values of the other tend to decrease	_____	negative
Relationship where, as values of one variable increase, related values of the other variable also tend to increase	_____	positive
Measure of whether a correlation was likely to have occurred by chance or not	_____	significance
Measure of the degree of matching measured by a correlation	_____	strength
Parametric measure of correlation	_____ _____-_____ _____	Pearson's product-moment coefficient
Diagram showing placement of paired values on a two-dimensional grid	_____	scattergram
Non-parametric, ordinal level measure of correlation; correlation of ranks	_____ ____	Spearman's rho

EXERCISES

1 (From an article in the *Times Educational Supplement*, 3 June 1988)

> ... teaching the sound and shape of letters can give preschool children a head start ... children who performed best at the age of seven tended to be those who had the most knowledge and understanding of the three Rs at the age of four.
>
> In the case of reading, the strongest predictor of ability among seven-year-olds was 'the number of letters the child could identify at the age of four-and-three-quarters' ... Tizard concludes that nursery teachers should give more emphasis to literacy and numeracy skills ...

a) What conclusion, other than the researcher's, could be drawn here?

b) Briefly describe a study which could help us decide between these alternative interpretations.

c) What sort of correlation must the researchers have found between number of letters identified at four and number of reading *errors* at seven – *positive* or *negative*?

d) Suppose the correlation between adding ability at five and mathematical ability at seven was +0.83 (Pearson). How would you describe the strength of this coefficient verbally?

e) What level of significance would the correlation of 0.83 be at (one-tailed) if the sample of children had numbered 33?

2 Several students in your group have carried out correlations, got their results, know what significance level they need to reach, but have sadly forgotten how to check in tables for significance. They agree to do calculations on your data if you'll just check their results and tell them whether to reject or accept their null hypotheses. The blank column in Table 12.3 overleaf is for you to fill in.

Table 12.3 *Question*

	Coefficient obtained	N =	Significance level required	Direction Predicted	Accept or reject H_0?
a)	$r = 0.3$	14	$p < 0.01$	+	
b)	$r = -0.19$	112	$p < 0.01$	−	
c)	$r_s = 0.78$	7	$p < 0.05$	+	
d)	$r = 0.71$	6	$p < 0.05$	+	
e)	$r_s = 0.9$	5	$p < 0.05$	+	
f)	$r = 0.63$	12	$p < 0.01$	no prediction made	
g)	$r = 0.54$	30	$p < 0.05$	−	

3 Spearman's correlation can always be calculated instead of Pearson's. Is the reverse of this true? Please give a reason.

4 A researcher correlates scores on a questionnaire concerning 'ego-strength' with measures of their anxiety level obtained by rating their verbal responses to several pictures. Which measure of correlation should be employed?

5 If a student tells you she has obtained a correlation coefficient of 2.79, what might you advise her to do?

WHICH TEST DO WE NEED?
CHOOSING AN APPROPRIATE TEST

Trying to choose an appropriate test can leave you with a floundering feeling because there are so many tests and there can be a lot of data and several hypotheses. The first golden rule is *not to panic*! Stay calm. Next . . .

- Take one hypothesis at a time
- Choose the test for this hypothesis
- Calculate the test
- Decide whether the result is significant

MAKING A CHOICE

So how do we choose the appropriate test? This really should be quite simple if you follow the three steps in Box 13.1 and use Table 13.1.

Box 13.1 *Steps in choosing the appropriate test*

Decision 1 Does the hypothesis predict difference or correlation?

Decision 2 At what level of measurement are the data?
  Note: If the level is interval and you wish to conduct a parametric test, check that your data satisfy the parametric test assumptions before proceeding. If the assumptions cannot reasonably be met, you will have to convert your data to ranked data.

  Parametric assumptions: if data are interval, check that:

  - Samples are drawn from a normally distributed population
  - Variances are homogenous (i.e. not significantly different) if using independent samples design with unequal participant numbers

  See chapter 11 for a fuller explanation

Decision 3 Is the design related or unrelated?

Table 13.1 *Choosing the appropriate test*

TESTS OF DIFFERENCE		
	Design is:	
LEVEL OF MEASUREMENT	UNRELATED	RELATED
CATEGORICAL		
NOMINAL	Chi-square[1]	(Binomial) Sign test
MEASURED		
ORDINAL	Mann-Whitney	Wilcoxon signed ranks
INTERVAL/ RATIO[2]	Unrelated *t*	Related *t*
TESTS OF CORRELATION		
ORDINAL		Spearman's *rho*
INTERVAL/ RATIO		Pearson

1 Chi-square is commonly known as a *test of association* and is something like a correlation for nominal data. However, it is included here as a *difference* test because, at this level, we usually use it to find whether one group *differs* from another across a given variable.

2 The shaded portions indicate parametric tests at interval level and are not currently included in A level syllabus question papers.

EXAMPLES OF CHOOSING A TEST

Take a look at Table 13.2. The data were produced by asking male and female 17-year-olds to estimate their own IQ, measuring their actual IQ, measuring their height and measuring their mothers' IQs.

Using Table 13.2, try to select the appropriate test for each of the following hypotheses:
  1 Male IQ estimates are higher than female estimates
  2 Female measured IQs are higher than male measured IQs
  3 The taller people are, the higher their IQ
  4 Female measured IQs are higher than their mothers' measured IQs

Table 13.2 *Male and female IQ data*

Males				Females			
Estimated IQ	Measured IQ	Height (cm)	Mother's IQ	Estimated IQ	Measured IQ	Height (cm)	Mother's IQ
120	107	160	100	100	97	155	105
110	112	181	105	95	92	165	97
95	130	175	102	90	104	177	115
140	95	164	97	110	112	162	96
100	104	163	120	85	130	173	100
120	92	158	131	100	95	159	120
110	97	172	115	105	107	164	102
105	101	171	96	100	101	165	131

Assume that mother and offspring can be treated as matched pairs.

Assume that estimated IQ cannot be treated as interval data.

Assume that this researcher will treat measured IQ as interval level data. Height is known to be normally distributed.

Hypothesis 1	Decision 1:	we are looking for a *difference*
	Decision 2:	we shall have to convert the estimated IQs to ranked, *ordinal* data
	Decision 3:	the design is *unrelated*; we have separate groups of males and females

Our choice is therefore **Mann–Whitney**.

Hypothesis 2	Decision 1:	we are again looking for a *difference*
	Decision 2:	these data are being treated as *internal* level
	Decision 3:	the design is *unrelated*, as before

Our choice is therefore a ***t*-test for unrelated samples** (independent *t*).

Parametric assumptions must be met:

- The interval level data assumption has been made.
- IQ tests are standardised to ensure that scores for the general population are normally distributed on them. Hence, the samples come from a normally distributed population.
- Using an 'eyeball' test, variances are not too different. This is not a problem anyway, because although we have an unrelated design, the numbers in each group are equal.

Hypothesis 3	Decision 1:	a positive *correlation* is predicted between height and IQ. We can treat male and female as one group
	Decision 2:	IQ is being treated as *interval*. Height is ratio level and therefore, at least *interval* level
	Decision 3:	correlations are automatically related designs

Our choice is therefore **Pearson's correlation coefficient**.

Parametric assumptions must be met:

- Arguments are the same as for **hypothesis 2** except that the design is related; height is known to be normally distributed.

Hypothesis 4   Decision 1:   a *difference* is predicted
     Decision 2:   measured IQ is being treated as *interval* level data
     Decision 3:   matched pairs are a *related* design

Our choice is therefore a **t-test for related samples** (or correlated *t*).

Parametric assumptions must be met:

- Arguments are covered above.

For each of the cases where a parametric test is chosen you could of course have chosen a non-parametric test, if you just wanted to use a simpler but possibly less powerful test.

   Here are some general hints to keep in mind when choosing tests:

- Correlations must always be related designs.
- χ^2 tests the *difference* between *observed* frequencies and *expected* frequencies. This is why it is placed where it is on Table 13.1. However, the net result is to tell us whether there is a significant *association* between one variable (say, being a smoker [or not] and having poor health [or not]). It is called a 'test of association'.
- If data appear as frequencies, in categories, a χ^2 test is indicated. Even though the numbers in the categories are real numbers, if it means that *all* you know is that, say 22 people are in one category, and you know no more about them and can't separate them in any way (by rank or score) the data are in frequency form and the categories concerned can be treated as a nominal scale.
- If a test or other psychological measure has been *standardised*, it can be treated as producing interval level data.
- If the results in question are in the form of scores or numbers produced by humans estimating or 'rating' events or behaviour, on some arbitrary scale, it is almost always safest to convert the numbers to ordinal level (by ranking them). The same goes for scores on an unstandardised questionnaire or opinion survey.
- Ordinal data appear as a set of ranks ('ord' for order).

EXERCISES

What tests should be carried out on the following data? Where there is a choice, select the more powerful test.

I Height (in cm) of girls bred on:

All Bran	Bread and dripping
172	162
181	172
190	154
165	143
167	167

The researcher was interested in whether one of the diets tended to produce taller girls.

2 Table 13.2 *Snooker players – position in league table*

Smoking and drinking players		Abstemious players	
Terry Davis	2	Steve Griffiths	8
Alex Hendry	6	Steve Higgins	1
Fred Longpole	10	Chris Cushion	5
Alf Garnett	9	Betty Baulk	3
Bob Black	4	Susan Swerveshot	7

In this case, we want to know whether abstemious players get significantly higher placings.

3 Table 13.3 *Language and position of Tour de France riders*

	English speaking	Non-English speaking	
In top half of Tour de France	19	67	86
In bottom half of Tour de France	10	76	86
	29	143	172

From these (fictitious) results what test would tell us whether English speaking riders are doing significantly better than the others in this year's Tour de France?

4 Students observe whether males or females do or don't walk under a ladder. They want to see whether one sex is more 'superstitious' than the other. What test do they need to use?

5 20 people perform a sensori-motor task in two conditions, one in a quiet room, alone, the other in a brightly lit room with a dozen people watching. An electronic timer takes an accurate record of the number of errors made in each condition.

   a) What test would be appropriate for investigating the significance of the differences in performance between the two conditions?

   b) Assume everybody deteriorates in the second condition. What test would be appropriate for seeing whether individuals tend to deteriorate by about the same amount?

6 A psychologist claims to have a very well standardised measurement scale. What statistical test would be used to check its test–retest reliability? What test would be used to check its validity on a criterion group who should score higher than a control group?

7 A set of photos of couples are rated for attractiveness by a panel of judges who rate the males separately from the females. The hypothesis tested is that people in couples tend to be of a similar level of attractiveness. What test would be used to compare the similarity of the two sets of ratings for male and female partners?

8 Two groups of people are selected. One has a very high 'initiative-taking' score, the other group's score is quite low. They are asked to select just one of three possible activities which they would prefer to do. The choices are: rock-climbing, dancing or reading a book. What test would demonstrate significant differences between their choices?

9 The time is recorded for the same group of participants to read out loud a list of rhyming words and a list of non-rhyming words. What test is appropriate for showing whether the rhyming words take significantly less time to read?

10 A group of management personnel undergo an intensive course on race issues. Essays written before and after the course are content analysed and rated for attitudes to race. What test would be appropriate for demonstrating a significant change of attitude as expressed in the essays?

11 A group of people attempting to give up smoking have been assessed for their progress on two occasions separated by six months. Raw scores have been discarded and we only know for each client whether they have improved, worsened or stayed about the same. What test would show any significant change over the period?

12 What test would show us how strongly students' levels of computer anxiety (assessed by a psychometric scale) are related to their marks in a computer competence test?

Ethics and practice

14

ETHICAL ISSUES AND HUMANISM IN PSYCHOLOGICAL RESEARCH

INTRODUCTION

The British Psychological Society (BPS) and the American Psychological Association (APA) have both agreed guidelines on the ethical issues involved in psychological research. The BPS currently has a booklet of statements (1993), covering a wide range of issues, and also a code of conduct (1985) adopted through a postal ballot of all its members. The 1992 revision of the 1978 principles is entitled *Ethical Principles for Conducting Research with Human Participants* and introduces 'with' as well as changing 'subjects' to 'participants' – not trivial amendments. The APA (1987) has a more comprehensive set of ethical principles comprising ten major categories, each with several sub-principles. The general public can bring complaints to the ethics committee who then adjudicate. The psychologist concerned can be reprimanded, dismissed or required to alter behaviour or attend relevant training. This breadth of principles and disciplinary power reflects the far wider application of psychology to the general public as consumers in the USA. Most of the major principles are similar to those which are relevant in the doctor–patient relationship.

The 1992 BPS *Principles* cover the following areas: consent, deception, debriefing, withdrawal from an investigation, confidentiality, protection of participants, observational research, giving advice (to participants) and monitoring of colleagues in the profession. Section 2 of the *Principles*, entitled 'General', runs as follows:

> In all circumstances, investigators must consider the ethical implications and psychological consequences for the participants in their research. The essential principle is that the investigation should be considered from the standpoint of all participants: foreseeable threats to their psychological well-being, health, values or dignity should be eliminated. Investigators should recognise that, in our multi-cultural and multi-ethnic society and where investigations involve individuals of different ages, gender and social background, the investigators may not have sufficient knowledge of the implications of any investigation for the participants. It should be borne in mind that the best judge of whether an investigation will cause offence may be members of the population from which the participants in the research are to be drawn.

Both the British and United States principles stress that psychological research should lead to better understanding of ourselves and to the enhancement of the human condition and promotion of human welfare. Both stress the need for an atmosphere of free enquiry in order to generate the widest, most valid body of knowledge. But both also stress that this free atmosphere requires a commitment to responsibility on the part of the psychologist in terms of competence, objectivity and the welfare of research participants.

Since 1987, the Royal Charter of the BPS has been amended, taking us some way towards the American model described above. The Society now maintains a 'register' of 'chartered psychologists'. These are people who practise psychology either in an applied or a research capacity. Members of the register use the formal letters 'C.Psychol', can be struck off for unprofessional behaviour and, it is hoped, will become recognised as bona fide 'trademarked' practitioners whom the general public can recognise and trust.

In the 1990s most research institutions now have an ethics committee to vet research proposals (of staff and students) for unacceptable procedures in any of the areas which we are about to consider.

PUBLICATION AND ACCESS TO DATA

Before taking a look at the rights and protection of individual participants, we can consider how psychologists are expected to commit themselves to freedom of information.

In general, a psychologist cannot claim to have demonstrated an effect and then withhold raw data or information on procedures and samples used. Persons who do this are generally considered to be charlatans. Where psychologists are prepared, as most are, to be completely open with their data, they would still not allow the alleged results of their work to affect people's lives, by policy formulation for instance, before the research community has thoroughly verified, evaluated and replicated results where possible. They should not 'rush to publish'.

There are occasions, in fact, when any scientist may feel that publication of results is potentially harmful or even dangerous. (One is reminded of the scientists who first became fully aware of the horrendous power of the nuclear fission process.) In such cases, the investigator is expected to seek the opinion of 'experienced and disinterested colleagues', an option recommended several times in the BPS statement for various dilemmas.

Findings on racial difference (in intelligence or personality, for instance) almost always stir up controversy, which is hardly surprising. For this reason some psychologists have been led to argue that a moratorium should be held on publication. They argue that, since race is always inextricably bound up with culture and socio-economic position, most responsible researchers would announce results with great qualification. However, they cannot then stop the lay racist or ignorant reader from using the unqualified information in discriminatory or abusive practices.

It has also been argued that professional psychological researchers should exercise integrity over the sources of their funding, increasingly likely to come from industry with an interest in the non-academic use of findings.

CONFIDENTIALITY AND PRIVACY

Apart from any ethical considerations, there is a purely pragmatic argument for guaranteeing anonymity for participants at all times. If psychologists kept publishing identities along with results, the general public would soon cease to volunteer or agree to research participation.

An investigator can guarantee anonymity or request permission to identify individuals. Such identification may occur through the use of video recordings as teaching materials for instance, as in Milgram's film *Obedience to Authority*. Research participants who have been seriously deceived have the right to witness destruction of any such records they do not wish to be kept. If records are kept, participants have the right to assume these will be safeguarded and used only by thoroughly briefed research staff. Usually, though, results are made anonymous as early as possible during analysis by using a letter or number instead of a name.

There are very special circumstances where an investigator might contravene the confidentiality rule and these are where there are clear, direct dangers to human life. An investigator conducting participant observation into gang life would have a clear obligation to break confidence where a serious crime was about to be committed. A psychiatric patient's plan to kill himself or a room-mate would be reported. The ethical principles involved here are broader than those involved in conducting scientific research.

The participant obviously has the right to privacy, and procedures should not be planned which directly invade this without warning. Where a procedure is potentially intimate, embarrassing or sensitive, the participant should be clearly reminded of the right to withhold information or participation. Particular care would be required, for instance, where participants are being asked about sexual attitudes or behaviour.

This principle is difficult to follow in the case of covert participant observation, and serious criticism has been levelled at users of this approach on these grounds.

Investigators would usually send a copy of the final research report to all participants, along with its justification and contribution to scientific knowledge and benefit to society in general. This procedure can be difficult where covert observation in a field situation has occurred, and expensive where a survey has used a very large sample.

MILGRAM – THE CLASSIC EXPERIMENT FOR ETHICAL DEBATE

Any discussion of ethical principles in psychological research inevitably throws up Milgram's famous demonstrations of obedience fairly early on in the debate. Several ethical issues are involved in this study so let me just describe it briefly and then ask you to think about what these issues are. Almost certainly you will have already heard about the experiment and fuller details are given in, for instance, Gross (1992).

> Volunteers were introduced to another 'participant' who was actually an experimental confederate. The volunteer became a 'teacher' who was asked to administer electric shocks, increasing by 15 volts for each mistake made by the confederate. 375 volts was described as 'Danger: severe

shock'. A tape recording of screams and refusals deceived the teacher–participant into believing the confederate was experiencing great pain and wished to end the session. The teacher–participant was pressured into continuing by 'prods' from the experimenter such as 'The experiment requires that you continue' and 'You have no choice but to go on'. To Milgram's surprise, 65% of participants delivered shocks to the end of the scale (450 volts) even though the confederate had ceased responding at 315 volts. Milgram had consulted 'experienced and disinterested colleagues' – psychiatrists predicted that no more than 0.1% would obey to the end. The teacher–participant often displayed extreme anxiety. One even suffered a seizure. An observer wrote:

> I observed a mature and initially poised businessman enter the laboratory smiling and confident. Within 20 minutes he was reduced to a twitching, stuttering wreck, who was rapidly approaching a point of nervous collapse. He constantly pulled at his ear lobe and twisted his hands. At one point he pushed his fist into his forehead and muttered, 'Oh God, let's stop it.' (Milgram, 1974)

The results of this experiment were used to argue that many ordinary people are capable of behaving in a manner, under pressure, which we might consider cruel. Atrocities are not necessarily carried out by purely evil persons.

List the aspects of this experiment which you consider to be unethical. Should the research have been carried out at all? Do the ends (scientific and surprising knowledge) justify the means?

Deception

Milgram's participants were quite grossly deceived. Not only did they believe they were shocking an innocent victim and that the victim suffered terribly, but also the whole purpose of the research was completely distorted as concerning the effects of punishment on learning.

DECEPTION, or at least the withholding of information, is exceedingly common in psychology experiments. Menges (1973) reviewed about 1000 American studies and found that 80% involved giving participants less than complete information. In only 3% of studies were participants given complete information about the IV. 44% of human psychological research today involves deception (Leavitt, 1991).

Some of this deception seems fairly innocuous. Some participants are told a baby is male, others that it is female, and their descriptions of it are compared. Participants performing a sensori-motor task, where the true aim is to record the effect of an observer on performance, are told that the observer is present to note details of the skilled behaviour involved. Children are told not to play with a toy because it belongs to another child who is next door. Students are told their experimental rats are 'bright'. Even the use of placebos is a deception.

Some deception is more serious. Participants have been told that test results demonstrate that they are poorly adjusted. Female participants are given feedback that they are considered attractive or unattractive by the men who will later interview them. Bramel (1962) gave male participants false feedback about their emotional reaction to photographs of men such that their responses seemed homosexually related. Participants in Latané and Darley's (1976) experiments thought they were overhearing an authentic epilectic seizure. The DV was the speed or occurrence of reporting the seizure.

So what can the investigator do if deception is to be used?

First, the 1992 BPS *Principles* recommend that, wherever possible, consultation should be conducted with individuals who share the social and cultural background of the participants.

Second, in some cases it is possible to obtain permission to deceive. Volunteers can be asked to select what sort of research they would be prepared to participate in from, for instance:

1 Research on recognition of commercial products.
2 Research on safety of products.
3 Research in which you will be misled about the purpose until afterward.
4 Research involving questions on attitudes.

Third, debriefing should be very carefully attended to.

DEBRIEFING

In all research studies, the investigator has a responsibility to debrief each participant. The true purpose and aims of the study are revealed and every attempt is made to ensure that participants feel the same about themselves when they leave as they did when they arrived. Where participants have been seriously deceived, this responsibility incurs a substantial effort in reassurance and explanation. The DEBRIEFING itself may have to involve a little more deception, as when children are told they 'did very well indeed' whatever the actual standard of their performance and when any suspicion that a participant really is 'poorly adjusted' is not communicated to them.

Applying this to Milgram's experiments, participants who went to the end of the scale were told that some people did this quite gleefully, in order that they could then compare their own unwillingness to proceed, and felt anxiety, fairly favourably. (Milgram has never reported that any participant *did* proceed at all happily.) However, at least 26 out of 40 participants knew, when they left, that they were capable, under pressure, of inflicting extreme pain, if not death, on an innocent human being. It seems hardly possible that these people left the laboratory feeling the same about themselves as before they entered. In Asch's (1956) classic paradigm, too, participants find they have 'conformed' to silly answers to simple problems because a group of confederates answered first. These participants also exhibited great anxiety during the experimental sessions.

DOES DEBRIEFING WORK?

Milgram sent a questionnaire to his participants after the study and 84% said they were glad to have participated, whereas only 1% regretted being involved, the remainder reporting neutral feelings. 80% believed more research like Milgram's should be carried out. 75% found the experience meaningful and self-enlightening.

Some writers discounted this broad range of appreciative and illuminating comments as an attempt by Milgram to justify an ethically unacceptable study. Ring et al. (1970) decided to evaluate the consequences to the participant in a study which, even though the investigators were critical of Milgram, not only included the deceptions of the original study but also used a dishonest primary debriefing before a second honest one. They showed that an initial, superficial debriefing dramatically reduces any negative participant evaluation of the research. However, they also found that one third of participants reported residual anger and disappointment with themselves even after the second, complete debriefing.

The fact that even a few participants felt quite negative about themselves well after the experiment, and that many participants felt extremely upset during it, has led many researchers to the position that deception and stress this extreme are ethically unacceptable.

Besides the question of ethics, it is unwise of investigators to indulge in a great deal of deception. Students very often suspect that the manifest structure and explanation of a study in which they participate is false. Ring et al. found that 50% of their participants claimed they would be more wary and suspicious of psychology experiments in the future. As Reason and Rowan (1981) put it 'Good research means never having to say you are sorry.'

STRESS AND DISCOMFORT

There is no argument against the principle that psychological investigators should guarantee the safety of their participants and that everything possible should be done to protect them from harm or discomfort. The difficulty comes in trying to decide what kind of stress or discomfort, physical or mental, is unacceptable. Humanists might argue that *any* traditional experimental research on 'subjects' is an affront to human dignity. At a lesser extreme, those who see value in the human experimental procedure have nevertheless criticised some investigators for going too far.

MENTAL STRESS

Examples of studies involving a possibly substantial degree of mental stress were given above. These involved deterioration of a person's self-image or the strain of feeling responsible for action in the Latané and Darley study. A further example, causing some dissent, is that in which a child was asked to guard the experimenter's pet hamster, which was removed from its cage through a hole in the floor when the child wasn't looking.

But not all mental stress emanates from deception. Participants may be exposed to pornographic or violent film sequences. Extreme psychological discomfort, in the form of delusions and hallucinations, was experienced by participants undergoing 'sensory deprivation' (deprived of sound, touch and sight) such that they often terminated the experience after three days. Zimbardo's (1972) simulation of authority and obedience had to be stopped after six days of the 14 it was supposed to run. Students played the part of aggressive, sadistic and brutal prison guards far too well. Their 'prisoners' (other students) became extremely passive and dependent. Within two days, and on the next few, participants had to be released, since they were exhibiting signs of severe emotional and psychological disorder (uncontrollable crying and screaming) and one even developed a nervous rash.

There is an obligation for investigators, not only to debrief, but also to attempt to remove even long-term negative effects of psychological research procedures. 40 of Milgram's participants were examined, one year after the experiment, by a psychiatrist who reported that no participant had been harmed psychologically by their experience. The 1992 BPS *Principles* urge investigators to ask participants to contact them should stress or other harm occur after participation.

PHYSICAL DISCOMFORT

Many psychological experiments have manipulated the variables of, for instance, electric shock, extreme noise level, food and sleep deprivation, anxiety or nausea producing drugs and so on.

Watson and Rayner (1920), as is well known, caused 'Little Albert', a young infant, to exhibit anxiety towards a white rat he had previously fondled quite happily, by producing a loud disturbing noise whenever he did so. Apparently Albert even became wary of other furry white objects. His mother moved away and so Albert was removed from the project before he could be deconditioned. The fear-inducing procedure developed into that of 'aversive conditioning' which is intended to rid willing clients of unwanted or destructive behaviour.

The term 'willing' creates difficulties. In the sensitive case of gay men submitting themselves to aversive therapy, it has been argued that treatment is unethical, since the men are succumbing to a conventional norm structure which treats their preference as undesirable or 'sick'. In general research work, a 'willing' participant may act under social pressure. They may wish to sustain a 'real man' image, to bear as much as, or 'beat', their peers. They may feel they are ruining the experiment or letting down the experimenter (the special power of the investigator is discussed below).

For these reasons, the investigator has a set of obligations to participants to ensure they do not suffer unduly or unnecessarily. These are outlined in the following section. In any research where discomfort might be expected the investigator is expected to seek opinion and advice from colleagues before going ahead.

THE RIGHT TO NON-PARTICIPATION

The investigator is obliged to:

1 Give the participant full information as to the likely level of discomfort and to emphasise the voluntary nature of the exercise and right to withdraw at any time.
2 Remind the participant of this right to withdraw at any point in the procedure where discomfort appears to be higher than anticipated.
3 Terminate the procedure where discomfort levels are substantially higher than anticipated and/or the participant is obviously disturbed to an unacceptable level.

Now we can see one of the most objectionable aspects of Milgram's study. His experimenter flagrantly contravened all three of these principles. The duty to respect the participant's right to withdraw and to remind the participant of this right are both stressed by the APA. Yet, contrary to this, each participant wishing to stop was commanded to continue in the interests of the research programme. Continuance was 'absolutely essential' and the participant had 'no choice but to go on'. The APA even stresses special vigilance when the investigator is in a position of power over the participant. This was, of course, the very position forcefully exploited and examined in the Milgram study.

It is usual to obtain the informed consent of research participants. As we shall see below, this isn't always possible before the research is conducted, though for laboratory experiments consent can always be obtained. In research with children, the informed consent of parents must first be obtained. For obvious reasons, children cannot be subject to great stress, even in the unlikely instance that parents agree (though there was little Albert).

Two factors working against informed consent are the investigator's need to deceive on some occasions, and the significant power attaching to the investigator *role*.

THE SPECIAL POWER OF THE INVESTIGATOR

In general, then, the investigator is obliged to give the participant every chance not to participate, both before and during the experimental procedure. Working against this, as we have just said, is the position of influence, prestige and power of the investigator. Torbert (1981) says:

> . . . the unilaterally controlled research context is itself only one particular kind of social context and a politically authoritarian context at that. It should not be surprising that some of its most spectacularly well-conceived findings concern persons' responses to authoritarianism.

An additional dimension to this power emerges when we consider the common position of United States' psychology undergraduates (and lately some in the United Kingdom) who often face an obligatory participation in a research project of their choice. In some cases an exemption is offered but it costs one additional term paper, making the choice more apparent than real.

A further issue for ethical concern has been the practice of obtaining prison inmates or psychiatric patients for stressful experimental studies, where inducements, such as a pack of cigarettes or temporary release from daily routines, are minimal and would not normally 'buy' participation outside the particular institution.

The 1992 BPS *Principles* lay particular emphasis on the way in which consent is obtained from detained persons and also on the special circumstances of children and adults with impairments in understanding or communication.

INVOLUNTARY PARTICIPATION

In participant observation studies, and in naturalistic (covert) observation, the persons observed are quite often unaware of their participation. This seems fairly unobjectionable where completely unobtrusive observation is made and each observee is just one in a frequency count; for instance, when drivers are observed in order to determine whether more males or more females stop at a 'stop' road sign.

In participant observation people's private lives may be invaded. Humphreys (1970) investigated the behaviour of consenting homosexuals by acting as a public washroom 'lookout'. Persons observed were completely unaware of the study and of the fact that their car registration numbers were recorded in order to obtain more background information later on.

Some field studies carried out in the public arena involve manipulations which interfere with people's lives. A street survey obviously delays each respondent but here consent is always sought first. In Piliavin et al.'s (1969) studies on bystander intervention, a person looking either lame or drunk 'collapsed' in a subway train. In one version the actor bit a capsule which produced a blood-like trickle on his chin. Predictably, the 'lame' person got more help than the drunk, with the 'blood' condition having a lowering effect on helping. Piliavin's study, in fact, contravenes the principles of openness (no deception), stress avoidance and informed consent before participation.

Doob and Gross (1968) delayed drivers at a traffic light in either a very smart, new car or an older, lower status one. Effects were predictable in that it took drivers longer to honk at the smarter car.

If these results are fairly unsurprising, couldn't willing participants simply be asked to imagine the situation and consider their likely response? Would simulation work here? Doob and Gross used a questionnaire as well, and found no difference between the reports of how long independent samples of students thought it would take them to honk at each car. Oddly, of the 11 students who said they would not honk, all six of those who would not honk at the low status car were male, and all five of those not honking at the high status car were female.

The 'as if' findings were so different from actual behaviour that the defenders of field research seemed vindicated in their claim to more realistic data. However, by 1991, a computer simulation had been devised, and this produced results confirming the original findings.

INTERVENTION

Some aspects of brief INTERVENTION with naïve participants have been dealt with above. Several studies have involved intervention on a substantial scale but with willing participation. For instance, psychologists have worked with parents and children in the home in an effort to demonstrate the beneficial effects of parental stimulation on the child's learning and intellectual performance. In these studies a control group is necessary for baseline comparison. In hospital experiments with new drugs, trials are halted if success is apparent on the grounds that it would be unethical to withhold treatment from the placebo and control groups. Unfortunately, in psychological intervention research, even if success is apparent, there would not usually be the political power and resources to implement the 'treatment' across all disadvantaged families. Ethical issues arise, therefore, in selecting one group for special treatment.

Where intervention occurs for research purposes only, and involves the production of behaviour usually considered socially unacceptable, ethical principles need very careful consideration. Leyens et al. (1975), for instance, raised levels of aggression in boys shown a series of violent films. They were observed to be more aggressive in daily activities compared with a control group shown non-violent films. Several other studies have produced the same effect, some with adults. It is quite difficult to see how debriefing alone could leave the boys just where they were before the study began.

RESEARCH WITH ANIMALS

There is nothing more certain of producing a lively debate among psychology students than the discussion of whether or not it is necessary or useful to experiment on defenceless animals. Many students are far more emotionally outraged about animal research than about some of the more questionable human studies, on the grounds that humans can refuse whereas animals have no such chance.

One cannot deceive animals, though one can fool them. Nor can they give their informed consent, be debriefed or ask for a procedure to be terminated, though only the most callously inhumane experimenter could ignore severe suffering. Animals can, however, be subject to exploitation, extreme levels of physical pain and mental stress.

Many students (unwisely) spend the whole of an essay on ethics discussing the plight of research animals, though Milgram will often be a secondary focus of attention. I don't intend to go through the innumerable examples of animals in pitiful situations in the psychological research laboratory. A list of situations is enough:

- severe sensory deprivation
- severe to complete social deprivation
- extirpation or lesion of the nervous system or body parts
- use of extremely aversive physical stimuli including electric shock, noise, poisonous or otherwise aversive chemicals, mood or behaviour altering chemicals
- starvation

Why have psychologists found it useful or necessary to use these methods?

THE CASE FOR ANIMAL RESEARCH

1 Animals can be used where humans can't. For instance, they can be deprived of their mothers or reared in complete darkness. This point of course completely begs the question of whether such procedures are ethical.

2 Great control can be exerted over variables. Animals can be made to feed, for instance, at precise intervals.

3 The whole process of development can be observed.

4 Several generations can be bred where species have short gestation and maturation periods. This is useful in studying genetic processes.

5 An effect shown or insight gained in animal studies, although not directly applicable to humans, may lead to fresh and fertile theories about human behaviour. Animal studies have contributed ideas to the debate on human adult–infant bonding and maternal separation, for example.

6 Comparisons across the phylogenetic scale are valuable for showing what humans *don't* have or *can't* do – what we have probably evolved away from or out of. Comparison is invaluable in helping us develop a framework for brain analysis based on evolutionary history. A seemingly useless or mystical piece of the nervous system may serve, or have served, a function disclosed only through the discovery of its current function in another species.

7 At a very elementary, physiological level, animals and humans have things in common. The nature of the synapse, neural connections and transmission for instance, are similar among higher primates.

8 Skinner argued that elementary units of learning would also be similar across most higher species. Hence, he mostly used rat and pigeon subjects in his research work, arguing that patterns of stimulus–response contingencies, schedules of reinforcement and so on were generalisable to the world of human behaviour.

THE CASE AGAINST ANIMAL RESEARCH

Theorists have argued that too much extrapolation from animal to human has occurred. Here are some reasons why such extrapolation is considered inappropriate.

1 Seligman (1972) has argued for the concept of 'preparedness' which implies that some animals are born especially prepared, through evolutionary processes, to learn easily certain behaviour patterns of survival value to the species. Likewise, some patterns are difficult or impossible to learn at all – the animal is 'contra-prepared'. This makes comparison between one species and another hazardous, let alone comparison between human and animal.

2 Kohler (1925) demonstrated in apes what he referred to as 'insight' learning – solving a novel problem with a sudden reorganisation of detail, much like we do when we spontaneously solve one of those annoying match-stick problems. If apes can do what humans certainly can, then the validity of comparing human learning processes with those of the rat, who *doesn't* exhibit 'insight', seems questionable.

3 The ethologists have shown that quite a lot of behaviour, subject to cultural variation and slow developmental learning in humans, is instinctive in animals, demonstrated as 'fixed action patterns'. Mating preludes and territorial defence are quite rigidly organised in a large number of species yet quite ungeneralised across the breadth of human cultures.

4 The ethologists, among others, have also questioned the validity of having animals do abnormal things in the laboratory and have concentrated on behaviour in the natural environment, only testing animals in the laboratory with variations of the stimuli which would be encountered normally outside it.

5 Language, strongly defined in terms of syntax and symbol, appears to be unique to humans. Language is the vehicle for transmission of cultural values, meanings and the individual's social construction of reality. Very much psychological research, consciously or not, assumes these values and meanings as integral to human awareness. The comparison with most animals seems at its weakest here.

The points above are all aimed at the rejection of animal research on *practical* grounds. It is argued that such research will not tell us what we want to know. Other arguments take a moral or humanitarian line.

6 Some argue that it is just categorically wrong to inflict pain and suffering on any living creature.

7 A more profound argument is that the experimenter's 'attack' on nature typifies the 'controlling' model of humankind associated with the psychologist as a hard, objective, neutral scientist. This image of the scientist is currently rejected, not just by humanist and many other psychologists, but by many scientists across the disciplines who wish to project a model of environmental care.

Supporters of the points above would argue that kittens need not be deprived of visual experience in order to study the nature–nurture issue in perception. Field studies on children who unfortunately *happen* to have been so deprived would be considered more valid and more ethical. Likewise, monkeys do not need to be deprived of their mothers. Plenty of children have been. The great debate in attachment theory has been over the number and quality of bonds necessary for optimum child development and here, monkey studies can hardly help us.

Whatever the rationale for animal studies, or the fierce, impassioned objections, it seems likely they will continue as an adjunct to psychological research, though perhaps not at their earlier intensity.

British research is carried out under guidelines issued by the BPS (1985). In these the following points are made:

- Knowledge to be gained must justify procedure; trivial research is not encouraged; alternative methods are
- The smallest possible number of animals should be used
- No members of endangered species should ever be used
- Caging, food deprivation and procedures causing discomfort or pain should all be assessed relative to the particular species studied. A procedure relatively mild to one can be damaging to another
- Naturalistic studies are preferred to laboratory ones, but animals should be disturbed as little as possible in the wild
- Experimenters must be familiar with the technical aspects of anaesthesia, pharmacological compounds and so on; regular post-operative medical checks must be made

The guidelines also direct the psychologist to the relevant laws under which animal research is conducted and to the need for various licences.

CONCLUSION

All in all, it looks difficult to conduct much research at all without running into ethical arguments. Certainly it seems impossible to proceed with anything before considering possible ethical objections. But this is as it should be. Other sciences too have their associations and committees for considering social responsibility in scientific research. They argue about the use to which findings might be put or the organisations from whom it would not be prudent to accept sponsorship. They consider the likely impact of their work on society as a whole.

Similarly, psychology has to make these considerations. But, since humans, as individuals in society, are also the focal point of research, it is hardly surprising that psychology, as a research society, has to be far sharper on its toes in spotting malpractice, abuse, thoughtlessness and lack of professionalism. If psychologists prefer not to have people take one step backwards at parties and say things like 'I bet you're testing me' or 'Is this part of an experiment?', they need to reassure the public constantly that some excesses of the past cannot now happen and that deception really *is* only used when necessary.

The humanists and 'new paradigm' researchers appear to have gained the moral high ground on these ethical issues, not just because they put dignity and honesty first, but because they see their collaborative or non-directive methods as the only route to genuine, uncoerced information. As Maslow puts it:

'. . . if you prod at people like things, they won't let you know them.'

Well, what do you think? You'll probably discuss quite heatedly, with co-students or colleagues, the rights and wrongs of conducting some experiments. I can't help feeling that the information from Milgram's work is extremely valuable. It certainly undermined stereotypes I had about whole cultures being inherently cruel. But I also can't help thinking immediately about those participants who went all the way. Can we be so sure we'd be in the 35% who stopped? Not even all these stopped as soon as the victim was clearly in trouble. How would we feel the rest of our lives? Should we inflict such a loss of dignity on others? I haven't made any final decision about this issue, as about many other psychological debates and philosophical dilemmas. Fortunately, I'm not in a position where I have to vote on it. But what do you think . . . ?

GLOSSARY

Informing participants about the full nature and rationale of the study they've experienced and removing any harm to self-image or self-esteem	_____	debriefing
Leading participant to believe that something other than the true IV is involved or, at least, not giving full information to the participant about the IV, DV or overall procedure	_____	deception
Research which makes some alteration to people's lives beyond the specific research setting, in some cases because there is an intention to remove disadvantage or make improvements of some kind in people's overall condition	_____	intervention
Effect of research which intrudes on people's personal lives	_____ __ _____	invasion of privacy
Taking part in research without agreement or knowledge of the study	_____ _____	involuntary participation

15

PLANNING PRACTICALS

If you are going to be devising and running your own practical work in psychology, good luck! It is great fun, and highly satisfying, to be presenting a report of work which is all your own, rather than of a practical which your tutor sets up and sends you all off to do. However, beware! Your tutor almost certainly has a lot of experience in planning such exercises such that you do not waste all your efforts and end up with useless data or find yourself running a project with hopeless snags or a completely inappropriate design.

Below I have jotted down most of the things I can think of which need attention before you start your data gathering. I've almost certainly missed some things but I hope these will be of some help. *Nothing I've written, however can substitute for very careful planning, preferably in a small group, before you start your data collection.*

Remember that the 'practical' doesn't start when you actually begin running your trials and testing your participants. That is a tiny part of the whole process. There is a large portion of time to spend planning and another large portion to spend analysing and (dare I say it) writing up your report!

Never gather data without first checking what statistical analysis you are going to use on them. It is very sad to see students with data that just won't demonstrate what they wanted to show and which may even be completely unanalysable. *Think ahead*, check with tutors, and adjust your data gathering strategy accordingly.

I have written these notes with the traditional, 'tight' hypothesis test in mind. Hence there is emphasis on strict definition of variables and thinking about the system of analysis before starting. This runs counter to the tenets of qualitative and 'new paradigm' research. However, most students will find that, through syllabus requirements or other forces, they will need to be familiar with this traditional design. Besides, since the 'old paradigm' is hardly likely to disappear overnight, I believe it is necessary to understand the approach fully in order to understand its weaknesses and to be able to take off in other directions.

The student wishing to conduct something more qualitative in design would need to consult thoroughly with their tutor in order to avoid ending up with a report which is fascinating but is seen as the work of a 'displaced novelist' and mainly anecdotal.

THE OVERALL AIM

- Did the idea just pop up in your head? It is worth checking to see if there is *related theory*. This might give you firmer ideas. You will probably be working to a syllabus which wants you to 'embed' the research aims in some background theory. There is nothing wrong in principle, however, in testing a personal idea which came to you unaided. Creativity is encouraging. However, it is likely that there *is* some related work on it, though perhaps hard to find in your college library. You can always phone up or write to other institutions or libraries, however, such as your local university.

• *Now* is the time to state your hypotheses very carefully, not when you come to write up the report!

THE DESIGN

• Do you need to quantify your variables because there is no existing measure? Can this be done sensibly? How will 'self-concept', for instance, be measured?
• In thinking of variables it will be useful to think about any *statistical analysis* you are going to employ. For instance, if you have been asked to use correlation then it is almost certainly intended that you should use Pearson or Spearman where both your variables should be measurable on at least an ordinal scale. Otherwise, if you tried to 'correlate sex with driving speed', for instance, you would end up with the *difference* between males and females, since sex is a nominal variable – it only has two qualitatively different values.

   Will you be able to develop a plausible rating scale for your variable(s)? Can people rate a photograph of a face on a scale of one to ten for 'happiness', for example? Using this approach, you will only be able to do a non-parametric test.

   If you measure driving ability by whether a driver stops or not, you can only achieve nominal level data. Is that what you want? Similarly, compare asking whether people passed their test first time with asking how long it took them to learn.
• Are you dealing with too many variables to keep statistical analysis simple enough? Say you wanted to see whether introverts improve on a task without an audience, whereas extroverts deteriorate. You'd like to see whether this is more true for males than for females and perhaps whether age has an effect too. Admirable thinking on interacting variables, but the statistical analysis will get very complicated.
• The last example would be very costly on participants. Could you get enough? In general, will you be able to get enough people for your chosen design? Remember, an unrelated design requires twice the number of people, to get the same number of differences as a repeated measures design. Will you be able to match pairs appropriately? You may not be able to obtain the information you need for this (e.g. social class). If you are going to use repeated measures, with tests on two different occasions, will everyone be available second time around?
• If you're testing whether people change their attitude having received some information, for instance, you will always need a *control group* who are also tested twice in order to see whether testing *alone* creates changes in your attitude measure.
• Is there a likelihood of any obvious confounding variables? If the general public are to be approached by researchers, will it matter that most of them are female? Some students I knew were going to say 'hello' to passers-by under two conditions, with and without a smile. It struck them that all of them were female and that there could be a differential response from male and female passers-by!
• Are conditions *equivalent*? If the experimental group have longer, more intricate instructions and introduction to their task, could this act as a confounding variable? Should the control group get equivalent but 'dummy' introduction and instructions, and/or equivalent time with the experimenters?

THE SAMPLE(S)

- Will you have to use the same old 'friends and acquaintances' or students in the college canteen? If so, will they be too much aware of your previous deceptions?
- Will they reveal the nature of the research to naïve participants?
- Even though the sample can't be truly random or representative, can you balance groups for sex, age etc.?
- Should you ask whether they've participated in this before? You can't ask beforehand, in many cases, such as, when you're showing an illusion. You'll have to ask afterwards and exclude them from the results if they weren't 'naïve'.
- If you suspected some participants of 'mucking around' or of already knowing the aim and perhaps trying to 'look good', you'll have to decide, having asked them afterwards, whether it is legitimate to drop their results. You can discuss this with colleagues.

THE MATERIALS

- Are they *equivalent* for both conditions? A group of students were doing a version of the Asch 'warm–cold' study. People in one group were shown a set of terms: *intelligent, shy, confident, warm, practical, quick, quiet.* The other group were shown the same terms except that '*cold*' was substituted for '*warm*'. The people had to judge other characteristics of the hypothetical person. One student had missed a class and had no '*cold*' forms, so she changed the word 'warm' in ink and photocopied. This gave a not-too-subtle clue to her second group as to what the important word in the set was.

  Can two memory word-lists be equivalent in word frequency? Are two sets of anagrams equally hard to solve? You can use *pre-testing* of the materials to show there is no real difference.
- Are instructions to participants *intelligible*?
- Are there too many units in the material? Will it take too long to test all on each participant? Can they be shortened?
- If you want to construct a questionnaire, see Chapter 6. Remember, a test of an attitude is often made, not with questions but with statements for people to agree/disagree with or say how far it represents their view. Don't say 'Do you believe in abortion/nuclear power/strikes?' These things exist! We want to know what people *think* about them.
- If you're unsure of the wording in the questionnaire, get the help of someone who's good with language. Respondents will not respect or take seriously a badly-written questionnaire.
- In all cases, *pilot*! Try out materials on friends and relatives.

It takes many years to train in the psychoanalytic interpretation of projective tests, such as the Rorschach and TAT. Their validity is very much questioned within the academic world. Therefore it would be unwise to attempt to incorporate the use of these instruments in a student practical.

If you are focusing on a specific group of people, such as a minority ethnic group, then please see the advice on page 67, and be extremely careful with your choice of language. If possible, check with members of the group concerned, other 'experts', your tutor and/or your classmates. This applies wherever a specific group is the focus, *whether members of that group will themselves be questioned or not* (e.g. a nationality, gay people, people with disabilities or specific illnesses or difficulties such as dyslexia, and so on).

THE PROCEDURE

- There may well be several of you going out to gather data. *Make sure you standardise your procedure exactly before you start.* The most common problem I have seen amongst a group of students doing a practical together is that they didn't have a final check that they had all got exactly the same steps of procedure. Don't be shy to ask your friends to do a final check before they rush off after a lot of hurried changes. Don't feel stupid if you don't feel confident about exactly what you have to do. Ask your friends or the tutor where appropriate. It's better to take a little more time, and admit you're not perfect, than to end up with results that can't be used or, worse, having to do things over again.
- *Record all the information on the spot.* If you decide to wait till later to record the age of your interviewee, you may well forget. Then the result may be wasted.
- Be prepared to put participants at their ease and give an encouraging introduction.
- Work out the *exact* instructions to participants. Have a simulated run through with a colleague. What have you failed to explain? What else might people need/ want to know?
- Decide how you will answer questions your participants might ask. Will you have stock answers or will you ask them to wait until after the testing?
- If the study is an observation:
  i) Will the observations really be unobtrusive? Check out the recording position beforehand.
  ii) Will recording be easy? Does talking into a tape recorder attract too much attention for instance? Does the coding system work? Is there time and ample space to make written notes?
  iii) Will more than one person make records in the interests of reliability?

Writing your practical report

If you carry out some practical work, you will find yourself faced with the onerous task of writing it all up. My first piece of advice is *don't put it off*! You'll find it much harder to come back to when any enthusiasm you had for the project will have worn off, and you won't be able to understand why certain precautions were taken or just what certain conditions were all about. You'll find essential details of data and analysis are missing and you may need the help of your class colleagues who've now lost their raw data or are too busy to help much.

What is the purpose of a report?

There are two main purposes, neither of which is to do with keeping your tutor happy. First, you are telling your reader just what you did, why you did it and what you think it adds to the stockpile of knowledge and theory development. Second, you are recording your procedures in enough detail for some of those readers, who are so inclined, to *replicate* your work. We have seen elsewhere why this is so important to scientific method.

Golden rule number one for report writing, then, is:

> **Make sure you write with enough depth and clarity for a complete stranger to repeat exactly what you did in every detail.**

What are the rules?

There are none. However, your tutor will often act as if there are when commenting on your work. This is because there *are* conventions fairly generally accepted. Most of these make sense and work in the interests of good report organisation and communication between researchers. Have a look at some journals in your college library, if that's possible, or ask to borrow a copy of one volume from a local academic institution. Your tutor may well have copies of old student work, though very often only the poorer work gets left. (Why this systematic bias?) The Associated Examining Board will send examples of marked work. I have included one fictitious report, with commentary, at the end of this chapter.

What follows, then, is the generally accepted format, around which most articles vary just a bit. Qualitative, inductive work will follow much the same format but will not have a specific hypothesis to test. However, it will have overall aims clearly set out. Another major difference will be that the 'results' section will tend to merge with the discussion. Otherwise, reporting of procedures and evaluation of findings, overall design and method should all be similar.

PLAGIARISM

Perhaps I was wrong about rules above. Plagiarism is copying directly from another's work *or* paraphrasing it so closely that it is recognisably similar. In official publishing this is illegal and people can be sued for it. On college courses, if coursework counts towards final marks then plagiarism is exactly the same as cheating in an exam. On many courses the ruling is stiff – one substantial piece of copying fails the entire work. The main point is that coursework must be your *own* (or, in some cases, your group's) work. The educational point is that we learn very little from copying, as you'll know from your psychological studies of memory and learning processes. The ethical point is that copying is stealing. So be very careful not to copy from texts. Of course you can't invent your ideas. Learning is about appreciating what has gone before, then, hopefully, adding to it. The best procedure is to read, make notes, close any books, ask yourself questions to see how far you've understood, *then* attempt to write out the ideas as you now see them. This is just as important in the introduction and discussion sections of practical reports as in any essay.

Box 16.1 shows a skeleton scheme of the various sections of a report.

Box 16.1 *Sections of a practical report*

```
            Title
Abstract/summary
Introduction/aims
    Hypotheses
Method:   Design
          Participants
          Materials/Apparatus
          Procedure
Results:  Description/Summary
          Analysis/Treatment

Discussion

Conclusion

References

Appendices
```

THE TITLE

This should be as concise as possible. You don't need 'An investigation to see whether...' or similar. You just need the main variables. Very often, in an experiment, you can use the IV and DV. For instance, 'The use of imagery and rehearsal methods in recall of verbal material' will adequately describe a (probably familiar) study. For a field investigation using correlation, 'The relationship between age and attitude to environmental issues' says enough.

ABSTRACT

Also known as the 'summary'. But why on earth does a summary come at the *beginning*? Well, suppose you were interested in whether anyone had done work on your proposed topic: anxiety and jogging behaviour in red-bearded vegetarian East Londoners. As you flip through dozens of journals looking for related work, how much easier it is to see the summary of findings right at the beginning of the article, without having to wade through to the end. The abstract contains the main points of the research report, 'abstracted' from it. Most of this century, volumes have been produced each month called *Psychological Abstracts*, containing only abstracts from articles in a huge variety of research journals. This eases the job of finding relevant work. Nowadays, this process has been speeded up enormously by the use of a CD-ROM database called Psychlit™.

Your abstract should stand out from the rest of the report by being in a box, in a different colour, indented or in a different (typed/word processed) font.

INTRODUCTION

I like to think of this as a funnel.

Start with the general psychological subject area. Discuss theory and research work which is relevant to the research topic. Move from the general area to the particular hypotheses to be tested via a coherent and logical argument as to why the specific predictions have been made. State the specific HYPOTHESIS

If you recall, way back in Chapter 1, we went through, very briefly, the reasons why a prediction was made that, when 'image linking' was used, more items from a word list would be recalled than when rehearsal only was used.

The introduction to a study testing this hypothesis need not contain a five-page essay on the psychology of memory, including Ebbinghaus' work and the perform-ance of eye-witnesses in court. The hypothesis test belongs within a specialised area of memory research.

We can move our reader through the introduction in the following steps:

- The concepts of short- and long-term memory stores
- Outline of the two-process memory model
- Some evidence for the two-process model
- Phenomena the model explains, such as primacy and recency in free-recall tasks
- Focus in on the model's emphasis on rehearsal as the process by which material is transferred to the long-term store
- Introduce the 'cognitive' objection that humans always attempt to construct meaning out of incoming sensory data. Give examples of what this means
- From this theory it follows that an attempt to give an unconnected word list some

'life', by visualising the items and connecting them, should be more successful in storing the information than simple rote repetition of each word
- Additional support could be given here, referring to previous similar studies and the work on imagery in the literature

We have argued through to our specific prediction. It only remains to state the aims and hypothesis in the clearest terms so there can be no doubt over what exactly were the results we expected.

STATING AIMS

One aim of our research is to demonstrate our hypothesis to be valid, using a free-recall experiment under two conditions. An overall aim is to challenge the traditional two-store memory model. Aims are what the research project is *for*, what it is supposed to do. In qualitative projects, aims may be far more wide ranging and less specific than those in a hypothesis-testing project. For this reason, particular care would be taken to specify aims at this point in qualitative research.

THE HYPOTHESIS

You may be expected to write either the *alternative hypothesis* (see Chapter 1) or your specific prediction for your study. For instance, the alternative hypothesis might be that mean recall scores are higher after 10 mg of caffeine than after no caffeine. The specific prediction for your study which will support this hypothesis is that mean recall scores after 10 mg of caffeine will be significantly higher than recall scores after no caffeine. Either way what is essential is that variables are *precisely defined*. It will be uninformative to say 'people will remember better after caffeine'. The hypothesis or prediction should *not* contain the underlying rationale. For instance we do not say, 'There is a correlation between self-esteem and academic achievement *because people feel better when they are successful* – this is more a description of the *aim* of the study. We simply hypothesise or predict a correlation between self-esteem scores and a precise measure of academic achievement – say, GCSE and A levels passes. Box 16.2 contains loose statements of the hypotheses from the Chapter 13 exercises along with possible wordings of the alternative hypothesis and prediction for the study. You might like to try writing out column two or three whilst only looking at column one.

Box 16.2 *Loose and precise wordings for hypotheses and predictions*

Vaguely worded	Alternative hypothesis	Prediction for study
More people of one sex avoid walking under a ladder because they are superstitious.	The proportions of men and women walking or not walking under the ladder are different.	The proportions of men and women walking or not walking under the ladder will be significantly different.
People will perform worse on the sensori-motor task in front of an audience.	Mean number of errors on the sensori-motor task when in front of an	The sample mean for errors made on the sensori-motor task in front

	audience is higher than the mean number made when alone.	of an audience will be significantly higher than the sample mean for errors made when alone.
Ratings on attractiveness will be similar for each member of a couple because like attracts like.	There is a positive correlation between ratings of male and female partners on attractiveness.	There will be a significant positive correlation between ratings of male and female partners on attractiveness.
Non-rhyming words are harder to read.	Mean time for reading non-rhyming words is higher than the mean time for reading rhyming words.	There will be a significant difference between mean reading times for rhyming and non-rhyming words, with the rhyming mean being higher.
Participants will improve in their attitude to race as a result of the training course.	Post-course essay ratings are higher than pre-course essay ratings.	A significant difference will be found between post-course and pre-course essay ratings with post-course ratings higher.
Smokers will have improved.	More smokers are assessed as 'improved' than are assessed as 'worsened' over the course.	The number of smokers assessed as 'improved' will be significantly higher than the number assessed as 'worsened'.

THE NULL HYPOTHESIS

The alternative or research hypothesis is often given the symbol H_1 and the null hypothesis gets H_0. Further hypotheses being tested get numbered logically, H_2, H_3 etc., each with their accompanying H_0. The null hypothesis gets stated directly after each hypothesis.

Note: it is a good exercise, in early psychological studies, to specify precisely what it is you are testing. Most tutors will ask you to state H_0, and the exam boards usually mention it. In published research reports, in fact, the null hypothesis is rarely mentioned or explicitly stated. Even hypotheses are not as dogmatically expressed as I've recommended. However, writers *do* make clear exactly what they're testing using well-developed writing styles.

THE METHOD

It is customary and convenient, but not absolutely necessary, to break the method used down into the following four subheadings. Materials and procedure may often be one heading.

DESIGN

This describes the 'skeleton' outline of the study – its basic framework. For instance, is it an experiment or not? If it is, what design is used (repeated measures, etc.)? What conditions are there, and how many groups are used? What is the purpose of each group (control, placebo, etc.)? How many participants are in each group (though this information can go in the 'participants' section below)? In many cases, describing the groups will be a way of describing the IV. In any case, both the IV and DV should be outlined here.

What controls have been employed? Is there counterbalancing and, if so, of what form?

In our experiment on imagery and rehearsal, we could say 'we used a repeated measures design with one group of 15 participants who were presented with a 20-item word list in two conditions, one with instructions only to rehearse each item, the other with instructions to use image-linking. Order of taking conditions was reversed for half the participants. The DV was number of items recalled under free recall conditions.' . . . and that's about enough.

You don't need to give any details of procedure or materials used, otherwise you'll find yourself laboriously repeating yourself later on.

If the study is non-experimental, its overall approach (e.g. observational) can be stated along with design structures such as longitudinal, cross-sectional, etc. Again there may be an (uncontrolled) IV and DV, for instance sex and stopping at an amber traffic light. Controls, such as measures of inter-observer reliability, may have been incorporated. Don't mention details here, just that the control was employed.

PARTICIPANTS

Give numbers, including how many in each group, and other details relevant to the study. If someone wishes to replicate your findings about 'adolescents' and their self-concepts, it is important for them to know exactly what ages and sex your participants were. These variables are less important in technical laboratory tasks, though general age range is usually useful and handedness may be relevant. Other variables, such as social class or occupation might be highly relevant for some research topics. Certainly important is how naïve to psychology participants were. Otherwise, keep non-relevant details to a minimum.

How were participants obtained? How were they allocated to the various experimental groups (if not covered in your 'design')?

MATERIALS/APPARATUS

Again, apply the golden rule: *give enough detail for a proper replication to be possible.* This means giving specifications of constructed equipment (finger-maze, illusion box) and source (manufacturer, make, model) of commercial items (tachistoscope, computer). Exact details of all written materials should be given here or in an appendix, including: word lists, questionnaires, lists people had to choose from, pictures and so on. You *don't* need to give details of blank paper or pencils!

In our memory study we would need two lists of words because we can't have people learning the same list twice without a mammoth confounding variable. We would state in this section how we justify our two lists being equivalent – selected from word frequency list, same number of concrete and abstract terms, etc.

It may be useful to include a diagram or photo of an experimental set-up or seating arrangements.

PROCEDURE

The rule here is simple. Describe exactly what happened from start to finish in testing. This must be enough for good replication. Any standardised instructions should be included here or in an appendix, including any standard answers to predicted questions from participants.

The exact wording used in training participants to use imagery in our memory experiment should be included, together with any practice trials and words used for these.

It is very tempting to 'skim' the materials and procedure sections and give far too little detail. My advice if you're not sure you've written enough is:

GIVE IT TO A FRIEND OR RELATIVE TO READ!

If your mother or boyfriend can understand *exactly* what happened, if they could go off and do it, then it's clear and enough. (They might not get on too well with the other sections without some psychological knowledge.)

RESULTS

DESCRIPTION

You must talk about and present the data you obtained *before* going on to analyse it with a test of significance. Large amounts of raw data go in an appendix. A summary table of these is presented in the results section, including frequencies, means, standard deviations or their equivalents. Any tables (appearing here *or* in the appendix) should be well headed. For instance, a table of our experimental findings starting like Table 16.1 is inadequate. What do the numbers stand for? We need a heading 'Number of words recalled in the stated condition'. If results are times, state 'seconds' or 'minutes'; if they are distance measurements, state the units.

Table 16.1 *Inadequate experimental results table*

Participant	Imagery	Rehearsal	
1	12	8	
2	15	12	
etc.	etc.	etc.	
:	:	:	

You might wish to present a graphical representation of your data, such as a histogram or scattergraph. Make sure these are clearly headed too, and that the vertical and horizontal axes have titles.

However, do not litter your results section with artistic charts which are not central to the description or analysis of results. Make sure charts are headed and have clearly titled axes. Tables and charts need numbering for reference purposes (e.g. 'Table 1').

ANALYSIS OR TREATMENT

If there are several hypotheses to test, or different treatments, take one at a time and divide this section into subsections ((a), (b), etc.) with a heading for each one stating what hypothesis is being tested in each case.

State which statistical test is being applied and *justify* this using the decision procedures outlined in Chapter 13.

State the result clearly and compare this with the appropriate critical value. Justify the choice of this critical value including N or degrees of freedom, number of tails, and the corresponding level of probability ('$p < \ldots$'). Box 16.3 is a quick exercise in noting what can be missing from statements of significance.

State whether the null hypothesis is being rejected or retained.

Calculations of your tests, if you wish to include them, should appear only in the appendix. Many calculations these days will be performed by computer or dedicated calculator. The software used, and intermediary results, can be mentioned in an appendix. Do *not* include miles of unexplained computer print-out.

If there are a number of test results, these could be presented in a clear summary table.

It is worth pointing out that actual journal articles never show calculations or include raw data and rarely justify the statistical test chosen. However, this information is always available through private correspondence. Students doing practical work are usually asked to substitute for the real-life situation by including these with their reports.

Box 16.3 *Incomplete significance statements*

Statements	What's missing
'The *t*-test showed that differences were significant'	At what level? How many degrees of freedom? How many tails?
'There was a strong correlation between the two variables'	But was it significant, and at what level? Was the correlation positive or negative? Was the prediction one- or two-tailed?
'There was a significant difference between the two conditions at the 1% level'	How many degrees of freedom? How many tails?

DISCUSSION

The first step here is to explain in non-statistical language just what has happened in the results section. These results must then be related to the hypotheses you set out to test, and to the original aims of the research. These in turn are then related to the background theory, showing support or a need to modify theory in the light of contradictory or ambiguous findings.

Unexpected findings or 'quirks' in the results can also be discussed as a secondary issue. From time to time, such 'oddities' lead in novel research directions. You can try to offer some explanations of these if you have good reasons.

EVALUATING THE METHOD

The conscientious researcher always evaluates the design and method, picking out flaws and areas of weakness. This isn't just to nitpick. A reader of the report might well come back and accuse the researcher of not considering such weaknesses. The researcher can forestall such criticism by presenting a good argument as to why the weakness should not have serious effect.

The emphasis of the evaluation depends partly on the outcome:

1   If we got the result we expected, we should look carefully at the design for possible confounding variables producing a type I error. If we were predicting that the null hypothesis would be supported, we should look for ways in which the design and procedures may have hidden differences or relationships.

2   If we failed to get what we predicted, we should look for sources of random variables (though research with a successful outcome may also have been affected by these). What aspects of the design, procedures and materials used did we find unsatisfactory? There could even be a confounding variable which *suppresses* our predicted effect.

3   Not everything in an experiment or investigation can be perfect. There is no need to talk about not controlling temperature or background noise unless there is good reason to suppose that variation in these could have seriously affected results. Usually this is quite unlikely.

Suggest modifications

Most research leads on to more research. From the considerations made so far you should be able to suggest modifications of this design, or quite new directions, which will follow up on, or check the points made.

CONCLUSION

Make summarising comments in terms of overall findings, their relationship to the relevant model or theory and implications for the future. Avoid repeating the abstract or the beginning of your discussion, however. A verbal summary of statistical findings may be useful where several tests in the results analysis were talked about one by one in the discussion.

REFERENCES

This is one of the most tedious aspects of writing a report, especially if you've referred to a lot of different research in your work. There is also often a lot of confusion over what exactly counts as a reference, what should be included.

Golden rule number 2 is:

> **If you referred to it directly somewhere in your text, include it. If you didn't refer to it, don't include it!**

If you wrote '. . . Gross (1992) argues that . . .'. this *is* a reference. The date means you're telling the reader where you got the information from. If you happened to read Gross' textbook whilst preparing your practical or trying to write it up – it may be where you got Bower (1977) from, for instance – then Gross is *not* a reference (but Bower will be, if you included it). Strictly speaking, if you read Bower *only* in Gross, you can say 'Bower (1977) plus reference details, as cited in Gross (1992) . . .' (etc.), giving the full Gross reference *and* page number(s). If you want to tell your reader what you read but didn't specifically refer to in your text, put these titles under 'Bibliography' if you like. In other words, your 'references' are what your text refers to, not what you read in total. Write references as at the back of this book. Notice that *journal articles* have the journal title in italics (you can use an underline). The article is in ordinary print. For *books* the book title gets special treatment. There can be a few awkward ones which were articles in someone else's collection of articles, government reports and so on.

APPENDICES

These might contain: calculations, instructions given to participants, memory list items, questionnaires and so on. These continue your normal page numbering. Separate topics go in separate, numbered appendices ('Appendix 1', 'Appendix 2', etc.).

GENERAL PRESENTATION

It is useful to have page numbering throughout. You might find it convenient to refer to pages in your text.

A title page sets the whole project off well and a contents page helps the reader go to specific sections. If you have presented a set of projects together, it might help to begin the whole set with a contents page and to have a 'header' on each page telling the reader what particular practical we're in.

CHECKLIST FOR WRITING A PRACTICAL REPORT

Note: some of these points will not apply to non-experimental or qualitative work.

Title
Does your title give a brief, but clear indication of the content?

Contents
Have you numbered every page? Have you included a contents page listing main sections of the report?

Abstract/summary
Does your summary cover the aims, IV, DV, participants, design, measures, main statistical results and conclusions of the research project? Does it convey a brief, essential impression of the research in less than 200 words?

Introduction
Have you given a brief general overview of the issues and concepts that are relevant to

the topic which places the research in context? Is there an account of similar or related studies? Have you explained why your study was undertaken? Have you explained the main aims of the investigation? Are hypotheses (if any) clearly stated in a straightforward, testable form with variables in clearly measurable operationalised terms?

Method

Will your readers have enough detail to repeat the study exactly as you did it? Have you chosen a suitable set of subheadings which organise the information clearly?

Design

Have you stated the main design form (field observation, repeated measures experiment, etc.)? Have you explained briefly why this design was selected? Have you explained the purpose of the different groups and given numbers in each? Have you identified the IV and DV and described conditions? Have you listed controls introduced ('blinds', counterbalancing)?

Participants

Is it clear who they were and how they were chosen or obtained? Have you provided any additional information which may be relevant to the research (age, sex, first language, naïvety)?

Materials/apparatus

Have you described these in sufficient detail for replication? Have you made use, where necessary, of drawings and diagrams? Have you described any technical apparatus? Have you included word lists, questionnaires etc.?

Procedure

Have you explained, in sequence, exactly what the experimenter/researcher did and what each participant experienced? Have you reported in full any important instructions given? (Copies in appendix.) Have you given a clear impression of the layout and arrangement of events?

Results

Is there a summary table of results giving totals, means, standard deviations or their equivalents? Are lengthy, raw data in an appendix? Have you exploited opportunities for visual presentation? Are all tables, graphs and charts fully and clearly labelled and numbered? Have you given each a title and are units clearly shown? Have you clearly explained any coding or rating systems, scoring of questionnaires or other ways data were manipulated before final analysis?

Analysis/treatment

Have you explained and justified your choice of statistical test for analysis? Have you listed the results of the tests, their significance, the degrees of freedom, number of tails? Are calculations in the appendix, or an explanation of how they were done (e.g. computer)? Are statements made about rejection or not of each null hypothesis?

Discussion

Is there a verbal (not statistical) description of results? Do you explain how the results relate to your hypotheses and any background theory or prior research? Can you explain any unexpected results? Have you evaluated the design and procedures used? Have you considered alternative explanations of results? Have you suggested modifications, extensions or new research to deal with these last three points?

References

Have you listed *all* the studies which you referred to (with a date in brackets) in your text? Have you used the standard format for references? i.e. last name, initials (date) *book title*, place published: publisher *or* last name, initials (date) article title, *journal title*, vol. page numbers.

Appendices

Have you labelled each appendix clearly? Do the appendices continue the page numbering? Are the appendices included on your contents page and referred to at appropriate points in the text?

COMMENTS ON A STUDENT PRACTICAL REPORT

What you see below is a *fictitious* student report. *It is not a good report,* so please use it carefully as a model, taking into account all the comments I've made beside it. My reasoning was this. If I include a perfect report the recent newcomer to psychology and its practical writing conventions would have little clue as to what typically goes *wrong* in report writing. To include *all* possible mistakes would be to produce an unreadable piece of work serving little purpose. The report below would be roughly in the mid-range at A-level, perhaps a little lower at first year degree level (I think) but its exact mark would depend upon the level or particular syllabus. Hence, I've refrained from assessing it formally. It contains quite a lot of omissions and ambiguities, but few outright mistakes. Too many of these might be misleading. I have marked the comments I would like to make with superscript numbers in the text. I have coded comments as follows:

✓ a good point
✗ an error, omission, ambiguity; in general, a point which would count to lower the overall mark for the report
? an ambiguity or odd point which would not lower the mark on its own but could contribute to an overall lower mark if it were repeated. Also used for grammatical and conventional style points which, again, are not terribly bad on their own but which may accumulate into a feeling of 'not quite so good' (but this *does* depend on your level of study)

Assume that materials mentioned as in appendices *were* included (often they aren't!).

AN EXPERIMENT TO SHOW WHETHER PEOPLE ARE[1] AFFECTED BY KNOWING A WRITER'S SEX WHEN THEY JUDGE A PIECE OF WRITING

ABSTRACT

We[2] set out to see whether people make sexist assumptions about an author when they read their writing. We asked 39 participants to read an article and told half of them (19) that the author was a man and the others that it was a woman. We did this by making the writer's name 'John Kelly' for one article and 'Jean Kelly' for the other.[3] Because of stereotyping we expected the 'Jean Kelly' group to think worse of the article's quality.[4] Results were not significant[5] and the null hypothesis was kept. It was thought that the article was too neutral and women might have been voted lower on a technical article and men lower on a child-care article. If results were valid this could be interpreted as a change in attitude since Goldberg's (1968) work.[6]

INTRODUCTION

People use stereotypes when they look at other people. When we perceive people it's like looking at things in the world. We look through a framework of what we've learnt and we don't see the real thing but our impressions of it are coloured by what we expect and our biases. Bruner (1957) said we 'go beyond the information given';[7] we use what's there as 'cues' to what we interpret is really there. For example, when we see a car on the road and a mountain behind it, the mountain might look only twice as high as the car but because we know how far away the mountain is we can estimate what size it really is. When we take a picture of a pretty sight we often get telephone wires in the way because we've learnt not to see what isn't important. Also, we take a shot of Uncle Arthur on the beach and he comes out really small because we thought he looked much bigger in the viewfinder because he's important to us. Bruner and his friends started the 'new look' in perception where they experimented with perception to show that we're affected by our emotions, motivation and 'set'. In one experiment they showed sweet jars to children that were either filled with sand or sweets.[8] The children saw the jars with sweets as larger, so we are affected by our past experience and what we *want*. (Dukes and Bevan, 1951.)[9]

To show that a small bit of information affects our judgement of persons Asch (1946) gave some people some words to describe a person. The words were the same except that 'warm' and 'cold' were different. This even works when the person is real because Kelley (1950) introduced students to a 'warm' or 'cold' person and they liked the warm one more. The 'warm' person was seen quite differently from the 'cold' one.

Sex differences are a myth.[10] Condry and Condry (1976) showed people a film of a nine-month-old child reacting to a jack-in-the-box. If they were told he was a boy the reaction was thought of as 'anger' but for a 'girl' it was thought of as 'fear'. Deux (1977) reviewed several studies and found females often explain their performance as luck, even if they do well, but men say their ability helped them. This was where the task they did was unfamiliar. This means that men and women accept their stereotype and go along with it in their lives.[11] Maccoby and Jacklin's experiment[12] in

1   ?   Don't need 'An experiment . . .'; title could be shorter, 'The effect of author's sex on assessment of an article'.

2   ?   Conventional reports are written in passive not personal mode; e.g. 'The theory was tested that author's sex affects judgement of writing.' '39 participants were asked . . .'

3   ✓   IV is clearly described.

4   ✗   DV is not at all defined. How will 'thinking worse of' be measured?

5   ✗   Results very poorly reported. What test was used? What data was/were the test(s) on? What *was* the null hypothesis? What significance level was chosen to reject at? (e.g. $p < 0.05$)

6   ✓   Some brief statement of conclusions included.

7   ✓   Quotation is in quote marks and attributed to an author, with date – this *must* be referenced at the end of the report.

8   (Poor children! – you wouldn't think they'd let psychologists do that sort of thing!)

9   ✓   A broad start about factors which affect judgement in perception. The introduction should now go on to introduce *person* perception and narrow down to sex-role stereotype effects.

10 ✗   !!! A gigantic and unjustified assumption made here; there are *some* differences (e.g. reading development rate); the claim needs qualifying with the use of 'some', 'many' or examples.

11 ✗   Another grand assumption here, following a very specific result; needs qualification.

12 ✗   It wasn't an experiment; it was a review of mostly correlational studies.

1974 showed that males describe themselves with independent terms (e.g. intelligent, ambitious) but females use more social terms (e.g. cooperative, honest).

A psychologist called[13] Goldberg (1968) got female students to read articles written by a man or a woman (they thought). The articles written by a man were rated as better. This is the experiment we're doing here.[14]

Hypothesis

People thinking an author is male will think some articles are better written than people thinking the author is female.[15]

H₀

There is no difference between the male and female author condition means.

METHOD[16]

Design

The experiment was independent samples.[17] There were two groups. The independent variable was the sex of the author and the dependent variable was the way they judged the article.[18]

Participants

We used a random sample of 39 participants from the college canteen.[19] Originally there were 20 in the male author condition and 20 in the female author condition but the results for one in the male author condition went missing. The participants were all students except for one who was a friend of one of the students.

Materials

We used an article from *The Guardian Weekend* magazine about travelling in Tuscany. This is in Appendix 1. It was 908 words long and was printed on two sheets of A4 paper. We also used a rating sheet (in Appendix 2) where participants recorded their rating of the article for quality and interest on a 10-point scale.[20,21] This also had some questions on it to make sure the participants had noticed the name of the author.[22]

Procedure

We sat each participant down and made them feel at ease. We told them there would be no serious deception and that they would not be 'tested' or made to feel stupid in any way. We said we just wanted their opinion of something and that their opinion would be combined with others and their results would be anonymous.[23] We then gave them the instructions shown below. All this was done in a standardised way.[24]

> 'We would like you to read the article we are about to give you. Please read it once quickly, then again slowly. When you have done that, please answer the questions on the sheet which is attached to the article. Try to answer as best you can but please be sure to answer all questions *in the order given.*'[25]

If the participant's number was odd they received the female author where the article was written by 'Jean Kelly'. The other participants were given 'John Kelly' sheets. In one case this order was reversed by mistake.[26]

Participants were then left to read the article and no questions were answered by the experimenters unless it did not concern the reading at all, for instance, if they

13 ? Don't need 'A psychologist called . . .'

14 ✗ The leap into the hypothesis is *far* too sudden here; we lurch from good background description straight into the hypothesis without some introduction to the (different) nature of the study being reported.

15 ✗ Hypothesis too vague; should specify the *operationalised* DV – rating (on the 10-point scale) of quality and of interest. Hence there are *two* hypotheses – ratings of quality for male author higher than for female author, and ratings of interest for male author higher than for female author. The specific prediction for the study would include reference to significance.

16 ✓ Good that all sections of the method are present and correctly titled.

17 ✓ Correct design and this *is* an experiment.

18 ✗ Again, DV not specified; it doesn't need complete description here but there should be an operational definition of the measure – 'quality was measured by scores given on a 10-point scale'. Other controls have not been specified.

19 ✗ Almost certainly not randomly selected from the canteen; no mention of the sex breakdown of participants and this might be important in this particular study.

20 ✓ Materials well described.

21 ✗ Notice that tucked away here is the first, and only, mention of the 10-point scale; we should have heard about this earlier; we still don't know which way the scale runs – is 10 high or low quality?

22 ✗ The technique of asking questions, including dummy ones, in order to ensure participants noticed the sex of the author deserves mention in the design (as types of 'control') and not to be tucked away in the materials section, along with the 10-point scale.

23 ✓ Ethical considerations well implemented here.

24 ? Ambiguity; was the initial rapport session standardised, or just the instruction giving?

25 ✓ Exact instructions given are included.

26 ✗ This system of allocation of participants might have been mentioned in the
    ✓ design; good that the mistake was reported however.

wanted the light turned on or heater turned off. Questions about the reading were answered 'Please answer as best you can and we can talk about ("that problem") after you've finished. That way, all our participants do exactly the same thing. Thank you for your cooperation.'

The experimenters kept a watchful eye to ensure that instructions were followed in the correct order.

RESULTS

Data obtained

The results from the two groups were collected and organised into the table of raw data shown in Appendix 3. The averages and standard deviations were calculated and these are shown in Table 1.

Table 1[27]

	Author	
	Female	**Male**
Quality		
Mean	6.7	6.3
SD	1.5	2.3
Interest		
Mean	4.3	5.2
SD	1.1	1.3

You can see from this Table[28] that the male got a lower rating on quality but a higher rating on interest. This may be because people think men *can* write more interestingly, in general, but women are more likely to be accurate and are generally better with language and the rules of grammar.[29]

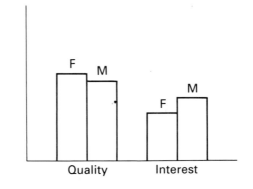

Figure 1[30]

Analysis

We decided to use an unrelated *t* test on this data to test for difference between the means. *t* tests are parametric and there must be a normal distribution from which the sample comes. Also, there must be homogeneity of variance and the level of measurement is interval.[31,32]

27 ✗ Table has no title; it does not state what the values 6.7 etc. *are*; should refer to 'points given by participants on a 10-point scale for the assessment indicated' or similar.

28 ? Should describe and summarise *for* the reader, not refer to them in this personal way.

29 ✗ Any interpretation or speculation should be conducted in the 'Discussion' section; here, just the factual results should be reported.

30 ✗ Chart has no title; 'M' and 'F' have no key (yes, it's obvious what they mean but clarity is the keyword here); the vertical scale has no values; the

　 ✓ chart is correctly drawn as a bar chart (not histogram); hair-splitters may argue that, since male and female are qualitatively separate, there should be space between the M and F bars, but the approach used here is common and usefully illustrative.

31 ✓ Good that parametric criteria are recognised and described fairly well.

32 ✗ The *use* of the *t* test here has not been justified – there should be an answer to the criteria given here, showing that *these* data are therefore suitable for a *t* test.

The calculation for t is shown in Appendix 4.

Our t was 0.97 for quality and 1.43 for interest. Neither of these is significant and in both cases we retained the null hypothesis.[33,34]

DISCUSSION

As we see above, there were small differences between the male and female author groups but the tests showed there was no significance. It could be that there is a difference but our design has failed to show this.[35] Or else there really is no difference in the way people judge this article according to the sex of the author. If this is true then we have contradicted Goldberg's results but these were done in 1968. Perhaps things have changed since then and people no longer judge according to sex on writing. First we will look at the things that could be wrong with our design.[36]

We asked participants to answer some 'dummy' questions so that we could be sure they'd noticed the sex of the author before they rated the article.[37] When we thought about it afterwards, we decided perhaps we should have got them to do the questions (or some of them) *before* they read the article so that they would be aware of the sex *while* they were reading it. This might have made a difference and we could do another study like this sometime.[38] We didn't take any notice of the sex of our participants but obviously this might make a difference.[39] Perhaps males would downrate female authors and maybe vice versa. In a future study we could take groups of men and women separately. Another problem was that not everybody would use our scale in the same way. 'Good' might be 7 to one person and 9 to another. We could perhaps have standardised by getting them to rate something else first and then discussing the points on the scale with them.[40] Also, we should have used more participants[41] and participants may have guessed what was going on and there may have been demand characteristics.[42]

We felt that the article used was on a very neutral subject. Goldberg used a selection of articles. Some were on traditionally male subjects and some of the subjects would be more associated with females. We could do the study again using, perhaps, an article on car maintenance and one on child-care to see whether this made a difference.[43]

If our result is genuine then perhaps times have changed since 1968. These days there are female bus drivers, fire-fighters and even matadors.

Bem sees sex stereotypes as a 'straight-jacket'[44] (Gross, 1992) and argues that society would improve with a shift towards 'androgyny'. This is where a person has the strengths of both traditional sex-roles. In order to 'discover' androgyny, it was necessary to see masculinity and femininity as not mutually exclusive but as two *independent* dimensions and to incorporate this into a new sort of test which would produce two logically independent scores. Bem developed such a test (1974).[45] It has been shown that people scoring high on Bem's Sex Role Inventory report higher levels of emotional well-being than others (Lubinski et al., 1981) and show higher self-esteem (Spence et al., 1975). Perhaps, from our results, we have shown that people are less likely today to take sex into account when judging the quality of writing because androgyny is more acceptable.[46]

REFERENCES[47]

Asch, S. E. (1946) Forming impressions of personality, *Journal of Abnormal and Social Psychology*, 4, 258–90.

Bem, S. L. (1974) The measurement of psychological androgyny. *Journal of Consulting and Clinical Psychology*, 42(2), 155–62.

33 ✓   Doing calculations helps understanding of the test (in some cases – perhaps not here) and mental effort, in general, is usually rewarded; however, not strictly necessary for A-level and in many other syllabuses; check whether you *need* to show working.

34 ✗   Where are critical values? What level of probability was referred to ($p < ?$)? How many degrees of freedom? Was the test one- or two-tailed?

35 ✓   Recognition that a type II error could have occurred and that the outcome, if genuine needs interpretation in the light of its contradiction of other work.

36 ✓   Deals with type II error possibility first, i.e. looks critically at the method.

37 ?   Again, role of dummy questions should have been made clear earlier but we have already taken this weakness into account in our assessment – not a double penalty.

38 ✓   Suggests modifications based on an analysis of the present study's outcomes and weaknesses.

39 ✓   Good! This point from our earlier debits has now been picked up so we can balance this in our assessment.

40 ✓   This point has also been picked up but it's a pity the implications for a parametric test aren't spotted here; should the data have been accepted as interval level then? Really, this is a partial ✗

41 ✗   Should avoid this knee-jerk point, unless there is a good reason to include it; there were a fair number of participants and with no reason given this is rather an empty point, 'thrown in'.

42 ✗
   ?   A difficult one; is the point that people may have guessed *and* there could have been 'demand characteristics'? If so, there should be an explanation of *why* the effect of demand characteristics is suspected; in what way? If people's guessing was meant *as* a demand characteristic, is this *feasible*? It must always be remembered in independent samples designs of this kind that *you* know what the IV is but how can the participants know? Why should *they* suspect that another author will be a different sex? This is an example of 'ego-centrism' to some extent, and being wise after the event.

43 ✓   Good extension of study proposed.

44 ✓   Has quoted and acknowledged Gross's specific term here.

45 ✗   !!! This suddenly technical and academic sounding piece of text, compared to most of the rest of the report, should set alarm bells ringing for the tutor. Most tutors, after only a little experience, can spot this kind of change and will lurch for the most likely textbooks to check for plagiarism. It is, in fact, cribbed straight from Gross (1992) page 696. This really would be a shame in an otherwise adequate report.

46 ✓   Good attempt to feed the result into general context. Some of these results are up to 20 years old. However, in some colleges it's difficult to get hold of more up-to-date research to relate to but try, if you can, to include more recent work.

47 ✓   Good references, put in conventional style and in alphabetical order.

Bruner, J. S. (1957) Going beyond the information given. In *Contemporary Approaches to Cognition: a symposium held at the University of Colorado*, Cambridge, MA: Harvard University Press.

Condry, J. and Condry, S. (1976) Sex differences: A study in the eye of the beholder. *Child Development*, 47, 812–19.

Deux, K. (1977) The social psychology of sex roles, in L. Wrightsman, *Social Psychology*, Monterey, CA: Brooks/Cole.

Dukes, W. F. and Bevan, W. (1951) Accentuation and response variability in the perception of personally relevant objects, *Journal of Personality*, 20, 457–465.

Goldberg, P. (1968) Are women prejudiced against women?, *Transaction*, April, 1968.

Gross, R. D. (1992) *Psychology: The Science of Mind and Behaviour*, Sevenoaks: Hodder and Stoughton.

Kelley, H. H. (1950) The warm–cold variable in first impressions of people. *Journal of Personality*, 18, 431–9. Lubinski et al. (1981) as cited in Gross, R. D. (above)[48].

Maccoby, E. E. and Jacklin, C. N. (1974) *The Psychology of Sex Differences*, Stanford, CA: Stanford University Press.

Spence, J. T., Helmreich, R. L. and Stapp, J. (1975) Ratings of self and peers on sex-role attributes and their relation to self-esteem and concepts of masculinity and feminity. *Journal of Personality and Social Psychology*, 32, 29–39.

Atkinson, R. L., Atkinson, R. C., Smith, E. E. and Bem, D. J. (1993) *Introduction to Psychology*, Fort Worth: Harcourt Brace Jovanovitch[49].

48 ✓ Yes! This one isn't in my current printing of Gross (though, by the time you read this, it may be). This is the way to refer to works you don't have/ can't get the original reference for but which you've seen referred to by another author.

49 ✗ 'Allo, 'allo! What's this one doing here? It's not in alphabetical order and, much more important, it *wasn't* referred to in the text of the report at any time. It's probably been read to do the report but it *isn't* a reference. It could be included as 'background reading' or, sometimes 'bibliography'. (But beware! Sociologists use 'bibliography' as psychologists use 'references'!)

STRUCTURED QUESTIONS

The following structured questions will give the reader practice in answering exam-type questions whilst noting that marks available indicate where longer answers are required.

QUESTION I

A psychologist wished to find out whether there was any relationship between the use of physical punishment by mothers and the levels of aggression in their children. Questionnaire scores were obtained on a scale from 0 to 20, for each mother's level of physical punishment use. Levels of aggression in the mothers' children were assessed using naturalistic observation at the children's schools at playtime. The correlation between physical punishment scores and aggression scores was 0.6.

Marks

a) State one advantage of the use of questionnaires in psychological assessment.   1

b) State one difficulty with the method of naturalistic observation as used in this study and explain why you think this is a difficulty.   2

c) The correlation found was *positive*. Explain what is meant by a positive correlation between two sets of scores.   2

d) A newspaper article described the research as showing that physical punishment caused aggression in children. Explain why this interpretation of the result is incorrect.

QUESTION 2

In a psychology experiment participants are asked to listen to a talk. During the talk a stranger holding an object bursts in and shouts at the speaker. In one condition the object is a gun while in the other condition it is a pen. Participants are later asked if they can recall the colour of the stranger's hair. It is predicted that less people would notice the stranger's hair colour when he is holding a gun. Results are shown below.

Table I *Number of people correctly recalling stranger's hair colour in gun and pen conditions*

Stranger holding	Participant recalled hair colour		
	Correctly	Incorrectly	Total
gun	17	33	50
pen	27	23	50
	44	56	100

		Marks
a)	What statistical test would determine whether the frequencies above are significantly different from those expected at a chance level of variation?	1
b)	What is the independent variable in this experiment? Give a reason for your answer.	2
c)	The experiment uses an *independent groups* design. Explain one advantage and one disadvantage of this design.	4
d)	State one ethical issue involved in the *design* of this study.	1

QUESTION 3

		Marks
a)	Describe what is meant by the *reliability* of a psychological measure.	2
b)	Describe what is meant by the *validity* of a psychological measure.	2
c)	State one major advantage of the use of interviews in psychological research compared with the use of structured questionnaires.	1
d)	Describe how content analysis could be used to deal with data gathered from informal interviews with hospital staff on the nature and causes of stress in their jobs.	3

QUESTION 4

In an experimental study which predicts that anagrams of uncommon words will take longer to solve, participants are given a list of anagrams containing 6 of common words and 6 of uncommon words. The two sets are mixed together randomly into one list of 12 anagrams. The researcher records the mean time taken by each participant to solve the two sets of anagrams.

		Marks
a)	State which is the independent variable and which is the dependent variable in this experiment.	2
b)	What type of experimental design is used in this study?	1
c)	Explain why the common and uncommon word anagrams are randomly mixed together.	3
d)	What is the null hypothesis for this study?	2

QUESTION 5

A researcher attempts to assess the effectiveness of two different programmes intended to improve children's reading ability. She matches each child in one class with a child in another class at the same school. All the children in both classes are 8 years old. Each class receives just one of the two programmes. After 6 months the children's reading scores are obtained and a comparison between the two groups is made.

Marks

a) State two *relevant* variables by which the children might be matched.   2
b) If the children's reading scores are ranked, what statistical test would be appropriate for testing the difference between the two classes? Give reasons for your choice.   3
c) Would the researcher conduct a one-tailed or a two-tailed test of her hypothesis?   1
d) One mother asks for specific information on how her child performed. Explain how the psychologist should react to this request.   2

QUESTION 6

An investigation is carried out to test the hypothesis that young teenage mothers are more controlling with their children than older mothers. Two groups of mothers, younger and older, are visited in their own home. A thirty-minute video tape recording is made of each mother at play with her two-year-old child. Several raters, unaware of the research hypothesis, are asked to rate the mothers' disciplining behaviour using a rigorous coding system. One of the measures is verbal control. The mean for the younger mothers on this variable is 35.8 and the standard deviation is 6.5. For the older mothers the mean is 28.6 and the standard deviation is 8.3.

Marks

a) Add all labels to the chart below which is intended to show the central tendency measures for the two groups.   3
b) What does the standard deviation tell us about a set of values?   1
c) Why are the raters kept unaware of the research hypothesis?   2
d) Explain why a 'rigorous coding system' is used to analyse the video-taped mothers' behaviour.   2

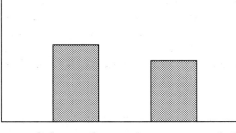

Mean verbal control scores for younger and older mothers

QUESTION 7

In an experiment the same group of participants is asked to perform a motor task, requiring care and concentration, under two different conditions. In the experimental condition they are given a strong cup of real coffee and in the control condition they are given decaffeinated coffee. These conditions are *counterbalanced*. Differences in performance are found to be significant with $p < 0.05$.

		Marks
a)	Give one advantage of the repeated measures design used in this study.	1
b)	What is meant by 'counterbalancing' and why is counterbalancing used in this design?	3
c)	Explain what is meant by the term 'significant with $p < 0.05$'.	2
d)	Explain why the participants are given decaffeinated coffee in the control condition.	2

QUESTION 8

Two groups of babies are observed in a play situation. One group has been reared in an institutional setting while the other group has been reared with two parents at home. The researchers are interested in how securely attached the babies are. All the babies have a female main carer. 'Attachment' is operationalised for this study in terms of their specific reaction to a stranger, their behaviour when their main carer departs, and their reaction on her return. In order to assess these reactions, procedures in the play situation are completely standardised.

		Marks
a)	What is meant by saying that the variable of attachment is 'operationalised' for this study?	1
b)	Explain what is meant by a 'standardised procedure' and why it is used in this study.	3
c)	One critic of the study argues that it very much lacks 'ecological validity'. What is meant by this term in this context?	2
d)	Each baby is given an overall 'attachment level' score. What statistical test would be appropriate for testing the difference between these two sets of scores? Give a reason for your choice of test.	2

QUESTION 9

Clients attending a drug rehabilitation unit are asked to take part in research aimed at improving the treatment offered. For technical reasons it is necessary to use a group attending on Mondays as the experimental group, who are trained in the special techniques of the programme, while a group attending on Wednesdays serves as the control group. At the end of the programme a measure is taken of each participants' 'self-esteem' on a 1 to 10 scale. The scores for the experimental group are given in the following table.

3	4	4	4	5	5	5	5	6	6	7	8

	Marks
a) Explain why this research design would be called a 'quasi-experiment' and the disadvantage it has compared with a true experiment.	3
b) What is the purpose of the control group used in this study?	2
c) What is the mode of the set of scores shown in the table above?	1
d) The variation ratio of the scores above is .67. Explain what is meant by the term 'variation ratio'.	2

QUESTION 10

In a study designed to compare sex-role stereotyping in television drama today and ten years ago, a researcher uses a 'content analysis' technique to analyse several hours of television film from both periods. Part of the analysis gives the frequencies shown in the table below for numbers of main character women in senior role positions (such as manager, prison governor and so on). The chi-squared test performed on these data produced a result which was not significant ($p > 0.05$).

Table 2 *Numbers of women shown in lead roles in television drama*

	Main characters in senior role	Main characters in non-senior role
1987	7	43
1997	15	38

	Marks
a) Describe how researchers use content analysis to obtain data from material such as television.	2
b) What factors might the researchers have to take into account when choosing the film to be analysed?	2
c) What test might be used on the data above in order to decide whether the change from 1987 to 1997 is significant? Give a reason for your choice.	2
d) What is meant by saying that the test result was not significant?	2

QUESTION 11

Mothers are interviewed in order to discover the quality of the diet they provide for their children and also the extent to which they provide extra vitamins. The research is aimed at the theory that extra vitamins and other dietary factors can enhance children's mental ability. The children's scores on a mental ability test are correlated with an overall 'healthy eating' score derived from the mothers' interview responses. The value of the correlation coefficient is 0.35 and is significant ($p < 0.05$). A local newspaper claims, in a report on the research, that 'healthy eating improves your child's mental ability'. The psychologist replies, in a letter, that this is only one possible conclusion from the research.

Marks

a) How would you describe the correlation of 0.35?   2

b) *Assuming the result is valid,* explain why the researcher argues that healthy eating may *not* improve a child's mental ability. Describe one other possible conclusion from the result, if it is valid.   3

c) A critic argues that 'social desirability' might have affected the validity of the interview data. What does 'social desirability' mean and how might it affect the validity of this study?   3

QUESTION 12

Participants are asked to perform a very difficult task requiring a great deal of concentration and patience. Even so, the task is made so difficult that few participants can complete it without a great deal of frustration. Times taken to complete the task are correlated with the number of errors made. These results are shown in the chart below. Immediately after the task is finished the participants are asked to complete a psychological test which is intended to assess levels of anger.

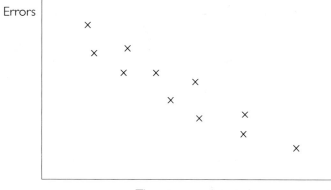

Marks

a) How would you describe the correlation shown in the scattergraph?   2

b) How might 'demand characteristics' affect the result concerning anger and frustration?   2

c) The person administering the anger test was kept unaware of the task results. Why might this precaution be taken?   2

d) The researchers predicted that there would be a correlation between levels of anger and time taken to complete the task. What would be the null hypothesis associated with this prediction?   2

QUESTION 13

A field experiment is conducted in which one group of factory workers is given a stress reduction training programme for two months. They are selected randomly from among all the workers in one large department. A second control group is also selected at random from the same department. Participants are asked to assess their stress levels both before and after the training period and the researchers use the median value of these assessments in their analysis.

Marks

a) Describe a method for selecting a sample at random from the department and explain the importance of doing this. 3
b) Explain fully what is meant by 'a field experiment'. 3
c) What advantage might a field experiment have over a laboratory experiment? 1
d) Why might the median be preferred to the mean as a measure of central tendency? 1

QUESTION 14

The aim of a research study is to confirm a prediction that the more experience people have had with computers the less anxious they will be. Psychology students are interviewed about their experience with computers and are then asked to complete a short computer anxiety scale. The raw scores on the anxiety test are given below.

Table 3 *Raw scores for computer anxiety (N = 26)*

1 2 2 3 3 4 5 5 6 6 6 7 7 7 7 7 8 8 8 8 8 8 9 9 9

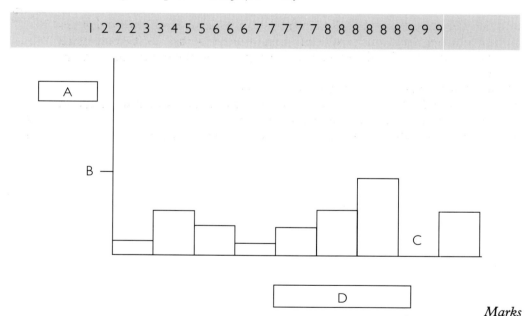

Marks

a) Name a statistical test which the researcher could use on the anxiety and experience scores in order to verify the prediction given as the aim of the study? 1
b) What is the range of the raw scores for computer anxiety? 1
c) Complete the histogram shown by adding information at points A to D. (Points A and D are labels; B is a value; and C is a column). 4
d) A local computer company is interested in the results and intends to use them in adjusting their recruitment policy. What limitations might there be in generalising the results to computer company applicants? 2

QUESTION 15

A clinical psychologist publishes results of a case study on one client who had received a programme of therapy designed to alleviate the problems he was experiencing in leaving his home and getting back to normal working life. Together, the therapist and client drew up a list of behaviour patterns which they intended to improve. They gave each of these behaviour patterns a rating from 1 to 10 at the start of the therapy and at the end of a three-month period. These patterns are labelled A to J in Table 4 below where the start and finish ratings are also shown.

Table 4

Behaviour pattern	A	B	C	D	E	F	G	H	I	J
rating at start	1	3	5	7	5	3	4	4	2	4
rating at end	3	5	5	9	4	7	8	8	6	5
improvement	+	+	0	+	−	+	+	+	+	+

Marks

a) The therapist decided to use a sign test on the start and finish ratings to see whether there was significant improvement across all the behaviour categories. Explain why this test is appropriate for the data in the bottom row. 2

b) What is the range of the 'rating at start' data? 1

c) State two ethical principles which the psychologist should observe before publishing the results of the therapy programme. 2

d) Describe the value of case studies in psychological research. 3

STATISTICAL TABLES

Table I *Random numbers*

```
03 47 43 73 86   39 96 47 36 61   46 98 63 71 62   33 26 16 80 45   60 11 14 10 95
97 74 24 67 62   42 81 14 57 20   42 53 32 37 32   27 07 36 07 51   24 51 79 89 73
16 76 62 27 66   56 50 26 71 07   32 90 79 78 53   13 55 38 58 59   88 97 54 14 10
12 56 85 99 26   96 96 68 27 31   05 03 72 93 15   57 12 10 14 21   88 26 49 81 76
55 59 56 35 64   38 54 82 46 22   31 62 43 09 90   06 18 44 32 53   23 83 01 30 30

16 22 77 94 39   49 54 43 54 82   17 37 93 23 78   87 35 20 96 43   84 26 34 91 64
84 42 17 53 31   57 24 55 06 88   77 04 74 47 67   21 76 33 50 25   83 92 12 06 76
63 01 63 78 59   16 95 55 67 19   98 10 50 71 75   12 86 73 58 07   44 39 52 38 79
33 21 12 34 29   78 64 56 07 82   52 42 07 44 38   15 51 00 13 42   99 66 02 79 54
57 60 86 32 44   09 47 27 96 54   49 17 46 09 62   90 52 84 77 27   08 02 73 43 28

18 18 07 92 46   44 17 16 58 09   79 83 86 16 62   06 76 50 03 10   55 23 64 05 05
26 62 38 97 75   84 16 07 44 99   83 11 46 32 24   20 14 85 88 45   10 93 72 88 71
23 42 40 64 74   82 97 77 77 81   07 45 32 14 08   32 98 94 07 72   93 85 79 10 75
52 36 28 19 95   50 92 26 11 97   00 56 76 31 38   80 22 02 53 53   86 60 42 04 53
37 85 94 35 12   83 39 50 08 30   42 34 07 96 88   54 42 06 87 98   35 85 29 48 38

70 29 17 12 13   40 33 20 38 26   13 89 51 03 74   17 76 37 13 04   07 74 21 19 30
56 62 18 37 35   96 83 50 87 75   97 12 25 93 47   70 33 24 03 54   97 77 46 44 80
99 49 57 22 77   88 42 95 45 72   16 64 36 16 00   04 43 18 66 79   94 77 24 21 90
16 08 15 04 72   33 27 14 34 90   45 59 34 68 49   12 72 07 34 45   99 27 72 95 14
31 16 93 32 43   50 27 89 87 19   20 15 37 00 49   52 85 66 60 44   38 68 88 11 80

68 34 30 13 70   55 74 30 77 40   44 22 78 84 26   04 33 46 09 52   68 07 97 06 57
74 57 25 65 76   59 29 97 68 60   71 91 38 67 54   13 58 18 24 76   15 54 55 95 52
27 42 37 86 53   48 55 90 65 72   96 57 69 36 10   96 46 92 42 45   97 60 49 04 91
00 39 68 29 61   66 37 32 20 30   77 84 57 03 29   10 45 65 04 26   11 04 96 67 24
29 94 98 94 24   68 49 69 10 82   53 75 91 93 30   34 25 20 57 27   40 48 73 51 92

16 90 82 66 59   83 62 64 11 12   67 19 00 71 74   60 47 21 29 68   02 02 37 03 31
11 27 94 75 06   06 09 19 74 66   02 94 37 34 02   76 70 90 30 86   38 45 94 30 38
35 24 10 16 20   33 32 51 26 38   79 78 45 04 91   16 92 53 56 16   02 75 50 95 98
38 23 16 86 38   42 38 97 01 50   87 75 66 81 41   40 01 74 91 62   48 51 84 08 32
31 96 25 91 47   96 44 33 49 13   34 86 82 53 91   00 52 43 48 85   27 55 26 89 62

66 67 40 67 14   64 05 71 95 86   11 05 65 09 68   76 83 20 37 90   57 16 00 11 66
14 90 84 45 11   75 73 88 05 90   52 27 41 14 86   22 98 12 22 08   07 52 74 95 80
68 05 51 18 00   33 96 02 75 19   07 60 62 93 55   59 33 82 43 90   49 37 38 44 59
20 46 78 73 90   97 51 40 14 02   04 02 33 31 08   39 54 16 49 36   47 95 93 13 30
64 19 58 97 79   15 06 15 93 20   01 90 10 75 06   40 78 78 89 62   02 67 74 17 33

05 26 93 70 60   22 35 85 15 13   92 03 51 59 77   59 56 78 06 83   52 91 05 70 74
07 97 10 88 23   09 98 42 99 64   61 71 62 99 15   06 51 29 16 93   58 05 77 09 51
68 71 86 85 85   54 87 66 47 54   73 32 08 11 12   44 95 92 63 16   29 56 24 29 48
26 99 61 65 53   58 37 78 80 70   42 10 50 67 42   32 17 55 85 74   94 44 67 16 94
14 65 52 68 75   87 59 36 22 41   26 78 63 06 55   13 08 27 01 50   15 29 39 39 43
```

Abridged from R. A. Fisher and F. Yates, *Statistical Tables for Biological, Agricultural and Medical Research*, (6th ed.) Longman Group UK Ltd (1974).

Table 2 *Areas under the normal distribution*

z	0 z	0 z	z	0 z	0 z	z	0 z	0 z
0.00	0.0000	0.5000	0.40	0.1554	0.3446	0.80	0.2881	0.2119
0.01	0.0040	0.4960	0.41	0.1591	0.3409	0.81	0.2910	0.2090
0.02	0.0080	0.4920	0.42	0.1628	0.3372	0.82	0.2939	0.2061
0.03	0.0120	0.4880	0.43	0.1664	0.3336	0.83	0.2967	0.2033
0.04	0.0160	0.4840	0.44	0.1700	0.3300	0.84	0.2995	0.2005
0.05	0.0199	0.4801	0.45	0.1736	0.3264	0.85	0.3023	0.1977
0.06	0.0239	0.4761	0.46	0.1772	0.3228	0.86	0.3051	0.1949
0.07	0.0279	0.4721	0.47	0.1808	0.3192	0.87	0.3078	0.1922
0.08	0.0319	0.4681	0.48	0.1844	0.3156	0.88	0.3106	0.1894
0.09	0.0359	0.4641	0.49	0.1879	0.3121	0.89	0.3133	0.1867
0.10	0.0398	0.4602	0.50	0.1915	0.3085	0.90	0.3159	0.1841
0.11	0.0438	0.4562	0.51	0.1950	0.3050	0.91	0.3186	0.1814
0.12	0.0478	0.4522	0.52	0.1985	0.3015	0.92	0.3212	0.1788
0.13	0.0517	0.4483	0.53	0.2019	0.2981	0.93	0.3238	0.1762
0.14	0.0557	0.4443	0.54	0.2054	0.2946	0.94	0.3264	0.1736
0.15	0.0596	0.4404	0.55	0.2088	0.2912	0.95	0.3289	0.1711
0.16	0.0636	0.4364	0.56	0.2123	0.2877	0.96	0.3315	0.1685
0.17	0.0675	0.4325	0.57	0.2157	0.2843	0.97	0.3340	0.1660
0.18	0.0714	0.4286	0.58	0.2190	0.2810	0.98	0.3365	0.1635
0.19	0.0753	0.4247	0.59	0.2224	0.2776	0.99	0.3389	0.1611
0.20	0.0793	0.4207	0.60	0.2257	0.2743	1.00	0.3413	0.1587
0.21	0.0832	0.4168	0.61	0.2291	0.2709	1.01	0.3438	0.1562
0.22	0.0871	0.4129	0.62	0.2324	0.2676	1.02	0.3461	0.1539
0.23	0.0910	0.4090	0.63	0.2357	0.2643	1.03	0.3485	0.1515
0.24	0.0948	0.4052	0.64	0.2389	0.2611	1.04	0.3508	0.1492
0.25	0.0987	0.4013	0.65	0.2422	0.2578	1.05	0.3531	0.1469
0.26	0.1026	0.3974	0.66	0.2454	0.2546	1.06	0.3554	0.1446
0.27	0.1064	0.3969	0.67	0.2486	0.2514	1.07	0.3577	0.1423
0.28	0.1103	0.3897	0.68	0.2517	0.2483	1.08	0.3599	0.1401
0.29	0.1141	0.3859	0.69	0.2549	0.2451	1.09	0.3621	0.1379
0.30	0.1179	0.3821	0.70	0.2580	0.2420	1.10	0.3643	0.1357
0.31	0.1217	0.3783	0.71	0.2611	0.2389	1.11	0.3665	0.1335
0.32	0.1255	0.3745	0.72	0.2642	0.2358	1.12	0.3686	0.1314
0.33	0.1293	0.3707	0.73	0.2673	0.2327	1.13	0.3708	0.1292
0.34	0.1331	0.3669	0.74	0.2704	0.2296	1.14	0.3729	0.1271
0.35	0.1368	0.3632	0.75	0.2734	0.2266	1.15	0.3749	0.1251
0.36	0.1406	0.3594	0.76	0.2764	0.2236	1.16	0.3770	0.1230
0.37	0.1443	0.3557	0.77	0.2794	0.2206	1.17	0.3790	0.1210
0.38	0.1480	0.3520	0.78	0.2823	0.2177	1.18	0.3810	0.1190
0.39	0.1517	0.3483	0.79	0.2852	0.2148	1.19	0.3830	0.1170

Table 2 *Continued*

z	0 z	0 z	z	0 z	0 z	z	0 z	0 z
1.20	0.3849	0.1151	1.60	0.4452	0.0548	2.00	0.4772	0.0228
1.21	0.3869	0.1131	1.61	0.4463	0.0537	2.01	0.4778	0.0222
1.22	0.3888	0.1112	1.62	0.4474	0.0526	2.02	0.4783	0.0217
1.23	0.3907	0.1093	1.63	0.4484	0.0516	2.03	0.4788	0.0212
1.24	0.3925	0.1075	1.64	0.4495	0.0505	2.04	0.4793	0.0207
1.25	0.3944	0.1056	1.65	0.4505	0.0495	2.05	0.4798	0.0202
1.26	0.3962	0.1038	1.66	0.4515	0.0485	2.06	0.4803	0.0197
1.27	0.3980	0.1020	1.67	0.4525	0.0475	2.07	0.4808	0.0192
1.28	0.3997	0.1003	1.68	0.4535	0.0465	2.08	0.4812	0.0188
1.29	0.4015	0.0985	1.69	0.4545	0.0455	2.09	0.4817	0.0183
1.30	0.4032	0.0968	1.70	0.4554	0.0446	2.10	0.4821	0.0179
1.31	0.4049	0.0951	1.71	0.4564	0.0436	2.11	0.4826	0.0174
1.32	0.4066	0.0934	1.72	0.4573	0.0427	2.12	0.4830	0.0170
1.33	0.4082	0.0918	1.73	0.4582	0.0418	2.13	0.4834	0.0166
1.34	0.4099	0.0901	1.74	0.4591	0.0409	2.14	0.4838	0.0162
1.35	0.4115	0.0885	1.75	0.4599	0.0401	2.15	0.4842	0.0158
1.36	0.4131	0.0869	1.76	0.4608	0.0392	2.16	0.4846	0.0154
1.37	0.4147	0.0853	1.77	0.4616	0.0384	2.17	0.4850	0.0150
1.38	0.4162	0.0838	1.78	0.4625	0.0375	2.18	0.4854	0.0146
1.39	0.4177	0.0823	1.79	0.4633	0.0367	2.19	0.4857	0.0143
1.40	0.4192	0.0808	1.80	0.4641	0.0359	2.20	0.4861	0.0139
1.41	0.4207	0.0793	1.81	0.4649	0.0351	2.21	0.4864	0.0136
1.42	0.4222	0.0778	1.82	0.4656	0.0344	2.22	0.4868	0.0132
1.43	0.4236	0.0764	1.83	0.4664	0.0336	2.23	0.4871	0.0129
1.44	0.4251	0.0749	1.84	0.4671	0.0329	2.24	0.4875	0.0125
1.45	0.4265	0.0735	1.85	0.4678	0.0322	2.25	0.4878	0.0122
1.46	0.4279	0.0721	1.86	0.4686	0.0314	2.26	0.4881	0.0119
1.47	0.4292	0.0708	1.87	0.4693	0.0307	2.27	0.4884	0.0116
1.48	0.4306	0.0694	1.88	0.4699	0.0301	2.28	0.4887	0.0113
1.49	0.4319	0.0681	1.89	0.4706	0.0294	2.29	0.4890	0.0110
1.50	0.4332	0.0668	1.90	0.4713	0.0287	2.30	0.4893	0.0107
1.51	0.4345	0.0655	1.91	0.4719	0.0281	2.31	0.4896	0.0104
1.52	0.4357	0.0643	1.92	0.4726	0.0274	2.32	0.4898	0.0102
1.53	0.4370	0.0630	1.93	0.4732	0.0268	2.33	0.4901	0.0099
1.54	0.4382	0.0618	1.94	0.4738	0.0262	2.34	0.4904	0.0096
1.55	0.4394	0.0606	1.95	0.4744	0.0256	2.35	0.4906	0.0094
1.56	0.4406	0.0594	1.96	0.4750	0.0250	2.36	0.4909	0.0091
1.57	0.4418	0.0582	1.97	0.4756	0.0244	2.37	0.4911	0.0089
1.58	0.4429	0.0571	1.98	0.4761	0.0239	2.38	0.4913	0.0087
1.59	0.4441	0.0559	1.99	0.4767	0.0233	2.39	0.4916	0.0084

Table 2 *Continued*

z	0 z	0 z	z	0 z	0 z	z	0 z	0 z
2.40	0.4918	0.0082	2.72	0.4967	0.0033	3.04	0.4988	0.0012
2.41	0.4920	0.0080	2.73	0.4968	0.0032	3.05	0.4989	0.0011
2.42	0.4922	0.0078	2.74	0.4969	0.0031	3.06	0.4989	0.0011
2.43	0.4925	0.0075	2.75	0.4970	0.0030	3.07	0.4989	0.0011
2.44	0.4927	0.0073	2.76	0.4971	0.0029	3.08	0.4990	0.0010
2.45	0.4929	0.0017	2.77	0.4972	0.0028	3.09	0.4990	0.0010
2.46	0.4931	0.0069	2.78	0.4973	0.0027	3.10	0.4990	0.0010
2.47	0.4932	0.0068	2.79	0.4974	0.0026	3.11	0.4991	0.0009
2.48	0.4934	0.0066	2.80	0.4974	0.0026	3.12	0.4991	0.0009
2.49	0.4936	0.0064	2.81	0.4975	0.0025	3.13	0.4991	0.0009
2.50	0.4938	0.0062	2.82	0.4976	0.0024	3.14	0.4992	0.0008
2.51	0.4940	0.0060	2.83	0.4977	0.0023	3.15	0.4992	0.0008
2.52	0.4941	0.0059	2.84	0.4977	0.0023	3.16	0.4992	0.0008
2.53	0.4943	0.0057	2.85	0.4978	0.0022	3.17	0.4992	0.0008
2.54	0.4945	0.0055	2.86	0.4979	0.0021	3.18	0.4993	0.0007
2.55	0.4946	0.0054	2.87	0.4979	0.0021	3.19	0.4993	0.0007
2.56	0.4948	0.0052	2.88	0.4980	0.0020	3.20	0.4993	0.0007
2.57	0.4949	0.0051	2.89	0.4981	0.0019	3.21	0.4993	0.0007
2.58	0.4951	0.0049	2.90	0.4981	0.0019	3.22	0.4994	0.0006
2.59	0.4952	0.0048	2.91	0.4982	0.0018	3.23	0.4994	0.0006
2.60	0.4953	0.0047	2.92	0.4982	0.0018	3.24	0.4994	0.0006
2.61	0.4955	0.0045	2.93	0.4983	0.0017	3.25	0.4994	0.0006
2.62	0.4956	0.0044	2.94	0.4984	0.0016	3.30	0.4995	0.0005
2.63	0.4957	0.0043	2.95	0.4984	0.0016	3.35	0.4996	0.0004
2.64	0.4959	0.0041	2.96	0.4985	0.0015	3.40	0.4997	0.0003
2.65	0.4960	0.0040	2.97	0.4985	0.0015	3.45	0.4997	0.0003
2.66	0.4961	0.0039	2.98	0.4986	0.0014	3.50	0.4998	0.0002
2.67	0.4962	0.0038	2.99	0.4986	0.0014	3.60	0.4998	0.0002
2.68	0.4963	0.0037	3.00	0.4987	0.0013	3.70	0.4999	0.0001
2.69	0.4964	0.0036	3.01	0.4987	0.0013	3.80	0.4999	0.0001
2.70	0.4965	0.0035	3.02	0.4987	0.0013	3.90	0.49995	0.00005
2.71	0.4966	0.0034	3.03	0.4988	0.0012	4.00	0.49997	0.00003

The left-hand column in each set of three shows the particular z-value. The centre column shows the area contained between the mean and this z-value. The right-hand column shows the area left in the whole distribution to the right of this z-value. The whole area is one unit and values shown are decimal portions of it. These are also the probabilities of finding a value within the area concerned. For percentages, multiply all area values by 100. For areas between −z and +z, double the values shown.

SOURCE: R. P. Runyon and A. Haber, *Fundamentals of Behavioral Statistics*, 3rd Ed. Reading, Mass.: McGraw-Hill, Inc. (1976) Used with permission. Artwork from R. B. McCall. *Fundamental Statistics for Psychology*, Second Edition, New York: Harcourt Brace Jovanovich, Inc. (1975).

Table 3 *Critical values in the Binomial Sign Test*

N	Level of significance for one-tailed test				
	0.05	0.025	0.01	0.005	0.0005
	Level of significance for two-tailed test				
	0.10	0.05	0.02	0.01	0.001
5	0	—	—	—	—
6	0	0	—	—	—
7	0	0	0	—	—
8	1	0	0	0	—
9	1	1	0	0	—
10	1	1	0	0	—
11	2	1	1	0	0
12	2	2	1	1	0
13	3	2	1	1	0
14	3	2	2	1	0
15	3	3	2	2	1
16	4	3	2	2	1
17	4	4	3	2	1
18	5	4	3	3	1
19	5	4	4	3	2
20	5	5	4	3	2
25	7	7	6	5	4
30	10	9	8	7	5
35	12	11	10	9	7

Calculated S must be EQUAL TO or LESS THAN the table (critical) value for significance at the level shown.

SOURCE: F. Clegg, *Simple Statistics*, Cambridge University Press, 1982. With the kind permission of the author and publishers.

Table 4 *Critical values of* χ^2

df	**Level of significance for a one-tailed test**					
	0.10	0.05	0.025	0.01	0.005	0.0005
	Level of significance for a two-tailed test					
df	0.20	0.10	0.05	0.02	0.01	0.001
1	1.64	2.71	3.84	5.41	6.64	10.83
2	3.22	4.60	5.99	7.82	9.21	13.82
3	4.64	6.25	7.82	9.84	11.34	16.27
4	5.99	7.78	9.49	11.67	13.28	18.46
5	7.29	9.24	11.07	13.39	15.09	20.52
6	8.56	10.64	12.59	15.03	16.81	22.46
7	9.80	12.02	14.07	16.62	18.48	24.32
8	11.03	13.36	15.51	18.17	20.09	26.12
9	12.24	14.68	16.92	19.68	21.67	27.88
10	13.44	15.99	18.31	21.16	23.21	29.59
11	14.63	17.28	19.68	22.62	24.72	31.26
12	15.81	18.55	21.03	24.05	26.22	32.91
13	16.98	19.81	22.36	25.47	27.69	34.53
14	18.15	21.06	23.68	26.87	29.14	36.12
15	19.31	22.31	25.00	28.26	30.58	37.70
16	20.46	23.54	26.30	29.63	32.00	39.29
17	21.62	24.77	27.59	31.00	33.41	40.75
18	22.76	25.99	28.87	32.35	34.80	42.31
19	23.90	27.20	30.14	33.69	36.19	43.82
20	25.04	28.41	31.41	35.02	37.57	45.32
21	26.17	29.62	32.67	36.34	38.93	46.80
22	27.30	30.81	33.92	37.66	40.29	48.27
23	28.43	32.01	35.17	38.97	41.64	49.73
24	29.55	33.20	36.42	40.27	42.98	51.18
25	30.68	34.38	37.65	41.57	44.31	52.62
26	31.80	35.56	38.88	42.86	45.64	54.05
27	32.91	36.74	40.11	44.14	46.96	55.48
28	34.03	37.92	41.34	45.42	48.28	56.89
29	35.14	39.09	42.69	49.69	49.59	58.30
30	36.25	40.26	43.77	47.96	50.89	59.70
32	38.47	42.59	46.19	50.49	53.49	62.49
34	40.68	44.90	48.60	53.00	56.06	65.25
36	42.88	47.21	51.00	55.49	58.62	67.99
38	45.08	49.51	53.38	57.97	61.16	70.70
40	47.27	51.81	55.76	60.44	63.69	73.40
44	51.64	56.37	60.48	65.34	68.71	78.75
48	55.99	60.91	65.17	70.20	73.68	84.04
52	60.33	65.42	69.83	75.02	78.62	89.27
56	64.66	69.92	74.47	79.82	83.51	94.46
60	68.97	74.40	79.08	84.58	88.38	99.61

Calculated value of χ^2 must EQUAL or EXCEED the table (critical) values for significance at the level shown.
Abridged from R. A. Fisher and F. Yates, *Statistical Tables for Biological, Agricultural and Medical Research*, (6th ed.) Longman Group UK Ltd (1974).

Table 5a *Critical values of U for a one-tailed test at 0.005; two-tailed test at 0.01* (Mann–Whitney)*

n_2 \ n_1	1	2	3	4	5	6	7	8	9	10	11	12	13	14	15	16	17	18	19	20
1	—	—	—	—	—	—	—	—	—	—	—	—	—	—	—	—	—	—	—	—
2	—	—	—	—	—	—	—	—	—	—	—	—	—	—	—	—	—	—	0	0
3	—	—	—	—	—	—	—	—	0	0	0	1	1	1	2	2	2	2	3	3
4	—	—	—	—	—	0	0	1	1	2	2	3	3	4	5	5	6	6	7	8
5	—	—	—	—	0	1	1	2	3	4	5	6	7	7	8	9	10	11	12	13
6	—	—	—	0	1	2	3	4	5	6	7	9	10	11	12	13	15	16	17	18
7	—	—	—	0	1	3	4	6	7	9	10	12	13	15	16	18	19	21	22	24
8	—	—	—	1	2	4	6	7	9	11	13	15	17	18	20	22	24	26	28	30
9	—	—	0	1	3	5	7	9	11	13	16	18	20	22	24	27	29	31	33	36
10	—	—	0	2	4	6	9	11	13	16	18	21	24	26	29	31	34	37	39	42
11	—	—	0	2	5	7	10	13	16	18	21	24	27	30	33	36	39	42	45	48
12	—	—	1	3	6	9	12	15	18	21	24	27	31	34	37	41	44	47	51	54
13	—	—	1	3	7	10	13	17	20	24	27	31	34	38	42	45	49	53	56	60
14	—	—	1	4	7	11	15	18	22	26	30	34	38	42	46	50	54	58	63	67
15	—	—	2	5	8	12	16	20	24	29	33	37	42	46	51	55	60	64	69	73
16	—	—	2	5	9	13	18	22	27	31	36	41	45	50	55	60	65	70	74	79
17	—	—	2	6	10	15	19	24	29	34	39	44	49	54	60	65	70	75	81	86
18	—	—	2	6	11	16	21	26	31	37	42	47	53	58	64	70	75	81	87	92
19	—	0	3	7	12	17	22	28	33	39	45	51	56	63	69	74	81	87	93	99
20	—	0	3	8	13	18	24	30	36	42	48	54	60	67	73	79	86	92	99	105

*Dashes in the body of the table indicate that no decision is possible at the stated level of significance.
For any n_1 and n_2 the observed value of U is significant at a given level of significance if it is *equal to or less than* the critical values shown.
SOURCE: R. Runyon and A. Haber (1976) Fundamentals of Behavioural Statistics (3rd ed.) Reading, Mass.: McGraw Hill, Inc. with kind permission of the publisher.

Table 5b *Critical values of U for a one-tailed test at 0.01; two-tailed test at 0.02* (Mann–Whitney)*

n_1

n_2	1	2	3	4	5	6	7	8	9	10	11	12	13	14	15	16	17	18	19	20
1	—	—	—	—	—	—	—	—	—	—	—	—	—	—	—	—	—	—	—	—
2	—	—	—	—	—	—	—	—	—	—	—	—	0	0	0	0	0	0	1	1
3	—	—	—	—	—	—	0	0	1	1	1	2	2	2	3	3	4	4	4	5
4	—	—	—	—	0	1	1	2	3	3	4	5	5	6	7	7	8	9	9	10
5	—	—	—	0	1	2	3	4	5	6	7	8	9	10	11	12	13	14	15	16
6	—	—	—	1	2	3	4	6	7	8	9	11	12	13	15	16	18	19	20	22
7	—	—	0	1	3	4	6	7	9	11	12	14	16	17	19	21	23	24	26	28
8	—	—	0	2	4	6	7	9	11	13	15	17	20	22	24	26	28	30	32	34
9	—	—	1	3	5	7	9	11	14	16	18	21	23	26	28	31	33	36	38	40
10	—	—	1	3	6	8	11	13	16	19	22	24	27	30	33	36	38	41	44	47
11	—	—	1	4	7	9	12	15	18	22	25	28	31	34	37	41	44	47	50	53
12	—	—	2	5	8	11	14	17	21	24	28	31	35	38	42	46	49	53	56	60
13	—	0	2	5	9	12	16	20	23	27	31	35	39	43	47	51	55	59	63	67
14	—	0	2	6	10	13	17	22	26	30	34	38	43	47	51	56	60	65	69	73
15	—	0	3	7	11	15	19	24	28	33	37	42	47	51	56	61	66	70	75	80
16	—	0	3	7	12	16	21	26	31	36	41	46	51	56	61	66	71	76	82	87
17	—	0	4	8	13	18	23	28	33	38	44	49	55	60	66	71	77	82	88	93
18	—	0	4	9	14	19	24	30	36	41	47	53	59	65	70	76	82	88	94	100
19	—	1	4	9	15	20	26	32	38	44	50	56	63	69	75	82	88	94	101	107
20	—	1	5	10	16	22	28	34	40	47	53	60	67	73	80	87	93	100	107	114

*Dashes in the body of the table indicate that no decision is possible at the stated level of significance.

For any n_1 and n_2 the observed value of U is significant at a given level of significance if it is *equal to* or *less than* the critical values shown.

SOURCE: R. Runyon and A. Haber (1976) Fundamentals of Behavioural Statistics (3rd ed.) Reading, Mass.: McGraw Hill, Inc. with kind permission of the publisher.

Table 5c *Critical values of* U *for a one-tailed test at 0.025; two-tailed test at 0.05* (Mann–Whitney)*

n_2	n_1 1	2	3	4	5	6	7	8	9	10	11	12	13	14	15	16	17	18	19	20
1	—	—	—	—	—	—	—	—	—	—	—	—	—	—	—	—	—	—	—	—
2	—	—	—	—	—	—	—	0	0	0	0	1	1	1	1	1	2	2	2	2
3	—	—	—	—	0	1	1	2	2	3	3	4	4	5	5	6	6	7	7	8
4	—	—	—	0	1	2	3	4	4	5	6	7	8	9	10	11	11	12	13	13
5	—	—	0	1	2	3	5	6	7	8	9	11	12	13	14	15	17	18	19	20
6	—	—	1	2	3	5	6	8	10	11	13	14	16	17	19	21	22	24	25	27
7	—	—	1	3	5	6	8	10	12	14	16	18	20	22	24	26	28	30	32	34
8	—	0	2	4	6	8	10	13	15	17	19	22	24	26	29	31	34	36	38	41
9	—	0	2	4	7	10	12	15	17	20	23	26	28	31	34	37	39	42	45	48
10	—	0	3	5	8	11	14	17	20	23	26	29	33	36	39	42	45	48	52	55
11	—	0	3	6	9	13	16	19	23	26	30	33	37	40	44	47	51	55	58	62
12	—	1	4	7	11	14	18	22	26	29	33	37	41	45	49	53	57	61	65	69
13	—	1	4	8	12	16	20	24	28	33	37	41	45	50	54	59	63	67	72	76
14	—	1	5	9	13	17	22	26	31	36	40	45	50	55	59	64	67	74	78	83
15	—	1	5	10	14	19	24	29	34	39	44	49	54	59	64	70	75	80	85	90
16	—	1	6	11	15	21	26	31	37	42	47	53	59	64	70	75	81	86	92	98
17	—	2	6	11	17	22	28	34	39	45	51	57	63	67	75	81	87	93	99	105
18	—	2	7	12	18	24	30	36	42	48	55	61	67	74	80	86	93	99	106	112
19	—	2	7	13	19	25	32	38	45	52	58	65	72	78	85	92	99	106	113	119
20	—	2	8	13	20	27	34	41	48	55	62	69	76	83	90	98	105	112	119	127

*Dashes in the body of the table indicate that no decision is possible at the stated level of significance.

For any n_1 and n_2 the observed value of U is significant at a given level of significance if it is *equal* to or less than the critical values shown.

SOURCE: R. Runyon and A. Haber (1976) Fundamentals of Behavioural Statistics (3rd ed.) Reading, Mass.: McGraw Hill, Inc. with kind permission of the publisher.

Table 5d *Critical values of U for a one-tailed test at 0.05; two-tailed test at 0.10* (Mann-Whitney)*

n_2 \ n_1	1	2	3	4	5	6	7	8	9	10	11	12	13	14	15	16	17	18	19	20
1	—	—	—	—	—	—	—	—	—	—	—	—	—	—	—	—	—	—	0	0
2	—	—	—	—	0	0	0	1	1	1	1	2	2	2	3	3	3	4	4	4
3	—	—	0	0	1	2	2	3	3	4	5	5	6	7	7	8	9	9	10	11
4	—	—	0	1	2	3	4	5	6	7	8	9	10	11	12	14	15	16	17	18
5	—	0	1	2	4	5	6	8	9	11	12	13	15	16	18	19	20	22	23	25
6	—	0	2	3	5	7	8	10	12	14	16	17	19	21	23	25	26	28	30	32
7	—	0	2	4	6	8	11	13	15	17	19	21	24	26	28	30	33	35	37	39
8	—	1	3	5	8	10	13	15	18	20	23	26	28	31	33	36	39	41	44	47
9	—	1	3	6	9	12	15	18	21	24	27	30	33	36	39	42	45	48	51	54
10	—	1	4	7	11	14	17	20	24	27	31	34	37	41	44	48	51	55	58	62
11	—	1	5	8	12	16	19	23	27	31	34	38	42	46	50	54	57	61	65	69
12	—	2	5	9	13	17	21	26	30	34	38	42	47	51	55	60	64	68	72	77
13	—	2	6	10	15	19	24	28	33	37	42	47	51	56	61	65	70	75	80	84
14	—	2	7	11	16	21	26	31	36	41	46	51	56	61	66	71	77	82	87	92
15	—	3	7	12	18	23	28	33	39	44	50	55	61	66	72	77	83	88	94	100
16	—	3	8	14	19	25	30	36	42	48	54	60	65	71	77	83	89	95	101	107
17	—	3	9	15	20	26	33	39	45	51	57	64	70	77	83	89	96	102	109	115
18	—	4	9	16	22	28	35	41	48	55	61	68	75	82	88	95	102	109	116	123
19	0	4	10	17	23	30	37	44	51	58	65	72	80	87	94	101	109	116	123	130
20	0	4	11	18	25	32	39	47	54	62	69	77	84	92	100	107	115	123	130	138

* Dashes in the body of the table indicate that no decision is possible at the stated level of significance.

For any n_1 and n_2 the observed value of U is significant at a given level of significance if it is *equal* to or less than the critical values shown.

SOURCE: R. Runyon and A. Haber (1976) Fundamentals of Behavioural Statistics (3rd ed.) Reading, Mass.: McGraw Hill, Inc. with kind permission of the publisher.

Table 6 *Critical values of* T *in the Wilcoxon Signed Ranks test*

	Levels of significance			
	One-tailed test			
	0.05	0.025	0.01	0.001
	Two-tailed test			
Sample size	0.1	0.05	0.02	0.002
N = 5	T ≤ 0			
6	2	0		
7	3	2	0	
8	5	3	1	
9	8	5	3	
10	11	8	5	0
11	13	10	7	1
12	17	13	9	2
13	21	17	12	4
14	25	21	15	6
15	30	25	19	8
16	35	29	23	11
17	41	34	27	14
18	47	40	32	18
19	53	46	37	21
20	60	52	43	26
21	67	58	49	30
22	75	65	55	35
23	83	73	62	40
24	91	81	69	45
25	100	89	76	51
26	110	98	84	58
27	119	107	92	64
28	130	116	101	71
29	141	125	111	78
30	151	137	120	86
31	163	147	130	94
32	175	159	140	103
33	187	170	151	112

Calculated T must be EQUAL TO or LESS THAN the table (critical) value for significance at the level shown.

SOURCE: Adapted from R. Meddis, *Statistical Handbook for Non-Statisticians*, McGraw-Hill, London (1975), with the kind permission of the author and publishers.

Table 7 *Critical values of t*

Degrees of freedom	Level of significance for a one-tailed test			
	0.05	0.025	0.01	0.005
	Level of significance for a two-tailed test			
	0.10	0.05	0.02	0.01
1	6.314	12.706	31.821	63.657
2	2.920	4.303	6.965	9.925
3	2.353	3.182	4.541	5.841
4	2.132	2.776	3.747	4.604
5	2.015	2.571	3.365	4.032
6	1.943	2.447	3.143	3.707
7	1.895	2.365	2.998	3.499
8	1.860	2.306	2.896	3.355
9	1.833	2.262	2.821	3.250
10	1.812	2.228	2.764	3.169
11	1.796	2.201	2.718	3.106
12	1.782	2.179	2.681	3.055
13	1.771	2.160	2.650	3.012
14	1.761	2.145	2.624	2.977
15	1.753	2.131	2.602	2.947
16	1.746	2.120	2.583	2.921
17	1.740	2.110	2.567	2.898
18	1.734	2.101	2.552	2.878
19	1.729	2.093	2.539	2.861
20	1.725	2.086	2.528	2.845
21	1.721	2.080	2.518	2.831
22	1.717	2.074	2.508	2.819
23	1.714	2.069	2.500	2.807
24	1.711	2.064	2.492	2.797
25	1.708	2.060	2.485	2.787
26	1.706	2.056	2.479	2.779
27	1.703	2.052	2.473	2.771
28	1.701	2.048	2.467	2.763
29	1.699	2.045	2.462	2.756
30	1.697	2.042	2.457	2.750
40	1.684	2.021	2.423	2.704
60	1.671	2.000	2.390	2.660
120	1.658	1.980	2.358	2.617
∞	1.645	1.960	2.326	2.576

Calculated *t* must EQUAL or EXCEED the table (critical) value for significance at the level shown.

SOURCE: Abridged from R. A. Fisher and F. Yates, *Statistical Tables for Biological, Agricultural and Medical Research*, (6th ed.) Longman Group UK Ltd (1974).

Table 8 *Critical values of Spearman's r_s*

	Level of significance for a two-tailed test			
	0.10	0.05	0.02	0.01
	Level of significance for a one-tailed test			
	0.05	0.025	0.01	0.005
$n = 4$	1.000			
5	0.900	1.000	1.000	
6	0.829	0.886	0.943	1.000
7	0.714	0.786	0.893	0.929
8	0.643	0.738	0.833	0.881
9	0.600	0.700	0.783	0.833
10	0.564	0.648	0.745	0.794
11	0.536	0.618	0.709	0.755
12	0.503	0.587	0.671	0.727
13	0.484	0.560	0.648	0.703
14	0.464	0.538	0.622	0.675
15	0.443	0.521	0.604	0.654
16	0.429	0.503	0.582	0.635
17	0.414	0.485	0.566	0.615
18	0.401	0.472	0.550	0.600
19	0.391	0.460	0.535	0.584
20	0.380	0.447	0.520	0.570
21	0.370	0.435	0.508	0.556
22	0.361	0.425	0.496	0.544
23	0.353	0.415	0.486	0.532
24	0.344	0.406	0.476	0.521
25	0.337	0.398	0.466	0.511
26	0.331	0.390	0.457	0.501
27	0.324	0.382	0.448	0.491
28	0.317	0.375	0.440	0.483
29	0.312	0.368	0.433	0.475
30	0.306	0.362	0.425	0.467

For $n > 30$, the significance of r_s can be tested by using the formula:

$$t = r_s\sqrt{\frac{n-2}{1-r_s^2}} \quad df = n-2$$

and checking the value of t in Table 7.

Calculated r_s must EQUAL or EXCEED the table (critical) value for significance at the level shown.

SOURCE: J. H. Zhar, Significance testing of the Spearman Rank Correlation Coefficient, *Journal of the American Statistical Association*, 67, 578–80. With the kind permission of the publishers.

Table 9 *Critical values of Pearson's r*

df	**Level of significance for a one-tailed test**			
	0.05	0.025	0.005	0.0005
df (N − 2)	**Level of significance for a two-tailed test**			
	0.10	0.05	0.01	0.001
2	0.9000	0.9500	0.9900	0.9999
3	0.805	0.878	0.9587	0.9911
4	0.729	0.811	0.9172	0.9741
5	0.669	0.754	0.875	0.9509
6	0.621	0.707	0.834	0.9241
7	0.582	0.666	0.798	0.898
8	0.549	0.632	0.765	0.872
9	0.521	0.602	0.735	0.847
10	0.497	0.576	0.708	0.823
11	0.476	0.553	0.684	0.801
12	0.475	0.532	0.661	0.780
13	0.441	0.514	0.641	0.760
14	0.426	0.497	0.623	0.742
15	0.412	0.482	0.606	0.725
16	0.400	0.468	0.590	0.708
17	0.389	0.456	0.575	0.693
18	0.378	0.444	0.561	0.679
19	0.369	0.433	0.549	0.665
20	0.360	0.423	0.537	0.652
25	0.323	0.381	0.487	0.597
30	0.296	0.349	0.449	0.554
35	0.275	0.325	0.418	0.519
40	0.257	0.304	0.393	0.490
45	0.243	0.288	0.372	0.465
50	0.231	0.273	0.354	0.443
60	0.211	0.250	0.325	0.408
70	0.195	0.232	0.302	0.380
80	0.183	0.217	0.283	0.357
90	0.173	0.205	0.267	0.338
100	0.164	0.195	0.254	0.321

Calculated r must EQUAL or EXCEED the table (critical) value for significance at the level shown.

SOURCE: F. C. Powell, *Cambridge Mathematical and Statistical Tables*, Cambridge University Press (1976). With kind permission of the author and publishers.

ANSWERS TO EXERCISES AND STRUCTURED QUESTIONS

For the end-of-chapter questions only direct and specific answers are given. They are not included where the reader is asked to conduct an exercise or give an open-ended description.

CHAPTER 2

1 a) Field investigation – sex is IV and this is not manipulated
   b) Laboratory investigation – number of brothers is IV and this is not manipulated
   c) Field experiment – if participants randomly allocated
   d) Laboratory experiment
   e) Quasi-experiment
   f) Field investigation
   g) Natural experiment/Quasi-experiment

2 a) a and c
   b) all
   c) all (in (a)), observer need not know that sex is the IV; in others people who rate recorded behaviour need not see original conditions

4 IV – complexity of patterns; DV – time spent gazing. Design – repeated measures (with randomisation of position and simultaneous presentation of conditions of the IV)

5 Add condition with same babies enticed over the shallow side – repeated measure; control group enticed over shallow side – independent samples

6 Repeated measures; randomisation of IV stimuli; avoids order effects

7 Repeated measures; counterbalancing; avoids order effects

8 Matched pairs

CHAPTER 3

1

IV	DV
a) Type of propaganda	Strength of attitude
b) Noise level	Work efficiency
c) Time of day	Attention span
d) Amount of practice	Level of performance
e) Smile given or not	Smile received or not
f) Level of frustration	Level of aggression
g) Order of birth	Personality and intellectual level
h) Presence or absence of crowd	People's behaviour (needs more specific definition)

2 Examples:
Noise: Hourly average decibel level
Attention span: Measured by number of 'blips' noticed on a radar-like screen
Smile: As recognised by a rater who doesn't know research aim, and lasting longer than 1 second

3 a) IV: preschool education or not   DV: cognitive skills and sociability
b) e.g. preschool children's parents more educationally concerned?
c) Match parents (on educational concern) in both groups

4 a) It has been found reliable since the correlation (agreement) is very high, hence it should be all right to use as far as reliability is concerned
b) Perhaps some recent well-publicised event, such as a nuclear accident

5 a) Compare results with interview data? Compare with strength of desire to return?
b) Can't carry out a test–retest check so can only test internally, e.g. split-half

6 Reliable, not necessarily valid

CHAPTER 4

1 Test participants, or an equivalent control group, *without* the confederates
2 Perhaps: area, number of children, educational background, age, etc.
3 Only volunteers; must read bulletin; no teetotallers
4 Only **c**
5 Placebo group – no special programme but given attention and parents given expectation that children might improve; raises ethical issues of course
6 For instance, left side students might be better at this problem-solving task

CHAPTER 5

4 The raters vary very much from each other, therefore poor reliability. Correlation is used for the comparison.

CHAPTER 6

1 *Advantages:* structured so easier to compare responses of different individuals; less variation in researcher procedure, hence less random error; can question many people more quickly.
Disadvantages: social desirability more likely as less time for relationship to become genuine and comfortable; can't obtain individual's personalised accounts and unique thoughts or behaviour patterns.

4 The sixth formers are volunteers. Only schools which agreed to the study can be sampled from. Those without telephones cannot be included. Those who use the youth club are more likely to be selected.

5 **a)** Question invites agreement
  b) Assumes children *should* be punished
  c) Is this easy to answer?
  d) Double barrelled – 'people *aren't* the same but should be treated with respect' is a possible response
  e) Double negative
  f) Item is ambiguous as extreme feminist and extreme sexist might well agree
  g) Technical term; will this be understood by all?

6 Use a ('blind') rater ignorant of research hypothesis and of who is in which group

CHAPTER 8

2 Ordinal

3 Nominal

4 **a)** Ordinal
  b) Ratio
  c) Interval-like but treat as ordinal
  d) Nominal

5 Box **b**

6 'Top' is a measure on an ordinal scale. We don't know how far ahead of the others she was. She may not be *far* better

7 Nominal – did/didn't hit kerb; Ordinal – rate smoothness on one to 10 scale; Interval/ratio – measure speed in race

8

Ordinal level	
Consistent	Inconsistent
6.5	11
9	17
1	11
2.5	4.5
16	18
2.5	4.5
6.5	8
11	14
13	15

Nominal level		
	Consistent	Inconsistent
above mean	4	7
below mean	5	2

9 a) Nominal
  b) Interval/ratio (because standardised)
  c) Ordinal
  d) Interval-like but best to convert to ordinal
  e) Interval/ratio
  f) Nominal (frequencies)
  g) Interval-like but best converted to ordinal
  h) Interval/ratio (because standardised)
  i) Interval/ratio if measured using rule
  j) Ordinal

CHAPTER 9

1 Males: mean = 171.6; median = 132. Females: mean = 367.2; median = 345

2 Males: 180.3; Females: 81.1

3 a) Data are skewed, therefore use median. Median = 79
  b) 74

4 Mean = 19.43

6 Since there is absolutely no variation, all scores must be the same; all scores are therefore 0.8 and the mean is 0.8

7 a) 115 **b)** about 2.3% **c)** 16% **d)** 130

8 Mode = 4, Variation ratio = 18/24 = .75.

CHAPTER 10

1 a) possibly one **b)** only two **c)** possibly one **d)** only two

2 a) 1% ($p < 0.01$) **b)** More likely

3

Decimal	Per cent	Fraction
0.01	1%	$\frac{1}{100}$
0.001	0.1%	$\frac{1}{1000}$
0.0005	0.05%	$\frac{1}{2000}$
0.1	10%	$\frac{1}{10}$
0.01	1%	$\frac{1}{100}$
0.001	0.1%	$\frac{1}{1000}$
0.005	0.5%	$\frac{1}{200}$

CHAPTER 11

1 $\chi^2 = 19.25$

2 Unwise because all expected frequencies are less than 5 and sample is very small

3 a) χ^2 'goodness of fit' – one variable, two categories
  b) $\chi^2 = 67.24$, $p < 0.001$
  c) Yes
  d) No. χ^2 cannot be performed on percentages. We require actual frequencies

4 $N = 8$; $S = 1$. Assuming a positive evaluation was predicted, a one-tailed test would be appropriate but this result has gone in the opposite direction even though it reaches the critical value required. With a two-tailed test the result does not reach the critical value. Hence, not significant either way.

5

	Sig.			Sig.	
	One-tail	Two-tail		One-tail	Two-tail
a)	0.01	0.02	**c)**	0.025	0.05
b)	0.005	0.01	**d)**	0.001	0.002

6 a) Table 11.11 – use Wilcoxon signed ranks: $T = 1$, $N = 12$, $p < 0.001$
  b) Table 11.12 – use Mann–Whitney: $U = 49$, $N_A = 13$, $N_B = 11$, $p > 0.05$, N/S

7 a) Variances obviously very different and unequal sample sizes with an unrelated design. Therefore unsafe. Use Mann–Whitney
  b) Variances different but this is a related design. Hence, safe to conduct t-test. Appropriate non-parametric test – Wilcoxon signed ranks

8 No. $df = 10$. cv (two-tailed) at $p < 0.01 = 3.169$

9 a) NS, keep null hypothesis
  b) 0.01, 1%, reject null hypothesis
  c) NS, keep null hypothesis

d) 0.005, 0.5%, reject null hypothesis

e) NS, keep null hypothesis

f) 0.01, 1%, reject null hypothesis

10 Distributions are skewed. As samples are large, the whole population may well be skewed too, and this is contrary to normal distribution assumption.

CHAPTER 12

1 a) Early letter recognition *correlates* with reading ability at seven years old but may not *cause* the superior reading. It may be related to something else that is responsible for better reading ability *or* children may differ innately in letter recognition and reading ability, in which case the greater emphasis would make little difference ˙

c) negative

d) strong/very strong

e) $p < 0.0005$

2 a) Accept **b)** Accept **c)** Reject **d)** Accept **e)** Reject **f)** Accept

g) Accept (wrong direction)

3 No. For Pearson, data must meet parametric requirements

4 Spearman. Data should be treated as ordinal because human judgement

5 Check her calculations – highest possible is 1

CHAPTER 13

1 Unrelated *t*; simpler alternative – Mann–Whitney

2 Mann–Whitney

3 Chi-square

4 Chi-square

5 a) Related *t*; simpler alternative – Wilcoxon Signed Ranks

b) Pearson's correlation

6 Pearson. Validity test – unrelated *t*

7 Spearman correlation

8 Chi-square

9 Related *t*; simpler alternative – Wilcoxon Signed Ranks

10 Wilcoxon Signed Ranks

11 Sign test

12 Pearson's or Spearman's correlation

STRUCTURED QUESTION I

a) Produce quantitative data/can be made reliable/standardised method of data collection/reduce researcher bias (compared with interview). (1 of these.)

b) Can't control observing situation/different children might or might not provoke aggression in observed child. In general, lack of control of extraneous variables.

c) Variables increase together/if one of a pair is high, tendency for the other to be high also and vice versa.

d) Correlation only shows a relationship, it doesn't account for the direction of cause and effect. Perhaps naturally aggressive children, or children who have learned to be aggressive at school, *provoke* physical punishment from parents.

STRUCTURED QUESTION 2

a) Chi-squared.

b) Gun or pen since this is the variable manipulated by the experimenter.

c) Advantage – no order effects which occur in repeated measures design where participants may improve through the unwanted variable of practice, for instance. Disadvantage – participant variables; groups may differ and this may be responsible for any differences found. (Note the request was *'explain'* not just *'state'*; 1 mark only for simple statements; also other advantages or disadvantages are possible – see text.)

d) Participants were deceived/*all* ethical issues (confidentiality, anonymity etc.) are *possibly* involved but deception is inherent in the *design* of this experiment).

STRUCTURED QUESTION 3

a) The measure is consistent. Could refer accurately to *internal* reliability, *external* reliability or *inter-rater/observer* reliability for the extra mark, e.g. people tend to score the same on it a second time as they did the first time.

b) That it measures what it is intended to measure. Could refer to any of the validity types (face, content, criterion etc.) for the extra mark, e.g. it successfully identifies differences between known groups.

c) Interviewer can clear up ambiguities, perhaps gain more relevant information/ questioning can be flexible/richer information may be obtained and so on – see text.

d) Researcher would need to identify appropriate categories and provide coding for placing information in each category. The coding might be carried out by coders unaware of the research hypothesis but certainly they would need to be well trained in the use of the coding system.

STRUCTURED QUESTION 4

a) Independent variable – common or uncommon words. Dependent variable – (mean) time taken for solution.

b) Repeated measures.

c) To avoid order effects from practice, fatigue or from guessing what the experiment is about.

d) There is no difference between mean times for common and uncommon word solutions.

STRUCTURED QUESTION 5

a) Initial reading level/other academic ability indicator/sex/socio-economic factors. (Note: sex is relevant because it is known that girls are generally superior in reading during the schools years. Variables *must* be relevant; there would be no *obvious* rationale for choosing race, height or distance lived from school.

b) Wilcoxon signed ranks. The data are ranked, the test is of differences between groups and the design is related (matched pairs).

c) Two-tailed. She does not predict the direction of the difference. Either programme might be more effective than the other.

d) Psychological ethics demand that participants be given full information on data collected about them. Therefore, unless there are prior restrictions agreed to by participants, the information should be made available along with any appropriate counselling or advice.

STRUCTURED QUESTION 6

a) Central tendency used was the mean. Hence taller column on chart should be labelled 'younger mothers' and the other column should be labelled 'older mothers' – both on horizontal axis at bottom of chart. The vertical axis should be labelled 'mean verbal control score' or similar.

b) The spread or *dispersion* of the set of values.

c) Avoids the possible criticism that they could be biased in their rating and help support the research hypothesis.

d) A rigorous system helps maintain objective assessment. It will at least aid in reliability if not validity of ratings.

STRUCTURED QUESTION 7

a) Differences between conditions cannot be the result of differences between two sets of participants (i.e. participant variables are ruled out).

b) Counterbalancing involves having some (half if there are two conditions) participants perform conditions in one order while the other half perform conditions in the opposite order. It reduces confounding from order effects – see 4c above.

c) If there were actually no difference in performance scores from coffee and decaffeinated conditions, then the probability of obtaining sample results this different is less than 0.05. Can't answer 'the null hypothesis is rejected' since this is a *result* of the significance decision, not the meaning of 'significant'.

d) To ensure *all* variables are as identical as possible *except* the independent variable. Here, only coffee content is absent from the control condition. All participants have a coffee-tasting drink.

STRUCTURED QUESTION 8

a) A general term is defined precisely in terms of what will be done to measure it for this particular study.

b) All procedures are exactly the same for each participant. This reduces any bias possible from researcher-participant interaction or error from extraneous variables which might cause differences in children's play behaviour.

c) The attachment behaviour is exhibited in a strange situation. The question is whether the findings would transfer to the children's natural environment. Perhaps this particular play set-up produces only behaviour special to the test situation, e.g. some element may be particularly frightening to some of the children.

d) Mann-Whitney. The children are given scores so data are at least ordinal and not just frequencies. The design is unrelated and we are testing for differences. (Note: *one* of these last two points would be sufficient for the single mark available.) (*t* test for unrelated samples is also appropriate if data meet parametric requirements for this test; data would have to be treated as being at least at interval level of measurement.

STRUCTURED QUESTION 9

a) Researcher is not able to allocate participants to conditions at random. Hence, any difference found *might* be the result of differences between the groups unrelated to the independent variable.

b) To provide a base-line measure. We can see whether self-esteem might have increased during the period *without* the special training and hence see whether the programme has any real effect.

c) 5.

d) It is a measure of dispersion and is the proportion of scores which are not of the modal value. (Note: two marks were available so best to make the general point about dispersion as well as giving a specific definition.)

STRUCTURED QUESTION 10

a) See answer to 3d.

b) Sampling would need to be representative and balanced across the two years. Samples would need to come from equivalent slots and would be chosen randomly within the slots.

c) Chi-square. Data are frequencies/we seek differences in role categories across time or an *association* between these two variables/the design is unrelated. (Note: only two of these reasons are required.)

d) The probability is greater than 0.05 that these frequencies would occur through random sampling if the null hypothesis is true (no association exists at all).

STRUCTURED QUESTION 11

a) Weak (possibly 'moderate') and positive.
b) Correlations do not indicate cause and effect. Perhaps families with higher mental abilities are more likely to see the value of healthier eating. Again, such families may be better off and can *afford* healthier eating habits. (Note: one reason will do.)
c) Conforming to social values and presenting oneself in this light. Here, mothers may have *said* they used healthier foods because they know this is socially desirable – the 'right thing to do'.

STRUCTURED QUESTION 12

a) Strong negative.
b) Participants might guess that the questionnaire has something to do with the emotional experience they have just had with the task. Hence this might affect the way they answer.
c) So that there can be no suggestion that knowing the desired outcome for the research, the test administrator could have biased the results, consciously or not.
d) The correlation between task time and anger level is zero.

STRUCTURED QUESTION 13

a) All names in box and shuffle; then pick sample/give each person a random number then take the highest/lowest 20 numbers if 20 required in sample/put all names in computer and let it generate random order. Take first 20 if 20 required. (Any of these three methods will do.) Reason: to make sure each person has an equal chance of being in sample – gives good chance of a representative group.
b) Study where researcher manipulates independent variable in non-laboratory situation – in 'real-life' situation where those studied would normally be found. (Note: 3 marks available so definition of experiment required as well as 'field').
c) Less artificial so behaviour more like that occurring in normal circumstances/ greater ecological validity/participants less inhibited by strange, formal situation and (possibly) demand characteristics (though these are possible in field studies too). (*One* of these points would do.)
d) Not affected by extreme scores in one direction.

STRUCTURED QUESTION 14

a) Spearman's rho/Pearson.
b) 9.
c) Point A – 'Frequency' (or similar); point B – '5'; point C – column should be just one unit higher than the column to its left; point D – 'Computer anxiety scores'.

d) Computer company applicants are not necessarily interested in psychology and are not students. Anxiety only assessed by paper test and not with live computers.

STRUCTURED QUESTION 15

a) The bottom row data are the signs (i.e. directions) of the differences between start and end ratings. Since we only have positive or negative signs the data are *nominal*. The design is *related*. We are looking for differences. (*Two* of these points would do.)

b) 7.

c) Any two of: clients should be assured of anonymity and confidentiality of any information on them/clients should be asked whether they are in agreement with publication/they should be able to check any data and to withdraw permission at any time before final publication/no information published should threaten their psychological health or make them feel uncomfortable. (Other points are possible.)

d) Three of the points on page 100, or two, with one expanded upon a little, should gain full marks here.

NOTE TO THE SECOND EDITION

In preparing the second edition of this book, prompted by the revision of the AEB A level psychology syllabus for commencement in 1996, it was decided not to discard material which would now no longer apply to that syllabus. This is because several other reader groups (for instance International Baccalaureate and nursing students) have found the book useful and might wish to use the material which would otherwise be dropped. However, for the benefit of the greater proportion of readers here is a list of items in this book which are *not* included in the draft version of the 1996 AEB A level psychology revision with reference to the Research Methods structured question sections.

- single participant design
- random and constant error
- specific types of validity of measures (face content criterion construct) though ecological validity and validity of experiments *are* included
- samples – specific strategies are not mentioned though 'selection of participants' *is* included. In this context, random and representative sampling are central concepts. It is necessary to understand these in order to carry out experiments for coursework. However, it is unlikely that questions could refer to the other specific sampling strategies covered in Chapter 4
- placebo group
- longitudinal and cross-sectional designs
- cross-cultural studies (though associated issues are included in theory sections)
- questionnaires – there is no mention of these in the draft syllabus material though interviewing (which could *use* a questionnaire) is included in general terms. Much of the technical detail in the questionnaire section of this book would not occur in the AEB's research methods questions. However, the material is included as a guide to students creating questionnaires for practical work
- levels of measurement – not included, although the student would need to recognise the major difference between *categorical* treatment of data and *measured* data in order to decide between appropriate use of chi-square/sign test or Mann-Whitney/Wilcoxon tests
- population parameters
- concept of cumulative frequency
- normal distribution, areas and z scores
- skewed distributions
- type I and type II error
- parametric tests (*t* tests and Pearson's correlation) and parametric assumptions
- qualitative methods in general are not included but qualitative analysis of data *is* mentioned. This refers to content analysis and interpretation of interviews, case studies and observations

REFERENCES

Ainsworth, M. D. S., Bell, S. M. & Stayton, D. J. (1971) Individual differences in strange situation behaviour of one-year-olds. In Schaffer, H. R. (ed.) (1971) *The Origins of Human Social Relations*. London: Academic Press.

Allport, G. W. (1947) *The Use of Personal Documents in Psychological Science*. London: Holt, Rinehart and Winston.

American Psychological Association (1987) *Casebook on Ethical Principles of Psychologists*. Washington: American Psychological Association.

Asch, S. E. (1956) Studies of independence and submission to group pressure. 1. A minority of one against a unanimous majority. In *Psychological Monographs*, 70 (9) (Whole No. 416).

Atkinson, R. C. & Shiffrin, R. M. (1968) Human memory: a proposed system and its control processes. In K. W. Spence & J. T. Spence (eds.) *The Psychology of Learning and Motivation*, vol. 2. London: Academic Press.

Baars, B. J. (1980) Eliciting predictable speech errors in the laboratory. In V. Fromkin (ed.) *Errors in Linguistic Performance: Slips of the Tongue, Ear, Pen and Hand*. New York: Academic Press, 1980.

Bandura, A. (1965) Influence of models' reinforcement contingencies on the acquisition of imitative responses. *Journal of Personality and Social Psychology*, 1, 589–95.

Barber, T. X. (1976) *Pitfalls in Human Research*. Oxford: Pergamon.

Becker, H. S. (1958) Inference and proof in participant observation. *American Sociological Review*, 23, 652–60.

Benedict, R. (1934) *Patterns of Culture*. Boston: Houghton Mifflin.

Berry, J. W., Poortinga, Y. H., Segall, M. H. & Dasen, P. R. (1992) *Cross-cultural Psychology: Research and Applications*. Cambridge: CUP.

Bramel, D. A. (1962) A dissonance theory approach to defensive projection. *Journal of Abnormal and Social Psychology*, 64, 121–9.

British Psychological Society (1985) A code of conduct for psychologists. *Bulletin of the British Psychology Society*, 38, 41–3.

British Psychological Society (1993) *Code of Conduct, Ethical Principles and Guidelines*, Leicester: British Psychological Society.

Brown, R. (1965) *Social Psychology*. New York: Free Press.

Brown, R., Fraser, C. & Bellugi, U. (1964) *The Acquisition of Language*. Monographs of the Society for Research in Child Development 29. 92.

Brunswick, E. (1947) *Systematic and Unrepresentative Design of Psychological Experiments with Results in Physical and Social Perception*. Berkeley: University of California Press.

Carlsmith, J., Ellsworth, P. & Aronson, E. (1976) *Methods of Research in Social Psychology*. Reading, Mass.: Addison–Wesley.

Charlesworth, R. & Hartup, W. W. (1967) Positive social reinforcement in the nursery school peer group. *Child Development*, 38, 993–1002.

Cook, T. D. & Campbell, T. T. (1979) *Quasi-experimentation: Design and Analysis Issues for Field Settings*. Chicago: Rand McNally.

Coolican, H. (1994) *Research Methods and Statistics in Psychology*. (2nd ed.): London: Hodder and Stoughton.

Cumberbatch, G. (1990) *Television Advertising and Sex Role Stereotyping: A Content Analysis* (working paper IV for the Broadcasting Standards Council), Communications Research Group, Aston University.

David, S. S. J., Chapman, A. J., Foot, H. C. & Sheehy, N. P. (1986) Peripheral vision and child pedestrian accidents. *British Journal of Psychology*, vol 77, 4.

Doob, A. N. & Gross, A. E. (1968) Status of frustration as an inhibitor of horn-honking responses. *Journal of Social Psychology*, 76, 213–8.

Duncan, S. L. (1976) Differential social perception and attribution of intergroup violence: Testing the lower limits of stereotyping of blacks. *Journal of Personality and Social Psychology*, 34, 590–8.

Elton, B. (1989) *Stark.* London: Sphere Books.

Eron, L. D., Huesmann, L. R., Lefkowitz, M. M. & Walder, L. D. (1972) Does television violence cause aggression? *American Psychologist*, 27, 253–63.

Eysenck, H. J. (1970) *The Structure of Human Personality.* London: Methuen.

Freeman, D. (1983) *Margaret Mead and Samoa: The making and unmaking of an anthropological myth.* Cambridge, Mass.: Harvard University Press.

Friedrich, L. K. & Stein, A. H. (1973) Aggressive and prosocial television programs and the natural behaviour of pre-school children. *Monographs of the Society for Research in Child Development.* 38(4, serial No. 51).

Ganster, D. C., Mayes, B. T., Sime, W. E. & Tharp, G. D. (1982) Managing organisational stress: a field experiment. *Journal of Applied Psychology*, 67(5), 533–42.

Gross, R. D. (1992) *Psychology: the Science of Mind and Behaviour.* (2nd ed.): London: Hodder and Stoughton.

Gross, R. D. (1994) *Key Studies in Psychology* (2nd ed.). London: Hodder and Stoughton.

Hampden-Turner, C. (1971) *Radical Man.* London: Duckworth.

Harré, R. (1981) The positivist–empiricist approach and its alternative. In Reason, R. & Rowan, J. (1981) *Human Inquiry: A Sourcebook of New Paradigm Research.* Chichester: Wiley.

Hatfield, E. & Walster, G. W. (1981) *A New Look at Love.* Reading, Mass.: Addison–Wesley.

Heather, N. (1976) *Radical Perspectives in Psychology.* London: Methuen.

Huff, D. (1954) *How to Lie with Statistics.* London: Gollancz.

Humphreys, L. (1970) *Tearoom Trade.* Chicago: Aldine.

Jowell, R. & Topf, R. (1988) *British Social Attitudes.* London: Gower.

Joynson, R. B. (1989) *The Burt Affair.* London: Routledge.

Jung, C. G. (1930) Your Negroid and Indian behaviour. *Forum*, 83, 4, 193–99.

Kagan, J., Kearsley, R. B. & Zelazo, P. R. (1980) *Infancy – Its Place in Human Development.* Cambridge, Mass.: Harvard University Press.

Kinsey, A. C., Pomeroy, W. B., Martin, C. E. & Gebhard, P. H. (1953) *Sexual Behaviour in the Human Female.* Philadelphia: Saunders.

Kohler, W. (1925) *The Mentality of Apes.* New York: Harcourt Brace Jovanovich.

Kuhn, T. (1962) *The Structure of Scientific Revolutions.* Chicago, Ill.: University of Chicago.

Latané, B. & Darley, J. M. (1976) *Help in a Crisis: Bystander Response to an Emergency.* Morristown, NJ: General Learning Press.

Leavitt, F. (1991) *Research Methods for Behavioural Sciences.* Dubuque, IA: Wm. C. Brown.

Leyens, J., Camino, L., Parke, R. D. & Berkowitz, L. (1975) Effects of movie violence on aggression in a field setting as a function of group dominance and cohesion. *Journal of Personality and Social Psychology*, 32, 346–60.

Likert, R. A. (1932) A technique for the measurement of attitudes, *Archives of Psychology*, 140, 55.

Marsh, P. (1978) *The Rules of Disorder.* London: Routledge.

Masling, J. (1966) Role-related behaviour of the subject and psychologist and its effect upon psychological data. In Levine, D. (ed.) (1966) *Nebraska Symposium on Motivation.* Lincoln, Neb.: University of Nebraska Press.

Mead, M. (1928) *Coming of Age in Samoa.* Harmondsworth Middlesex: Penguin.

Mead, M. (1930) *Growing up in New Guinea.* Harmondsworth Middlesex: Penguin.

Menges, R. J. (1973) Openness and honesty versus coercion and deception in psychological research. *American Psychologist*, 28, 1030–34.

Milgram, S. (1963) Behavioural study of obedience. *Journal of Abnormal and Social Psychology* 63, 371–8.

Milgram, S. (1974) *Obedience to Authority.* New York: Harper and Row.

Mixon, D. (1979) Understanding shocking and puzzling conduct. In Ginsburg, G. P. (ed.) (1979) *Emerging Strategies in Social Psychological Research.* Chichester: Wiley.

Ora, J. P. (1965) Characteristics of the volunteer for psychological investigations. Office of Naval Research Contract 2149(03), Technical Report 27.

Orne, M. T. (1962) On the social psychology of the psychological experiment: with particular reference to demand characteristics and their implications. *American Psychologist*, 17, 776–83.

Osgood, C. E., Luria, Z., Jeans, R. F. & Smith, S. W. (1976) The three faces of Evelyn: a case report. *Journal of Abnormal Psychology*, 85, 247–86.

Osgood, C. E., Suci, G. J. & Tannenbaum, P. H. (1957) *The Measurement of Meaning.* Urbana: University of Illinois.

Piliavin, I. M., Rodin, J. & Piliavin, J. A. (1969) Good samaritanism: an underground phenomenon? *Journal of Personality and Social Psychology,* 13, 289–99.

Raffetto, A. M. (1967) Experimenter effect on subjects' reported hallucinatory experiences under visual and auditory deprivation. Master's thesis, San Francisco State College.

Reason, P. & Rowan, J. (1981) (eds.) *Human Enquiry: A Sourcebook in New Paradigm Research.* Chichester: Wiley.

Ring, K., Wallston, K. & Corey, M. (1970) Mode of debriefing as a factor affecting subjective reaction to a Milgram-type obedience experiment: an ethical inquiry. *Representative Research in Social Psychology,* 1, 67–88.

Robson, C. R. (1993) *Real World Research.* Oxford: Blackwell.

Rokeach, M. (1960) *The Open and Closed Mind.* New York: Basic Books.

Rosenhan, D. L. (1973) On being sane in insane places. *Science,* 179, 250–8.

Rosenthal, R. (1966) *Experimenter Effects in Behavioural Research.* New York: Appleton-Century-Crofts.

Ross, H. L. (1973) Low science and accidents: The British Road Safety Act of 1967. *Journal of Legal Studies,* , 1–75.

Seligman, M. (1972) *Biological Boundaries of Learning.* New York: Appleton- Century-Crofts.

Thurstone, L. L. (1931) The measurement of social attitudes. *Journal of Abnormal and Social Psychology,* 26, 249–69

Torbert, W. R. (1981) Why educational research has been so uneducational: the case for a new model of social science based on collaborative enquiry. In Reason, P. & Rowan, J. (1981) *Human Inquiry.* Chichester: Wiley.

Valentine, E. R. (1992) *Conceptual Issues in Psychology* (2nd ed.). London: Routledge.

Watson, J. B. & Rayner, R. (1920) Conditioned emotional reactions. *Journal of Experimental Psychology,* 3, 1–14.

Weber, S. J. & Cook, T. D. (1972) Subject effects in laboratory research: an examination of subject roles, demand characteristics and valid inference. *Psychological Bulletin,* 77, 273–95.

Whyte, W. F. (1943) *Street Corner Society: the Social Structure of an Italian Slum.* Chicago: The University of Chicago Press.

Williams, J. E., Bennett, S. M. & Best, D. L. (1975) Awareness and expression of sex stereotypes in young children. *Developmental Psychology,* 11, 635–42.

Williams, J. E. & Berry, J. W. (1991) Primary prevention of acculturative stress among refugees: the application of psychological theory and practice. *American Psychologist,* 46, 632–41.

Zimbardo, P. G. (1972) Pathology of imprisonment. *Society,* April 1972.

INDEX

P261